Dedicated to Ronald C. Federico, January 9, 1941–October 2, 1992
a friend, scholar, and mentor

Contents

CHAPTER 3   THE DIMENSIONS OF HUMAN BEHAVIOR   69

CHAPTER 4   HUMAN BEHAVIOR THROUGHOUT
THE LIFE COURSE   129

CHAPTER 5 **FOCUSING ON PRACTICE**   **175**

ADDITIONAL PRACTICE TEXTS   **231**

EPILOGUE   **233**

Preface

As this book is being prepared to go into production, Congress is debating cutting the federal budget for school lunches and is working on a welfare reform package that will greatly diminish the resources of poor families in America. While discussing corporate and individual tax cuts, many in Congress are opposing an increase in the minimum wage. All indications suggest that an unbridled assault is underway on persons most in need in this country. If successful, this *Contract with America* will erode many, if not most, of the resources available to support persons and families in need.

It is in this context that the story of "Yummy" Sandifer, an 11-year-old child and gang member who killed and was killed, becomes all the more tragic (Gibbs, 1994: 54–59). It is, however, a much too familiar story in American life. Children's well-being is increasingly at risk because of poverty, violence, inadequate education, and exposure to drugs and crime. How do we begin to understand the actions of an 11-year-old murderer? Do we explore genetic anomalies, individual psychology, family relationships, or community life to discover an answer? Or do we look at a larger picture, in which social and political agendas create policies that disadvantage women, children, and minorities? How do we begin to understand the actions of politicians and those who elected them, who are presently seeking to dismantle many of the hard-won gains in care for the elderly, the poor, the disabled, women and children, and minorities?

Becoming an effective helping person involves understanding human behavior in its many forms. The horrifying and the heartwarming, the commonplace and the unique, the mean-spirited and the altruistic, are all part of the human situations in which people need help. Obviously, many of these situations are complex, made up of elements involving individuals, families, and a wide range of life experiences in a variety of social systems. Understanding them is a difficult task that requires much knowledge and considerable sensitivity.

The goal of this book is to help you to understand situations that require helping efforts. This task begins with your caring about others and your motivation to improve the quality of life for everyone. Underlying your impetus to help are knowledge, facts, and concepts about people and the systems in which they live. It is the application of your knowledge to specific people in need that will provide the base for your helping efforts. This book will focus on reviewing needed knowledge and provide you with a framework that you can use to integrate and apply that knowledge in practice. You will also learn how effective professional helpers use their knowledge within the context of human values and ethics.

DREAMS FULFILLED AND UNFULFILLED

This book is about what is important to people and how these things shape their lives. People in the helping professions are in the business of enabling others to attain their life goals. To do so effectively, we must first understand what is of value to people, because values and goals are closely related. Humans seek what they value, and they act in ways that are consistent with their values and perceptions of reality. Therefore, professional helpers must also understand what people consider appropriate strategies to attain their goals.

Many factors influence what individuals view as important and attainable. Some of these factors are concrete, as would be the case if a person who lacks formal education desires a job that requires this education. Such people would be excluded from the desirable jobs and would be forced to give up their dreams of work that they would find interesting and rewarding. Other factors are more intangible but, nevertheless, important. Religious beliefs may support a dream that says people can get along without racial conflict, even though such conflict presently occurs. This book will help you understand why people have their dreams, how their behavior is affected by them, and how these dreams get modified and, sometimes, destroyed. When you read the case of "Yummy" Sandifer at the end of the next chapter, you might wonder what dreams he may have had that will never be fulfilled. Was it a need for safety and security that led Yummy to join a gang, or was it a way of filling a need to belong? Although we can never truly know anyone's mind, we can attempt to understand the personal and social forces that impact people's lives.

Understanding requires knowledge. Because there are many factors that influence people's dreams and values, the knowledge needed is diverse and extensive. This book will help you review and place in context the knowledge that you already have and, when necessary, it will help you acquire useful new knowledge. In addition, you will learn how to use this knowledge as a professional helping person whose goal is to influence the human condition.

CLARIFYING AND ARTICULATING GOALS

In many cases the first task of the helping professional is to assist people in articulating their values and goals. Although deeply held, these values may rarely be made explicit in thought or speech. When people are helped to examine and to express their values and goals, it is easier for them to consider the means of attaining or modifying them. Of course, individuals sometimes want things that are impossible for them to attain. In these cases, acknowledging this reality with sensitivity and interpersonal support is part of what the helping professional brings to the helping process.

The values and goals that motivate human behavior are varied and often contradictory. Parents may envision their children becoming economically successful, yet also want them to be caring, honest people who are ethical and not too aggressive. Other parents may have the same dream but discourage their children from pursuing such a goal, because they do not believe that it is realistic. We all have hopes and related goals for ourselves and for others, but it is sometimes difficult to establish workable priorities among them and to sort out those that are likely to be attainable from those that are not. Professional helpers assist people as they express, clarify, and organize their dreams and goals. Professional helpers also act with, and on behalf of, people when they advocate policies that support basic needs.

TYPES OF KNOWLEDGE

There are many kinds of knowledge, and all are constantly developing. The sciences, the arts, and the humanities all attempt to explain and portray the mind, the body, and the nature of the human person. Each type of knowledge approaches this task differently. The sciences seek consistent, predictable, and quantifiable laws that will explain human behavior (Leshan and Margenau, 1982: 7). The arts look to human imagination to find a vision of the essentials of human existence, whereas the humanities examine cultural and historical traditions to find meaning in human life. Each of these approaches creates useful knowledge.

By understanding that there are many sources of knowledge, we can avoid unidimensional views of behavior. Fritz Perls (1969), the Gestalt psychologist, presents a useful metaphor to keep in mind as we embark on the study of human behavior. Borrowing from the language of art, he refers to the figure-ground dichotomy as we seek to understand behavior (Perls, 1969). If we attend to the apple (figure) on the table (ground), the table fades from attention. As we gaze into the night sky (ground) and imagine its immensity, we lose perspective of our place in it (figure). So also is it with our attempt to grasp the essence of human behavior. Each of the sciences, arts, and humanities has added something to our explanation of human behavior. Yet, by focusing on only parts of this total storehouse of knowledge, we tend to emphasize the figure (specific behavior of interest to us) and lose sight of the ground (the context within which the behavior occurs). In situations such as that of "Yummy" Sandifer, professional helpers could have provided individual help to him and his family. Professional helpers might also have sought to improve health care, housing, and employment in the community in which he lived. They might also have sought to lobby for adequate funding for schools, day care, job development, gun control, universal health care, and a variety of other social and economic supports that might have improved "Yummy's" life situation.

Human behavior is more than the sum of its parts. Despite all of our scientific knowledge, there is a mystery in human behavior. We can never know all of the variables that are responsible for any one person's actions at a given time. How, then, can we approach the study of human behavior? The answer is: With caution. Like the physical universe, the human person is governed by the ordered and the random. From the physical sciences we strive for predictability; from the social sciences we appreciate diversity; from the arts and the humanities we understand uniqueness and perspective. As helping professionals we must seek to learn all that is knowable while always being mindful of the incompleteness of the task. Science and mystery are not incompatible principles. They yield both knowledge and reverence.

This text develops a framework for approaching the study of human behavior that builds on an understanding of the sciences, the arts, and the humanities, one that is useful in practice. Discerning what knowledge is important for intervention is, to use Fritz Perls' analogy, a task of separating figure from ground. The framework is also firmly rooted in social work values and practice principles. It is, we believe, one that is useful to all helping professions. It is built on a health model of human behavior in which the human person is seen as striving for wellness and in the process of becoming.

Lest you become discouraged by the magnitude of the task, keep in mind that you already know a great deal about human behavior. In the courses you have taken in anthropology, psychology, sociology, political science, economics, and biology, you have learned much about various facets of people and their behavior. Building on this knowledge, the focus in this book will be on helping you review what you know, learn a framework for integrating that broad range of knowledge, and then develop skill in applying it to real-life situations that helping people commonly encounter. The end result of using this text, then, should be a very practical one. You should be more confident about what you know, and you should be able to use your knowledge to help yourself and others.

SUMMARY AND OBJECTIVES OF THIS BOOK

Let us summarize before you move on to Chapter 1. This book is intended to assist people in the helping professions to use knowledge in their practice. By understanding human behavior in its social context, helping professionals can make practice decisions more effectively. Several assumptions underlie this point of view:

1. Knowledge is fundamental for professionally responsible helping efforts.
2. Some knowledge is more useful for practice than other knowledge. In particular, knowledge that establishes a systems and human-diversity context for human development is most useful for understanding situations in which people need or want help.
3. To be of practical use, knowledge (in the form of concepts and data) must be learned, integrated, and applied to actual life situations. The practitioner must also know how to determine which concepts and data are most useful in specific practice situations. In addition to summarizing selected concepts, we will discuss their utility for practice.
4. The current state of our knowledge does not allow us to understand everything about human behavior. Thus, we encourage the reader to maintain a sense of awe and wonderment when confronted with the complexities of human action. This book attempts only to survey the types of knowledge available from the sciences, arts, and humanities. Knowledge is constantly expanding in the health and human services fields. As a result, theories about human behavior can be developed, used, critiqued, modified, and even abandoned in a relatively short time. This book will help your study of human behavior by providing useful screens from which to evaluate these theories and models. It should also assist you in contextualizing knowledge emanating from individual disciplines. Contemporary material from professional journals can be used to develop critical thinking further in regard to the framework presented in this text.

The book's three principal objectives derive from the assumptions above. They are summarized as follows:

1. *To review systematically and summarize concepts and data that have particular relevance.* Useful concepts exist in various disciplines in the biological, social, and behavioral sciences, especially sociology, psychology, political science, economics, anthropology, and human biology. In addition to summarizing selected concepts from these disciplines, their utility for practice will be discussed.
2. *To develop a framework that can be used to integrate the concepts relevant to understanding human behavior.* While individual disciplines concentrate on the teaching of discrete concepts and theories, this book will focus on finding relationships among them. This will make it easier to perceive and understand human behavior in its totality, rather than as discrete, or separate, actions.
3. *To demonstrate how integrated knowledge may be used by helping professionals.* In support of this objective, we will seek to establish a context for the analysis and decision making that are essential components for practice.

FEATURES OF THIS EDITION

The major framework in this edition remains the same as that in the three previous editions. We have continued to expand and update the material from the previous editions. Chapter 2 contains more information regarding systems theory and its criticisms. In Chapter 3, regarding the four sources of behavior, additional material is presented, especially in the areas of genetics, psychological theories, and social-structural institutions. Chapter 4, on the life course, has been expanded to include a discussion of personal narration and its importance to understanding individual behavior. Chapter 5 expands the discussion of the role of the professional helper and the helping process and elaborates on a strengths-based perspective in practice.

New study questions and exhibits have been added to this edition. These questions and exhibits are designed to challenge the student to acquire, integrate, and apply the concepts they have learned from this and previous texts. As in previous editions, key terms are listed for each chapter to help the reader review the central concepts and ideas presented.

Professor Ronald C. Federico, co-author of the first three editions of this text, died in 1992. His contributions to the field of social work will be missed. His influence on this text and its authors remains, however.

A new author, Professor Marilyn J. Rifkin from the University of Cincinnati, joins our team. Professor Rifkin brings 25 years of practice and teaching to this edition.

We hope you will find this book a helpful tool in your careers as students and practitioners.

ACKNOWLEDGMENTS

The authors wish to acknowledge the many persons who have contributed to this revised edition. As with previous editions many students, educators, friends, family members, and colleagues have offered suggestions, ideas, and comments that have added to the text's development and refinement.

We especially wish to thank Rosemary Schroeder and Mary Kay Martin-Heldman, both graduate students in the School of Social Work at the University of Cincinnati, who contributed original material used as Exhibits in Chapter 5. Our thanks also go to the authors and publishers who have graciously allowed us to use their material for this text.

We also wish to thank family members, especially Maria McBreen, for her patience and support during the writing of this text.

The technical assistance of the Longman staff has been especially helpful. George Hoffman, acquisitions editor, and Hillary Henderson, associate editor, have generously provided their technical assistance throughout this revision. Thanks are also extended to Linda Moser, production editor, for overseeing the production process, and to Linda F. Kurtz, Eastern Michigan University and

Dennis Saleebey, University of Kansas, for reviewing the manuscript and providing helpful suggestions.

REFERENCES

Gibbs, N. (1994). Murder in Miniature. *Time*, September 19, pp. 54-59.
Leshan, L. and A. Margenau (1982). *Einstein's Space and Van Gogh's Sky: Physical Reality and Beyond.* New York: Collier Books, p. 7.
Perls, F. (1969). *Gestalt Therapy Verbatim.* Lafayette, CA: Real People Press.

chapter **1**

Human Behavior and Effective Practice

*If this is a dream it is not my dream for how should I know the language
in which to dream it.*

Joyce Carol Oates*

*I concern myself with being only in so far as I have a more or less distinct
consciousness of the underlying unity which ties me to other beings of
whose reality I already have a preliminary notion.*

Gabriel Marcel**

OVERVIEW

That you are considering a career in social work or in a related human service
profession undoubtedly indicates your desire to be of service to people. This chapter
starts with the assumption that the foundation for professional helping indeed
begins with such a desire. The focus then shifts to why knowledge is important
for effective professional helping and discusses the kind of knowledge that is
most useful for the social work practitioner. A health- and strengths-oriented
model of social work practice is presented, and the implications of such a model
for the study of human behavior are discussed. The chapter also examines the
importance of an ecological perspective when working with persons to assess
problematic situations. Several different types of knowledge are proposed and

---

* Joyce Carol Oates (1990). *I Lock My Door Upon Myself.* New York: The Ecco Press, p. 75.
** Gabriel Marcel (1960). *The Mystery of Being: 2. Faith and Reality.* Chicago: Gateway Edition,
   Henry Regnery Company, p. 19.

examined. Finally, issues in selecting knowledge for practice are explored prior to examining the purposes of the generalist model of social work practice. Chapter 1, therefore, lays the groundwork for the remainder of the book by developing a perspective on human behavior content that is grounded in professional purpose and based on a health, ecological, strengths, and empowerment model of social work.

SOME WORDS ABOUT BEHAVIOR

Definitions of **behavior** are as diverse as the academic disciplines that seek to explain it and the professions that attempt to influence it. Even scientists and practitioners within these disciplines and professions vary greatly in their definitions and approaches to the understanding of human behavior. Some would define behavior in terms of specific acts. Behavior, according to such a perspective, is simply what one does. Others may suggest a broader perspective and include cognition and emotion in addition to action.

The *Social Work Dictionary* defines behavior as

> . . . any reaction or response by an individual, including observable activity, measurable physiological changes, cognitive images, fantasies, and emotion. (Barker, 1991: 22)

For the purposes of this book, we are adopting this perspective because it provides a set of parameters that help frame the subject under study. With such a broad definition, the practitioner is able to consider human behavior not only in terms of specific acts and their consequences but also the subjective states from which they arise.

This definition assists the social worker in gathering as much information as possible concerning the situations faced by those we seek to assist. In direct practice the practitioner may find questions such as "What influences, both internal and external, shape or affect a particular behavior?" The same question may be asked when the practitioner seeks to change the attitudes, beliefs, and behaviors of persons or groups that negatively impact the health and welfare of others as in the case of racial oppression. Behavior involves the interaction of three forces as the person encounters his or her environment:

the cognitive (what one thinks, believes, perceives, wills)

the affective (what one feels, including viscerally)

the behavioral (what one does)

At the end of this chapter is an account of the life of "Yummy" Sandifer, who at the age of 11 killed and was killed. In Yummy's short life he experienced more trauma than most of us can even imagine unless we have lived in similar situations. Life on Chicago's South Side has been described as a war zone. In trying to reconstruct and understand Yummy's life and the events, relationships, and social forces that led to his death, we are not attempting to assign blame. Social workers seek to understand how different factors influence behavior so that they can modify their intervention. Their goal is to allow people to grow and thrive, rather than lose control of their lives.

KNOWLEDGE, SKILL, AND COMMITMENT IN PRACTICE

The National Association of Social Workers' Code of Ethics states:

> The social worker shall have, maintain and endeavor periodically to update an acceptable level of knowledge and skills to meet the standards of practice. (NASW, 1973: Code of Ethics, 3.6)

The question that arises, of course, is, "What knowledge and skills does the social worker need to meet the standards of practice?" The answer becomes clear when we understand what constitutes social work practice. The National Association of Social Workers provides the following definition of social work practice:

> Social Work is the professional activity of helping individuals, groups, or communities to enhance or restore their capacity for social functioning and to create societal conditions favorable to their goals.
>
> Social work practice consists of professional application of social work values, principles, and techniques to one or more of the following ends: helping people obtain tangible services; providing counseling and psychotherapy for individuals, families, and groups; helping communities or groups provide or improve social and health services; and participating in relevant legislative processes.
>
> The practice of social work requires knowledge of human development and behavior; of social, economic, and cultural institutions; and of the interaction of all of these factors. (NASW, 1973: 3-4)

The National Association of Social Workers also delineates the primary goals of social work practice (NASW, 1982) as the attempt to:

1. enhance people's problem solving, coping, and developmental capabilities.
2. link people with systems that provide them with resources, services, and opportunities.
3. promote the effective and humane systems that provide people with resources and services.
4. develop and improve social policy.

As you reflect on the definition of social work and the goals of social work practice, you may begin to see that the depth and breadth of knowledge and skills required for effective practice is quite expansive. We can easily understand now why the NASW Code of Ethics mandates continued knowledge and skill acquisition in order to engage in effective professional practice. The helping professional needs a solid body of knowledge upon which to build a practice. Briar, commenting on the depth and breadth of this knowledge base, states:

> An expanding diversity characterizes many aspects of social work practice today. This is evident in the variety of fields of practice, the wide array of theoretical orientations and intervention approaches, and the increasing range of research tools to advance the knowledge base for practice. (Briar, 1987: 393)

Recent research (Saltman and Greene, 1993) indicates that the content of human behavior courses changes over time and reflects current thinking regarding which approach or approaches should be included in human behavior curricula. Interestingly, this research found that for practicing social workers the theoretical frameworks of human behavior and related practice models taught in their graduate education programs were maintained over time despite the introduction of new concepts in social work literature and practice. For example, the majority of practitioners surveyed, who received their Master of Social Work degrees in the 1960s, stated that they were using psychoanalytic or Neo-Freudian theory as the basis of their practice. Those respondents who graduated in the 1970s were also using psychoanalytic and Neo-Freudian theory, but they were using existential and systems theory more frequently. The 1980 graduates surveyed were predominantly using systems theory and Neo-Freudian theory as their base of practice. These researchers concluded that social workers need to learn multiple theories of human behavior in the educational process and that these should be taught in a context that includes an understanding of human diversity.

It is important to note, however, that not all theories of human behavior are complementary—some, in fact, contradict each other. Social workers may use a variety of theoretical approaches. These theories need to form a unified approach within a social work perspective. This perspective will be discussed later in this chapter.

The study of human behavior and its relationship to the social environment is the basis for all areas of social work practice. Human behavior is rich and complex. Many factors are involved when we consider any life situation. Social work practice ranges on a continuum from direct service with individuals to national legislative advocacy. Efforts to provide help must grow out of the ability to understand practice situations accurately. We must also be able to identify the resources available to resolve problems, as well as the obstacles that impair or prevent healthy functioning. Whether we are providing counseling to a depressed child, advocating increased mental health funding, or designing an effective child mental health delivery system, an understanding of persons and their interaction with their social and physical environment is essential to the process.

Although this book will focus primarily on knowledge as a component of effective helping, knowledge is only one of four essential components of helping. These essential components are: (1) having a commitment to helping others; (2) having and using the knowledge needed to understand all significant aspects of a practice situation; (3) showing **competency** in the use of intervention skills; and (4) using knowledge and skill in ethical ways within the value base of the helping professions.

In addition to knowledge, the practice of social work requires commitment. The complexity of the personal and social problems people face today makes many demands of the person who wishes to provide help to those seeking it. First, we must be committed to helping those in need. This commitment cannot be taught, but it can be learned through the process of living. It must come from within the helping person and is related, at least in part, to one's ability to be empathetic and caring. Without such a commitment, the problems our clients present, and the obstacles we encounter in our helping efforts, may leave us feeling hopeless. Second, we must be committed to lifelong professional growth, which includes continually seeking opportunities to increase our professional knowledge and skills. Effective helping skills are developed through continued education, supervision, and practice.

When social workers interact with or on behalf of a person, they become a part of that person's social environment and in doing so have a direct or indirect impact on their lives. The knowledge and skills social workers acquire in conjunction with the role they play as helpers places them in an influential position in relation to that person. Given that social workers are in such a position, the profession mandates that they use the knowledge and skills they have acquired in an ethical manner. As social workers continue their professional education, they find that social work values, methods, and knowledge will assist them in their development as competent and ethical practitioners.

Exhibit 1 at the end of this chapter provides an opportunity for reflection upon the personal and social forces that combined to create the tragic life and death of Yummy Sandifer. What can account for a child who is capable of acts of great kindness and equal cruelty? Alex Kotlowitz, in his book *There Are No Children Here* (1991), provides a moving narrative of the lives of two boys growing up in Chicago's Henry Horner Homes. Children like Yummy grow up in extremely difficult and dangerous circumstances. Singer and co-workers (1995: 481), in studying adolescents' exposure to violence, found "that substantial percentages of adolescents had been exposed to violence as either victims or witnesses, and such exposure was reliably associated with psychological trauma (depression, anxiety, dissociation, and posttraumatic stress)." DuRant et al. (1994) found that symptoms of depression and hopelessness were found to be associated with self-reported use of violence within a sample of urban African-American adolescents. Further research demonstrates the link between emotional problems of children and the social-environmental (poverty, violence, discrimination) context in which they live and suggests the need for the person-in-the-environment perspective as necessary to assist troubled children (Proctor et al., 1993). Could the fate of Yummy and his victims have been changed? If it had been possible, it would have required an understanding of the multiple social forces that resulted in these children's deaths and the commitment and skill to alter them. The study of human behavior is the basis for both individual helping and social policy directed at changing detrimental social structures that create poverty, racism, and other forms of oppression.

SOCIAL WORK PERSPECTIVES

The profession of social work seeks to understand human behavior by utilizing particular theoretical perspectives. Social work theory and practice utilize an **ecological perspective**, such as the one suggested by Germain and Gitterman (1986), Hartman and Laird (1983), and Pardek (1988). Using this approach, social workers view human behavior from an holistic perspective as developing from a complex interplay of biological, psychological, social, economic, political, and physical forces. Human beings develop and adapt through transactions with all elements in their environment. People are involved in dynamic and reciprocal interactions with persons and forces within their environment (Zastrow, 1995: 24). These transactions are not always mutually beneficial or entered into with equal power and status. From a social work perspective, therefore, theories of human behavior must take into account these interacting influences in order to be useful.

The profession of social work has historically focused on person–environment transactions. Social work promotes the interaction between individuals and their environment for the betterment of both. Therefore, the focus of social work intervention can be with the individual, the environment, or the interaction between the two. The person-in-environment perspective of social work requires a **holistic view of human behavior.** Such an approach attempts to understand an event or behavior in its larger context. In other words, the social worker attempts to understand the interplay of personal, interpersonal, and social factors that affect the current situation. For instance, to have helped Yummy Sandifer, or the thousands of other traumatized children in similar situations, would have required the holistic approach of social work to address his needs for nurturance, emotional support, housing, education, health care, and financial well-being. A social work approach would also address the similar needs of Yummy's caregivers and his community. Social work also mandates that the professional understand and change the larger political, social, and economic forces that have converged to place Yummy at risk. In such a situation a social worker would attempt to put together a package of services to address all of these needs, through intervention at multiple levels. Specific resources, such as medical care or housing, would be provided by other helping professions in conjunction with social work services. Making sure that all of these professionals work together in an integrated fashion would be the task of the social worker.

Social work also grounds practice in a health perspective that focuses on the interaction between people and their environment (Weick, 1986). The health perspective views people as agents of change who need resources, support, and knowledge so that they can make choices that will better enable them to function in their environment. It articulates a belief in the capacity of people to become more fully human and in the dignity that is inherent in this capacity. The health perspective emphasizes a growth orientation and assumes that the person strives for a state of wellness. The health perspective is understood better when compared with a biomedical model, upon which some human development theories and intervention practices are based. The medical model, for example, locates problems primarily within the person. The health perspective locates problems in people–environment transactions (Kagel and Cowger, 1984). In Table 1.1, comparing the two perspectives, you can see that the biomedical model seeks a specific cause (disease) for a problem that is solved by experts who are problem-focused. Whereas the biomedical perspective has a narrow focus and considers professionals to be the primary agents of change, the health

TABLE 1.1 The medical and health models compared

	Biomedical Model	Health Model
Primary emphasis	Study of treatment of disease	Study and promotion of health
Orientation toward	Diseases as derangement of body	Ill health as expression of imbalance among interacting environments
	Health as absence of disease	Health as expression of optimal well-being
Causality	Attempt to locate specific cause in biochemical and organic functioning of body (reductionist)	Recognition of patterns among levels of influence (holistic)
Nature of intervention	Provision of externally produced cure	Stimulation of internal healing capacity
Role of professional	The agent of externally produced cure	The facilitator of healing process
Role of patient	Passive but cooperative recipient of medical intervention	Active director of the healing process
Role of society	Disease is a private business; society shoulders some of the costs in its welfare function	Health is the public's business; society is responsible for creating healthy environments

From: Ann Weick, "The Philosophical Context of a Health Model of Social Work," *Social Casework,* Nov. 1986, Families International, Inc. Reprinted by permission of publisher.

perspective views people themselves as able to manage their own lives. The role of the professional is to provide the resources people need, whether they be personal (such as information or counseling) or environmental (such as access to job training or housing).

We now turn our attention to the **strengths**-based practice in social work. Ann Weick (1992) outlines three assumptions that form the core of a strengths perspective. First, every person has an inherent power that may be characterized as life force, transformational capacity, life energy, spirituality, regenerative potential, or healing power. Second, a strengths perspective assumes that these powers are a strong form of knowledge that can guide personal and social transformation. Third, a strengths-based practice assumes that when people's positive capacities are supported, they are more likely to act on their strengths. By focusing upon people's resources, talents, experiences, and aspirations, the probability of positive growth is enhanced. Weick contrasts the strengths perspective with the traditional problem-solving model that has dominated much of social work practice. The focus of the problem-solving model is to restore a client's problem-solving abilities. This model differs from the strengths perspective in that it assumes the client has impaired or undeveloped problem-solving skills and places the social worker in an educational and restorative role. Weick also suggests that inherent in the problem-solving model is the premise that the practitioner must diagnose the problem and provide a cure. In contrast, the strengths perspective suggests that "each person already carries the seed for his or her own transformation" (Weick, 1992: 25) and the social worker's gift is a steadfast belief in that potential. It should be noted here, however, that the social work perspective does not suggest that the primary focus of work is on changing the individual. The social work axiom of "starting where the client is" should not be misinterpreted to suggest that we accept the client as deficient in his or her present state and in need of our assistance in becoming something more. Social work practice focuses upon assisting clients in negotiating their environment, which may or may not necessitate personal change. Social workers support clients as they seek to meet their goals. In many situations, the client is only in need of a specific resource. In other situations, where clients may have been denied resources because of discrimination, the focus is on assisting the client through advocacy.

The sociologist C. Wright Mills (1971) made a distinction between private troubles and public issues. The concept of *private troubles* refers to those inter- or intrapersonal experiences that are problematic, such as relationship conflicts, death of a family member, or the stress of a family without housing. *Public issues* refers to those problems related to the larger society, its policies and institutions. Circumstances such as high unemployment, lack of affordable housing, and health care fall into the realm of public issues. Social workers frequently deal with private troubles that are at least in part due to public policy. The child welfare worker who insists that an angry and acting-out child who has had multiple workers and foster care placements must learn to adjust within the system is suggesting that the deficit is in the child's coping abilities and not within the child welfare system. That worker is placing the burden of change on the child and not on the system that promotes the acting-out behavior. A strengths perspective might view this child as having tremendous perseverance in spite of well-intentioned but ineffective systems of care. Social work has a dual role of assisting the person in utilizing personal and social resources while simultaneously changing oppressive systems that have a negative impact on individuals and their development. A final note regarding strengths-based practice is provided by Saleebey when he states:

> Social work, like so many other helping professions, has constructed much of its theory and practice around the supposition that clients become clients because they have deficits, problems, pathologies, and disease; that they are, in some critical way, flawed or weak. This orientation is rooted in the past where certainties and conceptions about the moral defects of the poor, the despised, and the deviant held thrall. More sophisticated terms prevail today, but the metaphors and narratives that guide our thinking about our clients are essentially negative constructions that are fateful for the future. The diction and symbolism of weakness or deficit shape how others regard clients, how clients regard themselves, and how resources are allocated to groups of clients; in the extreme, they may lead to punitive sanctions. (Saleebey, 1992: 3)

Some of the terms that are common in our practice today are co-dependent, dysfunctional family, adult children of . . . , unwed mothers, parentified child, borderline personality, conduct disorder, and adjustment disorder. This list goes on and on. Terry Grundy, a United Way planner in Cincinnati, recently suggested in a lecture that when we cannot utilize any of these labels, we employ the catchall phrase of "at risk," which usually means that while no problem presently exists, professionals have found that a sufficient number of indicators are present to suggest that a problem is likely to occur. This orientation is clearly visible within most social history and service plan formats that focus most of our attention on problems, deficits, and failings and then append a small section called "*strengths.*" This format orients the client's and worker's focus more on what the client does not do or does poorly, rather than on what the person does well. To maintain a strengths perspective in light of the vast amount of deficit-based theories and practice methodologies is quite difficult for both the beginning and the experienced social work practitioner.

The strengths and health perspectives, within the context of an ecological model, lead to the concept of **empowerment**. Labonté (1990) suggests a transitive and intransitive definition of empowerment. The transitive use of the verb indicates a bestowing of power from one person to another. The intransitive verb usage means to gain or assume power. Empowerment exists on three levels: on the intrapersonal level, it is the experience of a potent sense of self, enhancing self-esteem and self-efficacy; interpersonally, it is the construction of knowledge and social analysis based upon personal and shared experiences; and within communities, it is the cultivation of sociopolitical gains. The following list from the Heart Health Inequalities II Workshop (Health Promotion Directorate, 1989) provides a continuum of empowerment activities in which persons and professional helpers may be involved to promote personal transformation and social change:

Personal empowerment
Small group development
Community organization
Coalition advocacy
Political action

Labonté (1992: 10) lists the following helping strategies that support the empowerment continuum activities as they relate to health care:

Personal empowerment:	Developmental casework
	Enhancing personal perceptions of control and power
Small group development:	Improving social support
	Promoting personal behavioral change
	Providing support for life style change
Community organization:	Developing local action on community-defined health issues
	Critical community/professional dialogue
	Raising conflict to the conscious level
Coalition advocacy:	Lobbying for healthier public policies
	Achieving strategic consensus
	Collaboration and conflict resolution
Political action:	Support for broad-based social movements
	Creating a vision of a sustainable, preferred future
	Enhancing participatory democracy

The empowerment process is not necessarily a linear process moving from personal empowerment to political action. For example, a person who becomes involved in a community organizing effort to clean up his or her neighborhood may become aware of personal strengths and talents, and in the process feels more capable. In another situation, a man who joins a support group for gay males becomes aware of the need for coalition building and political action.

The empowerment perspective, coupled with the strengths perspective, gives rise to radically different concepts of human development and the social work role. These concepts coincide and lend support to much of the postmodern and feminist perspectives on theory and practice in social work literature.

Saleebey asserts that the empowerment agenda is critical in social work with the vulnerable and marginalized people whom we serve.

> The empowerment agenda is not based on returning power to the people, but on discovering the power within the people (individually and collectively). To discover that power, we must subvert and abjure pejorative labels; provide opportunities for connection to family, institution, and community; assail the victim mindset; forswear paternalism (even in the most benign guises); and trust people's intuitions, accounts, perspectives, and energies. Empowerment is aimed not only at reducing the sense and reality of individual and community powerlessness, but also at helping people discover the considerable power within themselves, their families, and their neighborhoods. (Saleebey, 1992: 8)

Social workers, however, must be cognizant of the considerable power held by systems that victimize people. Even when joined with others in efforts to combat injustice, competent people may not have the power to overcome the oppressive power held by persons, groups, and organizations.

In summary, the perspectives discussed above are the basis of contemporary social work practice. Theories of human behavior and intervention should possess these elements:

1. A health orientation, in which people, groups, or communities are seen as striving for health and wholeness.
2. A growth orientation, with people, groups, or communities seen as positively goal-directed.
3. An ecological perspective, with people, groups, or communities seen as influenced by multiple and interacting factors.
4. A strengths perspective, in which people, groups, or communities are seen as possessing all that they need for their own transformation.
5. An empowerment perspective, focusing on an interactional process in which all parties discover, support, and enhance personal and communal power and growth.

ISSUES IN SELECTING KNOWLEDGE

Each person's behavior, including his or her thoughts and emotions, is the result of many experiences and influences both from the past and the present. Therefore, all knowledge may be potentially useful, but because we are capable of accessing and assimilating only a fraction of all available knowledge, we need tools to use in selecting knowledge upon which to build our practice. The authors suggest the framework below for organizing types of knowledge so that the role of each type in practice can be appreciated.

Types of Knowledge

Empirical	Personal	Communal	Philosophical
	Specialist	Generalist	
	Explanatory	Interventional	

All of these types of knowledge will be discussed in this chapter and referenced in later chapters.

Empirical Knowledge

Empirical knowledge is based on the scientific method of inquiry. It relies on our senses—things we can hear, taste, touch, see, and smell. Empirical knowledge is that which we can measure in some concrete way. For example, we can measure the volume of water in a glass, the number of people who answer yes to the same question, or the accuracy with which a person views an eye chart.

People tend to use empirical knowledge when they want to "prove" something. In everyday life we argue over what was in a newspaper article and resolve the dispute by getting the paper and looking at what was written. The disputed statement is either there or it is not. The scientific method is employed when we wish to verify consistency of phenomena. The sciences adopt this same basic approach, although with considerably more sophistication. The biological, physical, social, and behavioral sciences all attempt to measure objects of interest so that they can be accurately perceived and counted. Biologists count the number of white cells in blood, physicists measure the speed of light, and sociologists determine what health care services a particular group of persons is most likely to utilize. All are efforts to measure the behavior of objects in the real world. Empirically measured information is usually called data and is considered to be fact when repeated measurements yield the same result. Because of its emphasis on measurable fact and proof, the empirical approach is sometimes also called a positivist approach.

The sciences use measurement to find predictable patterns of behavior in the physical and social worlds. It is these patterns upon which decisions are based. People who have a reduced number of white blood cells may have a particular illness; this is based on voluminous research that has shown a predictable relationship between reduced white blood cells and a particular illness. Learning that millions of people lack health insurance has led to repeated attempts for government provision of universal health care coverage. The argument for government-subsidized universal health care coverage might be based upon sociological and epidemiological research demonstrating that those who do not have affordable access to routine health care are more likely to become ill; and left untreated, these cases will be more costly than if preventative health care services had been provided. Employers might find it less costly to provide health insurance to their employees than to lose worker production time when they become seriously ill.

Helping professionals use empirical knowledge extensively. We have clients fill out questionnaires to provide basic demographic information, such as age, race, income, educational level, and marital status. This information is often used in social research to determine if certain demographic variables are correlated with a particular behavior, cluster of behaviors, or unmet needs. Social workers also study the literature to learn how others have solved problems that they may be facing; they examine research data so that they are sensitized to existing problems and needs. Is the incidence of teenage pregnancy increasing or decreasing? What variables are related to such an increase or decrease? What interventional methods or policy initiatives might be most effective in reducing teenage pregnancy if that is the desired social outcome? What resources are needed by young parents and their children in order to lead fulfilling lives? Practitioners also count events in their own practice so that they can fill out reports for the agencies for whom they work, or they collect data that they can use to advocate for particular legislation. Funders of social service initiatives, wishing to determine a program's effectiveness, may utilize various research methods and tools. The utilization of the scientific method can be an important means of protecting persons from ineffectual or harmful treatment whether considering a new medicine in the treatment of an illness or the practice methods of a helping profession. Empirical data, then, are of great importance in social work practice, both in the area of understanding human behavior and in the development of effective helping strategies. Empirical research and the knowledge based on it are not free of subjective bias, however. Research decisions about what subject will be studied and how it will be examined already contain elements of subjectivity and choice. As we will see in Chapter 2, when discussing systems theory, the preconceptions of the researcher will determine not only the research design but also the eventual findings. The interpretation of data is another area in which the biases and preconceptions of the researcher can influence summary findings. Additional concerns regarding the limits and abuses of scientific knowledge will be discussed in the following section.

Philosophical, Personal, and Communal Knowledge

Philosophical knowledge attempts to understand universal and individual experience through reflective thought rather than through the measurement of actual behavior of people or objects. Philosophical knowledge is possible because of the unique ability of human beings to think and to be conscious of themselves. Freire (1993: 3) suggests that "to be human is to engage in relationships with others and the world. It is to experience that world as an objective reality, independent of oneself, capable of being known. . . ." He further suggests that people are beings of relationships and that they apprehend reality through critical reflection, and through that reflection discover their own temporality: "Transcending a single dimension, they (humans) reach back to yesterday, recognize today, and come upon tomorrow. The dimensionality of time is one of the fundamental discoveries in the history of human culture" (Freire, 1993: 3).

Philosophical knowledge is possible because our consciousness of ourselves as beings in historical time allows us to remember, retell, perceive present reality, and await future events. Philosophical knowledge is our attempt to provide a context for these human, historical events.

The ability to reflect allows human beings to process their own images of reality and to construct its meaning. For example, Victor Frankl, in *Man's Search for Meaning* (1959), notes that the atrocities inflicted on the inmates in Nazi concentration camps were designed not only to annihilate the body but also to destroy the human spirit. Yet men and women were able to rise above their suffering and to live and die with dignity, even when no dignity was afforded them. Through their minds they created a spirit that did not exist in the empirical, measurable world, but which nonetheless sustained them.

It is important to note that the Nazis used Darwin's scientific thought to justify the extermination of "non-Aryan" people. Shipman states: "Human evolution had been politicized in Germany as early as the first introduction of Darwin's words into that nation. . . . race science, as some called it, took on a momentum of its own, gathering speed and power as it was appropriated by the Nazi party. Medical practitioners and physical anthropologists became race scientists . . . transforming warped beliefs about race into terrible implementation of 'public hygiene measures' that marched, inexorably toward the ultimate evil" (1994: 145). In such situations, philosophical knowledge could provide an important balance to scientific knowledge. Philosophical knowledge may be utilized to place scientific endeavors in context, as in the case of genetic engineering.

Social work and other helping professions have access to a vast amount of intervention and helping knowledge. However, the act of social helping is based upon certain philosophical assumptions. Reamer states:

> The principal aims of any profession rest on core assumptions about missions, methods, and conceptual orientation. In short, the heart of any profession consists of a philosophically oriented statement of purpose and perspective. . . . In some respects the pursuit of philosophical questions and issues may seem like an exercise in intellectual gynmnastics, removed from the immediate, pressing, and daunting demands faced by contemporary social workers. . . . In the end, however, we cannot ignore the primary questions, questions that move social workers in the first place to be concerned about starving children, or any other vulnerable group. If social work is to enhance its own knowledge base as it continues to mature as a profession, it is essential for the profession to examine, shape, and clarify its key philosophical assumptions. (Reamer, 1993: xii–xiii)

At the heart of many social policy debates are basic philosophical differences about the nature of people and the individual's relationship to the state, usually termed the *social contract*. The recent promotion of the Republican party's "Contract with America," for example, is based upon a belief that individuals are

1 / HUMAN BEHAVIOR AND EFFECTIVE PRACTICE

responsible for their own lives, and the state has minimal obligations to support or intervene with individuals. A series of philosophical questions may pertain to the issue of genetic engineering. What are human persons? What part of our humanness is genetic? Do we have a right or an obligation to alter our genetic makeup? Who should decide these questions—individual persons, the scientific community, or the state? Questions of ethics, of personal rights and responsibilities, of social obligation, and of the nature of human persons are just a few of the philosophical issues that provide a foundation for social work practice.

Although they are quite different, an important link exists between empirical and philosophical knowledge. It is the ability of people to think logically, reflectively, creatively, and intuitively about themselves and their environment that makes it possible to imagine previously unknown links among elements of the real world. In some instances, once these ideas have been generated, empirical methods can be used to determine whether the relationship actually exists. The testing of new treatment possibilities for diseases results from the systematic thinking about what curative agents might be effective. Of course, there are still relationships that can logically be deduced as true but that cannot be proven empirically because of limitations in our measurement tools.

Roberta Wells Imre illustrates how philosophical and empirical knowledge is vital to social work practice. She points out, however, that the philosophical base for social work practice has been sorely neglected in the literature. Referring to the philosopher Martin Buber's I-Thou and I-It thinking about relationships, she states:

> Human beings of necessity move back and forth between the worlds of I-It and I-Thou. It is the uniquely human quality of I-Thou relationships, however, that can be overlooked and quite possibly jeopardized in social work practice when only that which can be perceived within a conceptual framework acceptable to a positivist science (e.g., the empirical approach) is considered to be knowledge. . . . Social workers need to awaken out of acceptance of the basically positivistic position that there can be a clear-cut separation between knower and what is known, between facts that tell how the world is and what is considered to be good and valuable. In human lives empirical evidence counts; it is not all that matters. A profession intrinsically concerned with human beings requires a philosophy of knowing capable of encompassing all that is human. The language of philosophy is needed in order to address questions about what it means to be human. (Imre, 1984: 44)

In this statement, Imre notes that relationships between people are of critical importance to them and to our efforts to understand people. It is not just people in relationship to the physical world or to formal structures that are important. Furthermore, many questions can only be pondered, not proven. What is the meaning of life? What should the fundamental relationship of people be to each other? What is right or wrong in daily living? These questions may be addressed quite differently by persons, cultures, and legal structures. The answers, however, remain "unprovable" through empiricism. Although we cannot measure and prove these dimensions of existence, their importance cannot be ignored. Philosophical knowledge enables us to think about such issues in constructive ways, and Imre implores us not to limit our thinking only to that which is empirically provable.

Personal knowledge is the body of knowledge that develops from one's own experience. Communal knowledge may be viewed as knowledge that is jointly held by a group of persons and is often contained within that group's culture. The validity of such personal and communal knowledge is often suspect in that it lacks the objectivity of the scientific method. These sources of knowledge, however, are becoming the focus of current social work literature. This body of literature grows out of postmodern thought. The modern, or Enlightenment, era of Western Europe, beginning with the astronomer Galileo and the philosopher Descartes, attempted to understand the universe in rational, mathematical, and empirical terms. Beginning with new discoveries in the physical sciences, the "postmodern era" of the mid-twentieth century soon influenced literature, theology, philosophy, and the social sciences. Quantum mechanics theory, the relativity theory, and the chaos theory have challenged preexisting rationalist notions of the stability and predictability of phenomena. In physics, the Heisenberg Uncertainty Principle suggests that the act of observing alters the behavior of what is being observed (Spielberg and Anderson, 1987). A similar phenomenon was discovered in the social sciences in the 1920s. Elton Mayo and his colleagues were studying the physical features of the work setting (lighting and rest periods) that might affect worker productivity at Western Electric Company's Hawthorne plant. The researchers found that the most important factor that improved productivity was that the workers felt that they were receiving special interest from the company (Mayo, 1945). The Uncertainty Principle and the Hawthorne effect suggest that many research designs contain within them the contaminating effect of the observer's presence.

Michel Foucault's analysis of both historical texts and social institutions demonstrates the relativity of all knowledge (including research) and suggests that both are constructed in a manner that maintains the power of the dominant culture. Foucault asserts that the main texts (writings, philosophies, theories, and institutional structures) available are products of those in power. The result is that differing "texts" or visions of reality become subjugated and, therefore, are considered of little value. He states:

> Subjugated knowledges are thus those blocs of historical knowledge which were present (at any given time) but disguised with the body of functionalist and systematizing theory. . . . I believe that by subjugated knowledges one should understand something else, something which in a sense is altogether different, namely, a whole set of knowledges that have been disqualified as inadequate to their task or insufficiently elaborated; naive knowledges, located low down on the hierarchy,

beneath the required level of cognition or scientificity. I also believe that it is through the re-emergence of these low ranking knowledges (such as that of the psychiatric patient, or the ill person, or the nurse, or the doctor—parallel and marginal as they are to the knowledge of medicine) and which involve what I would call a popular knowledge . . . a local, regional knowledge, a differential knowledge incapable of unanimity. . . . (Foucault, 1980: 82)

Gorman (1993: 249) suggests that a parallel shift has occurred in the social sciences—a pervasive turn away from methodological approaches designed to establish the "truth" of propositions toward a more relativist stance, which encourages the exploration and expression of multiple voices and multiple realities that were marginalized by the modernist search for a "grand theory" that could explain all physical relationships. Instead, Hartman states: "We (social workers) must enter into a collaborative search for meaning with our clients and listen to their voices, their narratives, and their constructions of reality. It is significant that studies grounded in the subject's experience, that speak in the voices of oppressed people, and that promote the insurrection of subjugated knowledge become classics" (1992: 484). Referring to personal and communal knowledge, Graff (1979: 32-33) proposes that emotions, intuition, speculation, personal experience, musing, metaphysics, myths, magic, and mysticism—all devalued by the modernist emphasis on rationality—take on renewed importance.

Reamer summarizes the main tenets of a *naturalistic approach* to social work indicative of postmodern inquiry.

1. *The nature of reality.* There is no single reality. Rather, multiple realities exist that can be understood from varying perspectives.
2. *The relationship between observer and observed.* The relationship between the observer and the observed (researcher–subject, helper-person being helped) is interactional and reciprocal. The process of observation changes both the observer and the observed.
3. *The limits of generalizability.* Research in the area of human behavior is inherently limited. Human diversity does not allow for predictability of individual behavior.
4. *The limits of causal connections.* Straightforward, asymmetrical, and linear causal relationships are nonexistent. Given the complexity of causal connections among the entities that social workers study (clients, interventions, organizations, communities, and demographic trends), it is difficult to distinguish causes from effects.
5. *The relevance of values.* Values influence the initial choice of which problem to investigate (or with whom to intervene), the methods and theoretical framework used to conduct inquiry (or intervention), and the analysis and interpretation of results (or information gathered from persons being helped). (Reamer, 1993: 145-146)

There are many implications of postmodernism for social work sources of knowledge, theory, practice and research. These will be discussed in greater detail in later sections.

Polanyi (1958: 18) states that personal knowledge (what he calls tacit knowledge) is the basis of all objective knowledge (what he calls explicit knowledge). He believes that personal knowledge is gained through true creativity. In other words, it is similar to empirical knowledge because it depends on our sensorial experience. It is, nonetheless, different in that it is not always measurable. Three kinds of personal knowledge are especially important: sentient, experiential, and a priori. Let us consider each one briefly.

Sentient knowledge is defined by Zuboff (1988: 61) as an action-centered skill based upon the sensory information derived from physical cues. It is knowledge held by the body, and such activities as sewing, throwing a curve ball, painting a watercolor, driving a car, typing, and mountain climbing are all possible because of sentient knowledge. In this highly technological age, Zuboff suggests, skills are being lost because of automated production processes as well as through the use of labor-saving devices. Her text asserts that the loss of sentient skills is a profoundly disorienting experience, because they are an extremely important way for human beings to relate to their world.

Child development experts believe that the basis of all subsequent cognitive and abstract learning is sensory experience. Children know the sense of roundness long before they have the language to express it, or before they are able to know abstractly that balls, wheels, balloons, and pies are all round. In Zuboff's study, when workers no longer needed their sentient skills and knowledge in a new "hands off" computerized work world, they became disoriented and alienated from their work. Sentient knowledge is vital to physical and mental functioning and growth. In Polanyi's words, "To be aware of our body in terms of the things we know and do is to feel alive. This awareness is an essential part of our existence as sensuous active persons" (1958: 31). Sentient knowledge is a means of learning about ourselves and our world. It is also an important means of expressing our creativity in work and play.

Experiential knowledge is closely akin to sentient knowledge in that it is derived from contact with the environment. It differs in that the experiences are processed through the conscious mind and need not have been actually experienced by the "knower." For example, people who have been burned by a match know that they will experience similar pain if they enter a burning building. Experiential knowledge allows a person to extrapolate information from one experience to a similar experience. It is also the basis of empathy, an essential element of the social worker-client relationship. Experiential knowledge permits people to relate to another person's perceptions, feelings, and actions, based upon mutual experiences.

A priori knowledge is similar to philosophical knowledge in its attempts to understand both universal and individual experience. It differs from formal philosophical knowledge in that it exists beyond reflective thought, although rational thought may be used to explain a priori knowledge. Campbell (1986: 27) suggests that a priori knowledge is within us from birth. Jung (1968: 50), however, believes that in addition to personal conscious and unconscious processes there exists a collective unconscious. This is comprised of symbols and images rooted in the human psyche. He suggests that the similarities among symbols and myths found in various cultures is evidence of the presence of a collective unconscious shared by humankind. Thus, symbols such as the tree of life and serpents or legends such as the mythic hero, death and resurrection, and feral children speak to a body of knowledge common to all people.

The knowledge contained in symbols and myths may embody a universal understanding of the nature of relationships: person to person, person to nature, and person to the supernatural. This collective knowledge seems to contain within it the "wisdom of the ages." While a priori knowledge can only be inferred by examination of universal symbols and myths, it should be acknowledged as one aspect of personal knowledge. Mythical tales and symbols constantly repeat themselves in literature and art because they convey not only personal but also universal meaning.

Social work practice requires an understanding and utilization of empirical, personal, communal, and philosophical sources of knowledge in relation to the study of human behavior.

Generalist Knowledge

Undergraduate social work education prepares the practitioner for **generalist social work practice**. The generalist nature of this work is due to the purpose of social work, described by Baer and Federico:

> Social work is concerned and involved with the interactions between people and the institutions of society that affect the ability of people to accomplish life tasks, realize aspirations and values, and alleviate distress. These interactions between people and social institutions occur within the context of the larger societal good. (Baer and Federico, 1978: 68)

Utilizing this description of the purpose of social work and joining it with social work perspectives previously discussed, we can state that social work activities generally:

1. Support the problem-solving, coping, and inherent developmental capabilities of people.
2. Promote the effective and humane operation of the systems that provide people with resources, services, and opportunities.
3. Link people with the systems that provide them with resources, services, and opportunities.

This holistic view of human behavior and generalist social work practice flows from the person–environment perspective discussed above. Human life is seen as a totality in which biological, psychological, cultural, and social-structural elements are in constant interaction. It is this complex interaction that social workers use to find the resources that will make possible the desired outcome. This view begins to define the knowledge required so that the complex web of human life is understandable. This concept will be addressed in further detail in the next chapter.

The **generalist** addresses the needs of the whole person and tries to find the package of resources that will address them. In helping someone about to have surgery, for example, the generalist might assist in selecting a competent surgeon, making financial arrangements, finding adequate child care, explaining the need for and procedure of the surgery, providing emotional support to the individual and his or her family, and arranging for posthospital care upon discharge. A social worker may also find it necessary to suggest changes in hospital policies and practices that would further support the patient's well-being. For example, a hospital might better serve its patients through a more flexible visiting schedule for out-of-town visitors or the provision of an interpreter for a non-English-speaking patient or a signer for a deaf patient.

Generalist social workers utilize a wide range of systems and resources in their work, and the knowledge they need is extensive. Zastrow (1995: 81) lists the following areas of required knowledge:

Behavioral factors

Biophysical factors

Cognitive factors

Cultural factors

Emotional factors

Environmental factors

Family systems

Motivational factors

Multifarious systems: economic, legal, educational, medical, religious, social, interpersonal

These same factors form the basis of our understanding of human behavior and will be addressed in the next chapter.

Specialist Knowledge

A **specialist** provides specific kinds of helping services in particular types of situations. For example, a surgeon performs surgery on people who have certain kinds of illnesses. Lawyers often specialize in particular practice areas, such as criminal, civil, or corporate law. Specialized knowledge is needed to provide specialized services. None of us would entrust our body to someone who had not had specialized training to perform the kind of surgery we needed.

Because the focus of the intervention of specialists is fairly narrow, the knowledge they need is easier to identify. Selecting knowledge begins with a specification of the actual tasks that the practitioner will have to perform. A psychiatrist, for example, writes prescriptions, supervises students in training, and practices psychotherapy, which mandates that psychiatrists have medical training, knowledge of teaching and supervisory skills, and a command of theories of psychotherapy. They are not likely to need to possess other kinds of knowledge—resources available for homeless children, how to organize a rent strike, or how to form a self-help group for parents and children with learning disabilities. Specialists, then, focus their search for knowledge in areas related to their practice. A social worker whose practice is primarily with the elderly may need to have specialized knowledge in the physiology of the elderly; medicines and their side effects; personal, family, and social issues facing the elderly; social programs and social services supportive of older persons; and health financing systems. As social workers narrow the focus of their practices with specific populations, they are likely to need more focused knowledge in areas related to that population. It is important to note that the lines distinguishing generalist from specialist social work knowledge are becoming less clear in practice. Generalist social workers often find themselves in a work setting that deals primarily with a specific population. Agencies may have as their mission to serve distinct client populations, such as the elderly, children, families, the homeless, persons with disabilities, and so forth. In these situations the generalist practitioner must know much information about that particular group of persons in order to provide competent service. However, the same values, perspectives, and approaches are consistent in all forms of social work practice.

ACQUISITION, INTEGRATION, AND APPLICATION

Knowledge about human behavior that guides practice is drawn from empirical, personal, communal, and philosophical sources. However, practitioners also utilize explanatory and intervention knowledge.

Explanatory knowledge seeks only to explain a phenomenon, not to change or alter it. The academic disciplines generally seek this kind of knowledge in pursuit of their primary goal: to explain and/or predict human behavior. Applied disciplines, such as social work, do not have as their main focus the explanation of behavior, although explanatory knowledge informs intervention strategies. Social workers primarily seek intervention knowledge that can be used to influence or change human behavior.

Both types of knowledge are useful in practice. Explanatory knowledge guides the professional in answering "why" questions. Why are some people more likely than others to misuse alcohol or drugs? Why do some communities organize to expel the homeless, while others organize to help them? Why are many social welfare benefits so low that they force recipients to continue living in poverty?

Intervention knowledge is called upon in addressing *how* and *what* questions. It is integrated with explanatory knowledge and prior experience so that some change becomes possible. How can self-help groups be organized to help people who are drug and alcohol dependent? What support do communities require when addressing the needs of homeless persons? What financial policies need to be developed to provide a level of income to people so that they can live with dignity? What are the best methods to combat racism, sexism, ageism, homophobia, and discrimination against persons with disabilities? The social worker has a societal mandate not only to understand the human condition, a task shared with the academic disciplines, but also to use that understanding in a disciplined and planned way to influence and change the behavior of (and toward) persons, groups, and communities. Social workers often practice in situations in which the client's participation in the service is not voluntary. Child protective and juvenile justice services, offenders programs, and involuntary psychiatric hospitalizations are examples of practice situations in which the social worker acts as an intermediary between the client and society. In such situations clients may or may not wish to change their behavior, and yet society mandates such change. In these situations social workers find themselves in the paradoxical situation of balancing the profession's practice of supporting the client's right to self-determination and society's expectation of behavioral change or control. Most clearly, in these situations the social worker plays a dual role of support and social control. These roles are not necessarily contradictory, but they are exceedingly difficult to negotiate, requiring not only skillful intervention but also respect of the client's rights. One of these practices is that of "informed consent." In these practice situations the social worker needs to inform the client of the nature of the service to be provided, the roles of the client and the worker, the client's right to refuse services, and the possible consequences of service refusal. Work with involuntary clients often requires specialized intervention knowledge. In other practice situations social workers are called upon to protect and advocate for clients who are being harmed by the many forms of oppression.

Explanatory and intervention knowledge are also closely related in research. Issues that arise from practice situations (intervention) often become the questions upon which future research (explanation) builds. The relationship between knowledge and practice is a reciprocal one. The application of existing knowledge in practice often yields a measure of its accuracy and can serve to identify gaps and weaknesses in our existing knowledge. In return, existing knowledge directs and informs interventions and helps assess why such efforts were or were not helpful.

Knowledge shapes and focuses the social worker's understanding of human behavior and the social environment in three interrelated and cumulative ways:

1. *Acquiring Knowledge.* Knowledge of biological, social, and behavioral science concepts helps to explain the multifaceted dimensions of

individual, group, and social-structural behavior. These concepts come from human biology, anthropology, economics, political science, psychology, and sociology.

2. *Integrating Knowledge.* A holistic view of human behavior results from the integration of concepts from the multiple sources noted above.

3. *Applying Knowledge.* Identifying concepts with particular utility for practice enables integrated knowledge to be applied to concrete situations as part of practice and guides intervention efforts.

The interrelated and cumulative tasks of acquiring, integrating, and applying knowledge give form and substance to the professional's understanding of the dimensions of human behavior. They become the steps through which knowledge about the biological, psychological, cultural, and social-structural bases of behavior directs practice activities.

SUMMARY

This chapter has emphasized the close ties between knowledge and skills that are important to social workers. No matter how much one wants to help others, the development of professional skills grows out of knowledge about the goals people have for themselves, about ways of attaining these goals, factors influencing people's behavior, and the helping process. The discussion of the types of knowledge utilized in social work practice has important implications. Empirical knowledge is a vital source of information in social work in that it provides measured data to support both explanatory and intervention knowledge. It is important to note, however, that empirical research is not without its own particular biases and that these biases often have negative consequences for individuals and groups. Of concern to the social worker is the utilization of empiricism to develop theories of **normalcy** when speaking of human behavior. When a particular behavior is defined as normal, those nonconforming behaviors are often referred to as **deviant** and abnormal. As Foucault (1980) and Hartman (1992) point out, normal and abnormal are usually defined by the dominant culture and can give rise to oppression. It is especially important for social workers to seek to hear and understand the alternative voices of all people and to see them as valid sources of knowledge. The generalist approach to helping emphasizes the person-in-situation, takes a holistic view of behavior, and adopts health, growth, strength, and empowerment perspectives in the helping process. Effective helping occurs only when the many dimensions of the client's situation are understood, considered, and addressed—a perspective that results from the social worker having acquired a wide range of biological, behavioral, and social science knowledge. This range of knowledge will be the focus of the next chapter.

STUDY QUESTIONS

1. One of the best ways to utilize this book is to think of your own life when studying the material. Begin now by asking yourself, "Why am I taking this course?" What events, values, life experiences, social influences, and so forth have come together to bring you to this course? You may use the "why" question to work backwards from the initial question. It may begin something like this:

> "Why am I taking this course?"
> Because it's required to earn my degree.
> "Why do you want your degree?"
> Because . . .

   This exercise may begin to help you understand that many factors (personal, family, social, economic, and cultural) have come together to bring you to this point, and in doing so, help you to appreciate the ecological perspective in the study of human behavior.

2. In order to arrive at this point in your life, you have probably had to overcome many obstacles. Attending to the rigors of academic life also makes it difficult to balance the many demands on your time. What resources (personal, social, familial, economic, emotional, and spiritual) have you had to use in order to accomplish your goals?

3. Read the following scenario and then answer the question that follows.

   A person whose short-term memory begins to fail finds that he is having difficulty remembering appointments, meetings, and work deadlines. He utilizes his extraordinary organizational skills to compensate for his memory loss by keeping an engagement calendar, writing notes to himself, and using a tape recorder while driving in his car to record reminders about work to be done.

   Question: What implications do you think this scenario may reveal for a strengths-based social work practitioner?

4. Read Exhibit 1 at the end of this chapter. Then try to identify the knowledge needed to adequately understand "Yummy" from a person-in-situation perspective. Go on to identify the knowledge needed to intervene in Yummy's situation. Share your ideas with others in the class. Do others share or differ in their ideas and perspectives? Did the sharing process expand or change your perspective? If so, what may the implications be for the client-social worker relationship?

5. In this chapter reference was made to Foucault's concept of "subjugated knowledge" (1980). What do you think some of the implications of this concept might be for the social worker's study of human behavior?

KEY TERMS

Behavior. Any action or response, including observable activity; measurable, physiological changes; cognitive images; fantasies; and emotions.

Competency. The ability to perform a function skillfully.

Deviant. Being different, especially from the norm, usually defined by the dominant culture.

Ecological perspective. A perspective that focuses on the interaction of people and environments.

Empirical knowledge. Knowledge based on direct observation or gained through the scientific method.

Empowerment. Strengthening the ability of people to achieve control of their own lives.

Generalist. A professional helper who addresses the needs of the whole person and tries to find the package of resources that will address the range of needs that people have.

Generalist social work practice. Social work that focuses on the interactions between people and the institutions of society that affect the ability of people to accomplish life tasks, realize aspirations and values, and alleviate distress.

Health perspective. A perspective that views people as agents of change who need resources, support, and knowledge to improve their social fuctioning.

Holistic view of human behavior. A person-in-situation view that sees human behavior as the result of complex interactions among biological, psychological, social-structural, and cultural factors.

Normalcy. The common or natural condition, form, or degree, usually defined by the dominant culture.

Specialist. A professional helper who provides specific kinds of helping services in particular types of situations.

Strengths-based practice. Social work practice that focuses attention on the real strengths of persons, groups, or communities rather than on real or perceived weaknesses or deficits.

REFERENCES

Baer, B. and R. Federico (1978). *Educating the Baccalaureate Social Worker,* Vol. 1. Cambridge, MA: Ballinger.

Barker, R. (1991). *Social Work Dictionary.* Silver Spring, MD: National Association of Social Workers, p. 22.

Briar, S. (1987). *The Encyclopedia of Social Work,* 18th edition, Vol. 1. Silver Spring, MD: National Association of Social Workers.

Campbell, J. (1986). *The Inner Reaches of Outer Space.* New York: Harper & Row.

DuRant, D., C. Cadenhead, R. A. Pendergast, G. Slavens, and C. W. Linder (1994). Factors Associated with Use of Violence among Urban Black Adolescents. *American Journal of Public Health,* Vol. 84, pp. 612–617.

Foucault, M. (1980). *Power/Knowledge: Selected Interviews and Other Writings (1972-1977),* edited by Colin Gordon. New York: Pantheon Books.

Frankl, V. (1959). *Man's Search for Meaning.* New York: Washington Square Press.

Freire, P. (1993). *Education for Critical Consciousness.* New York: Continuum Publishing.

Germain, C. and A. Gitterman (1986). The Life Model Approach to Social Work Practice Revisited. In *Social Work Treatment: Interlocking Theoretical Approaches,* 3rd edition, edited by F. Turner, pp. 618-643. New York: Free Press.

Gibbs, N. (1994). Murder in Minature. *Time,* September 19, pp. 54-59.

Gorman, J. (1993). Postmodernism and the Conduct of Inquiry in Social Work. *Affilia,* Vol. 8, No. 3 (Fall).

Graff, G. (1979). *Literature Against Itself.* Chicago: University of Chicago Press.

Hartman, A. (1992). In Search of Subjugated Knowledge. *Social Work,* Vol. 37, No. 6, pp. 483-484.

Hartman, A. and J. Laird (1983). *Family Centered Social Work Practice.* New York: Free Press.

Health Promotion Directorate (1989). *Heart Health Inequalities II.* Ottawa: Health and Welfare Canada.

Imre, R. W. (1984). The Nature of Knowledge in Social Work. *Social Work,* Vol. 29, No. 1, pp. 41-45.

Jung, C. (1968). *Analytic Psychology: Its Theory and Practice.* New York: Vintage Books.

Kagel, J. and C. Cowger (1984). Blaming the Client: Implicit Agenda in Practice Research? *Social Work,* Vol. 29, No. 4 (July-August), pp. 347-351.

Kotlowitz, A. (1991). *There Are No Children Here.* New York: Doubleday.

Labonté, R. (1990). Empowerment: Notes on Professional and Community Dimensions. *Canadian Review of Social Policy,* No. 26, pp. 64-75.

Labonté, R. (1992). Determinants of Health: Empowering Strategies for Nursing Practice, A Background Paper. *New Directions for Health Care.* Vancouver, B.C.: Registered Nurses Association of British Columbia, p. 10.

Mayo, E. (1945). *The Social Problems of an Industrial Civilization.* Cambridge, MA: Harvard University Press.

Mills, C. W. (1971). *The Sociological Imagination.* New York: Penguin Books.

National Association of Social Workers (1973). *Standards for Social Service Manpower.* Washington, DC: NASW.

National Association of Social Workers (1982). *Standards for the Classification of Social Work Practice.* Washington, DC: NASW.

Pardek, J. (1988). An Ecological Approach to Social Work Practice. *Journal of Social Welfare,* Vol. 15, No. 2, pp. 133-145.

Polanyi, M. (1958). *The Study of Man.* Chicago: University of Chicago Press.

Proctor, E., N. Vosler, and E. Sirles (1993). The Social-Environmental Context of Child Clients: An Empirical Exploration. *Social Work,* Vol. 38, No. 3 (May), pp. 256-262.

Reamer, F. (1993). *The Philosophical Foundations of Social Work.* New York: Columbia University Press.

Saleebey, D. (1992). *The Strengths Perspective in Social Work Practice.* New York: Longman, pp. 3, 8.

Saltman, J. and R. Greene (1993). Social Workers' Perceived Knowledge of Human Behavior Theory. *Journal of Social Work Education,* Vol. 29, No. 1 (Winter), pp. 88-98.

Shipman, P. (1994). *The Evolution of Racism: Human Differences and the Use and Abuse of Science.* New York: Simon and Schuster.

Singer, M., T. Anglin, L. Song, and L. Lunghofer (1995). Adolescents' Exposure to Violence and Associated Symptoms of Psychological Trauma. *Journal of American Medicine,* Vol. 273., No. 6 (January), pp. 477-482.

Spielberg, N., and B. Anderson (1987). *Seven Ideas That Shook the Universe.* New York: John Wiley and Sons.

Weick, A. (1986). The Philosophical Context of a Health Model of Social Work. *Social Casework,* Vol. 67, No. 9, pp. 551–559.

Weick, A. (1992). Building a Strengths Perspective for Social Work. In *The Strengths Perspective in Social Work Practice,* edited by D. Saleebey, pp. 18–26. New York: Longman.

Zastrow, C. (1995). *The Practice of Social Work,* 5th edition. Pacific Grove, CA: Brooks/ Cole Publishing Company.

Zuboff, S. (1988). *In the Age of the Smart Machine: The Future of Work and Power.* New York: Basic Books.

exhibit 1.1

Murder in Miniature: The Story of "Yummy" Sandifer

This story is reprinted from "Murder in Miniature" by Nancy R. Gibbs, Time Magazine, *September 19, 1994, pp. 69-73. Copyright © 1994 by Time/Warner Incorporated. Reprinted by permission.*

On a bright September afternoon last week, the mothers of Chicago's South Side brought their children to a vigil for a dead boy they had never met. They wanted their kids to see the scrawny corpse in the loose tan suit lying in a coffin, next to his stuffed animals, finally harmless. The big kids dragged the little kids up to look at the stitches on his face where the bullets fired into the back of his head had torn through. The only picture the family could find for the funeral program was a mug shot. "Take a good look," said the Rev. Willie James Campbell. "Cry if you will, but make up your mind that you will never let your life end like this."

Parents hoped to haunt their children; maybe fear would keep them safe. Lynn Jeneta, 29, took her nine-year-old son Ron. If he got scared enough, she decided, "maybe then he wouldn't be lying there himself one of these days." She pushed him right up to the coffin. Ron tried to stay calm. "Some kids said Yummy looked like he was sleeping, but he didn't look like he was sleeping to me." What exactly then did he look like? "Kind of like he was gone, you know?" His composure melts. "When Mama pushed me forward, I thought I was going to fall right in the damn coffin. That gives me nightmares, you know? Can you imagine falling into a coffin?"

Many who knew Robert ("Yummy") Sandifer better mourned him less. "Nobody didn't like that boy. Nobody gonna miss him," said Morris Anderson, 13. Anderson used to get into fistfights with Yummy, who received the nickname because of his love of cookies and Snickers bars. "He was a crooked son of a bitch," said a local grocer, who had barred him from the store for stealing so much. "Always in trouble. He stood out there on the corner and strong-armed other kids. No one is sorry to see him gone."

Nor, it seems, was anyone very surprised. The neighborhood was still grieving its other dead child, the girl Yummy allegedly killed two weeks ago, when he was supposed to fire on some rival gang members but shot 14-year-old Shavon Dean instead. Police descended on the gang, and Yummy became a liability. So he became a victim too. When he was found dead in a bloody mud puddle under a railway viaduct three days later, an entire city shuddered and clutched its children and looked for lessons.

The major of Chicago admitted that Yummy had slipped through the cracks. Just what cracks where those? The sharp crevices that trap children and break them into cruel little pieces. Chicago's authorities had known about Yummy for years. He was born to a teenage addict mother and a father now in jail. As a baby he was burned and beaten. As a student he often missed more days of school than he attended. As a ripening thug he shuttled between homes and detention centers and the safe houses maintained by his gang. The police arrested him again and again and again; but the most they could do under Illinois law was put him on probation. Thirteen local juvenile homes wouldn't take him because he was too young.

Before they grow up, these children can become walking weapons. One very mean little boy didn't grow up, so he became an icon instead. The crimes he committed—and those he suffered—shook the country's conscience in a way that violent acts with far larger body counts no longer do. "If ever there was a case where the kid's future was predictable, it was this case," says Cook County public guardian Patrick Murphy. "What you've got here is a kid who was made and turned into a sociopath by the time he was three years old." Yummy's mother Lorina called him, without irony, "an average 11-year-old." The courts and cops and probation officers and psychologists who tracked his criminal career all agree. "I see a lot of Roberts," says Cook County Circuit Judge Thomas Sumner, who handled charges against Yummy for armed robbery and car theft. "We see this 100 times a week," says Murphy.

The proof is in the paperwork—worn folders inches thick, filed at the public guardian's office, the courts, the police headquarters and now the medical examiner's office. Yummy's files are indistinguishable from the records of thousands of other urban American kids. The evidence—if more evidence is really necessary—is overwhelming: when a child's brain is flooded, the child eventually drowns.

That was the verdict of a psychiatric evaluation last November. "Robert is emotionally flooded," the confidential report reads. "His response to the flooding is to back away from demanding situations and act out impulsively and unpredictably." The examiner asked him to complete the sentence "I am very . . ." "Sick," Yummy replied. The examiner saw a child full of self-hate, lonely, illiterate, wary. When he heard a walkie-talkie down the hall, he jumped from his seat, afraid of police. "You tryin' to trick me," he accused the examiner. There was not much doubt about how he came to be that way—only about whether anyone or anything could save him.

Yummy's mother was the third of 10 children from four fathers—she never knew her own. When she was 15 she had her first son Lorenzo, then Victor, then Yummy and eventually five more. She dropped out of 10th grade, found an apartment, went on welfare and nursed a crack habit. For a while she tried living with Yummy's father Robert Akins, who was convicted of drug and weapons charges. They soon split because he had "a rather angry and hot temper," she told a social worker.

So, apparently, did she. The first charge of child neglect was filed in 1984, when Lorina failed to follow doctors' orders for treating two-year-old Victor's eye condition. He eventually went blind. The following year 22-month-old Yummy arrived at Jackson Park Hospital covered with scratches and bruises. A few months later it was his sister, this time with second- and third-degree burns on her genitals. Lorina explained that the toddler had fallen on the radiator. An emergency-room nurse told the court that the injuries did not quite match the story. Someone probably held the child on the heater, the nurse testified.

The courts finally moved in a year later, when neighbors told police that the five children were routinely being left at home alone. By the time they removed the kids, Yummy was a bundle of anger and scars. He had long welts on his left leg; police suspected he was beaten with an electrical cord. There were cigarette burns on his shoulders and buttocks. "I never beat my kids," Lorina insists to this day. She says the scars were caused by chicken pox, not cigarettes. "I gave him all the attention I could," she says of Yummy, but admits there were distractions. Now 29, she has been arrested 41 times, mainly for prostitution.

"He shouldn't be dead," she says, sitting in her living room the day after his funeral. There is a white bucket in the corner with a live frog he caught a few weeks ago. "He liked to fish," she says. "People think he was a monster, but he was nice to me." She says she saw him regularly; he called her Reen instead of Mom, and, she admits, "he was always blaming me" for his problems. "They could have saved him and rehabilitated him," she insists. "When he started taking cars, they should have put him away then and given him therapy."

From early on, the child-welfare workers had little hope for Lorina as a parent. "There is no reason to believe that Lorina Sandifer will ever be able to adequately meet her own needs, let alone to meet the needs of her growing family," a psychiatrist reported to the juvenile court in 1986. And so Yummy and his brothers and sister were placed with his grandmother, Janie Fields, whom Yummy took to calling Mama. Her prognosis as a care giver was not much more promising. The psychiatric report described Fields as "a very controlling, domineering, castrating woman with a rather severe borderline personality disorder."

Neighbors in the black working-class neighborhood called Roseland still remember the day Janie Fields moved into a two-story, three-bedroom house with her brood: nearly all her 10 children and 30 grandchildren lived with her at one time or another. "They are dirty and noisy, and they are ruining the neighborhood," complained a neighbor. Residents launched an unsuccessful petition drive to force Fields out. "All those kids are little troublemakers," said Carl McClinton, 23, who lives down the street. "This is the kind of neighborhood where we all look after each other's kids, but they are a rougher breed."

The neighborhood kids describe two different Yummy Sandifers. There is the bully, the extortionist, the fierce fighter who would take on the big kids and beat them. "Yummy would ask you for 50¢," says Steve Nelson, 11, "and if he knew you were scared and you gave him the money, he'd ask for another 50¢." Erica Williams, 20, a neighbor, says, "You really can't describe how bad he really was. He'd curse you completely out. He broke in school, took money, burned cars."

Others recall a sweeter side. Lulu Washington sells discount candy out of her house, just across from Yummy's. "He just wanted love," she says. For that, he could be disarmingly kind. "He'd say thank you, excuse me, pardon me." He loved animals and basketball and had a way with bicycles. He once even merged two bikes into a single, working tandem. Those were the good times. "It always meant trouble when he was with a group," says Ollie Jones-Edwards, 54. "If he was alone, he was sweet as jelly."

Yummy liked great big cars, Lincolns and Cadillacs, says Micaiah Peterson, 17. "He could drive real well. It was like a midget driving a luxury car." Sometimes he hung out at the local garage, learning about alternators and fuel injectors. When he wasn't stealing cars, he was throwing things at them or setting them on fire. "What could you do?" asks McClinton. "Tell his grandmother? She'd yell at him, and he'd be right back on the street. If the police picked him up, they'd just bring him back home because he was too young to lock up. He was untouchable, and he knew that."

His odds of reaching the age of 12 dropped sharply when he fell in with the local Black Disciples gang. Several thousand or so gang members in Chicago are spread out across separate fiefdoms, led by "ministers" in their 30s and 40s who are always recruiting children. There is plenty of work for everyone: car theft, drug running, prostitution, extortion, credit-card fraud. Police suspect that gang leaders use the little ones as drug runners and hit men because they are too young to be seriously punished if they are caught.

On the other hand, they aren't likely to last long. "If you make it to 19 around here, you are a senior citizen," says Terrance Green, 19. "If you live past that, you're doing real good." A Black Disciple named Keith, 17, describes the role the youngest members play: "He's this small little punk but wants a name, right? So you make him do the work.

'Hey, homey, get me a car. A red car. A red sports car. By tonight. I'm taking my woman out. Or hey, homey, go find me $50. Or hey, little homey, you wanna be big? Go pop that nigger that's messing with our business."

Yummy averaged a felony a month for the last year and a half of his life; 23 felonies and five misdemeanors in all. Ann O'Callaghan, a lawyer and assistant public guardian, met Yummy once, last December in court. She was astonished by his size and demeanor. "Some of these kids we represent are ominous characters. But I had to bend over, and I was like, 'Hi! My name is Ann, and I'm your lawyer.' I couldn't believe it." Yummy wasn't the least bit intimidated by the courtroom. "It was like he was just sitting there waiting for a bus."

Last fall Yummy was placed with the Lawrence Hall Youth Services, which runs homes for troubled teenagers. He ran away in February and went back to his grandmother until June, when he spent two weeks in a detention facility. In July, Yummy and his cousin Darryl went on a church trip to Six Flags Great America, an hour north of the city. "Yummy couldn't get on most of the rides," Darryl says. "He was too small." On another day a neighbor, Ida Falls, took Yummy and 12 other kids to the local police station to see a film on crime. The cops asked her not to bring him back because he got into fights with other children. On Aug. 15 he was charged in another burglary. By Aug. 28 he would be firing the fatal bullets—and it would be too late.

Falls' niece Shavon Dean lived around the corner from Yummy and had known him growing up. One August Sunday night she was sitting in the kitchen eating Doritos, while her mother Deborah was out back grilling ribs and chicken for a family barbecue. Shavon slipped out for a few minutes to walk a friend home. She never made it back.

George Knox, a gang researcher at Chicago State University, believes Yummy was sent on a specific mission of revenge sparked by a drug feud or a personal insult. "If it was just an initiation ceremony, he'd do it from a car. But to go right up to the victims, that means he was trying to collect some points and get some rank or maybe a nice little cash bonus." Yummy opened fire with a 9-mm semiautomatic into a crowd of kids playing football. Sammy Seay, 16, was struck in the hand. "I hit the ground," says Seay. "It was the second or third shot before I knew I had been shot. So I got up and I just ran, trying to save my life." Shavon was struck in the head and died within minutes. "Shavon never got a chance, never got a chance," her mother says.

Yummy spent the last three days of his life on the run. Gang members shuttled him between safe houses and abandoned buildings as police swooped down on the neighborhood, searching for the shooter, followed by a flock of reporters. Gang leaders felt the pressure. "He was like a trapped animal with everyone after him," says Knox. "He was the hunter, and then he was the prey."

Maybe Yummy figured out that the gang's protection was not worth much. Janie Fields last spoke to Yummy Wednesday afternoon before he died. "He said, 'What is the police looking for me for?' I said, 'I'm coming to get you.' I had clothes with me 'cause I knew he was probably filthy and dirty. My heart was racing. I said, 'You ain't done nothing wrong, just let me come and get you.'" The phone went dead. She went to 95th Street, where he said he would be. "He wasn't there."

But he appeared that night on a neighbor's porch, visibly frightened, asking that she call his grandmother so he could turn himself in. He asked if they could say a prayer together. The neighbor went to make the call, and when she came back, he was gone. The police can only guess what happened next. Derrick Hardaway, 14, and his brother Cragg, 16, both honor students and fellow gang members, found Yummy and promised that they could help him get out of town. They drove him to a railroad underpass, a dark tunnel marbled with gang graffiti. Yummy's body was found lying in the mud, with two bullet wounds in the back of his head.

Now it's the Hardaway brothers' turn. Authorities say gang leaders, who can easily order hits in any prison in the state, may have the Hardaways targeted next. Both boys were arrested and are being held in protective custody. As for the other children in Yummy's neighborhood, when they are asked what would make them feel safer, most give the same answer: getting a gun. Among other things, it would protect them from the children who already have them.

There were those who were missing Yummy last week, those who had seen the child and not the killer. "Everyone thinks he was a bad person, but he respected my mom, who's got cancer," says Kenyata Jones, 12. Yummy used to come over to Jones' house several times a month for sleep-overs. "We'd bake cookies and brownies and rent movies like the old Little Rascals in black and white," says Jones. "He was my friend, you know? I just cried and cried at school when I heard about what happened," he says, plowing both hands into his pants pockets for comfort before returning to his house to take care of his mother. "And I'm gonna cry some more today, and I'm gonna cry some more tomorrow too."

chapter **2**

The Integrating Framework

Upon this age, that never speaks its mind,
This furtive age, this age endowed with power
To wake the moon with footsteps, fit an oar
Into the rowlocks of the wind, and find
What swims before his prow, what swirls behind—
Upon this gifted age, in its dark hour,
Rains from the sky a meteoric shower
Of facts . . . they lie unquestioned, uncombined.
Wisdom enough to leech us of our ill
Is daily spun; but there exists no loom
To weave it into fabric; undefiled
Proceeds pure Science, and has her say; but still
Upon this world from this collective womb
Is spewed all day the red triumphant child.

Edna St. Vincent Millay*

OVERVIEW

An intake social worker in a family planning clinic interviews a 35-year-old
woman and her 14-year-old pregnant daughter. The mother is crying and explaining that she has tried to raise her daughter properly but fears she has failed.
She is unsure how to help her daughter, or how she can afford to support
another child in the home.

---

* "Upon this age, that never speaks its mind," by Edna St. Vincent Millay. From *Collected Poems,*
Harper Collins. Copyright © 1939, 1967 by Edna St. Vincent Millay and Norma Millay Ellis.
Reprinted with permission of Elizabeth Barnett, literary executor.

A social worker in a community center that serves a primarily low-income Hispanic population experiences concern regarding a proposed urban renewal project that threatens existing housing in the neighborhood. The residents are becoming increasingly angry over the situation, and tensions are rising.

A social worker with a multiservice agency that provides latchkey services to neighborhood children is confronted with the closing of the program. Agency priorities are being redirected to other programs that are "fundable" under the state's managed-care system.

A social worker working in a home for the elderly is informed by the Residents' Rights Council of the council members' concerns. The Council believes that many of the elderly are not receiving adequate nursing care, that some are being overmedicated, and that the nursing home is not providing an opportunity for residents' personal and social development.

The above examples are representative of the range of practice situations encountered by social workers. Being effective in addressing such diverse problems and needs requires an understanding of the forces, events, and processes that underlie them. In Chapter 1, we raised the question of what knowledge and skills are necessary for beginning generalist social work practitioners to practice effectively in the diverse situations they will encounter. We also discussed the social work perspectives of holism (an ecological approach), health, and strengths as they relate to practice.

In this chapter, we will further develop these concepts and provide a basic framework with which to view the study of human behavior. The framework is a **model**—a way of organizing related concepts and theories. Remember that a model attempts to reflect reality. It is not reality itself. A model in social science endeavors to conceptualize or construct a means of understanding individual and social reality. An inherent danger in attempting to apply models to social reality is a tendency for the observer to see what he or she wants to see or only what the model allows them to see. A clear example of this tendency can be seen in the science of physics and its attempts to understand the physical nature of light. For those who believe that light is a wave phenomenon, experiments can be set up that will prove light has the properties of waves. Conversely, theorists who view light as particles can construct equally valid experiments to prove their hypothesis. A problem arises, however, because within Newtonian physics light can be either a wave or a particle but not both. Later in this chapter, we will discuss the "co-dependency" model and how it frames our perception of a "problem's" origins and its implications for "treatment."

We have presented a model in this chapter to take related concepts from the social, biological, and behavioral sciences and apply them to the situations that social workers encounter in their daily practice—situations such as those described in the short anecdotes that open this chapter. We will also introduce four sources of behavior—the biological, psychological, social-structural, and cultural (including spiritual)—and discuss basic concepts related to each of them. These sources of behavior will be explored further in later chapters. Upon completing this chapter, you will have an assortment of specific concepts and theories to consider. In addition, you will have a way of relating these concepts and theories to each other so that they can be applied in practice situations. As a result, you will be able to view practice situations holistically.

The following example will illustrate why professionals need to integrate knowledge from diverse sources to intervene effectively:

> Mai is a widowed 63-year-old Vietnamese woman who came to the United States in 1987. She lives with her daughter and two teenage grandchildren; her son-in-law was unable to leave Vietnam.
>
> Mai's daughter took her to the neighborhood health clinic, concerned about her withdrawal from the family, except for intermittent outbursts of anger. Mai told her daughter that she had found a lump on her breast several weeks earlier but that she was fearful of discussing it with anyone or seeking treatment. She was also worried about the cost of such treatment. Upon first discovering the lump, Mai used herbal tonic and balms, in the hope that the lump would go away. Finally, her daughter convinced her to seek medical attention.

This vignette illustrates the importance of the practitioner knowing about the interrelated aspects of Mai's situation so that he or she could make an accurate assessment of the issues and intervene in an effective and informed manner. Consider the following dimensions that may influence Mai's situation:

biological (age, gender, physical symptomology)

psychological (fears about treatment and its cost, anxieties about disfigurement, coping strategies)

cultural (beliefs about the use of medicine; the meaning of illness, suffering, and healing);

social-structural (the absence of an adult male in the family unit who, in Vietnamese culture, might be expected to help with such crises; the impact of illness on the family and the community; the availability of culturally acceptable medical treatment; the access to resources to pay for treatment; and the medical establishment's possible lack of personnel who are fluent in her language)

These are all important aspects that need to be considered in making an accurate assessment. To separate one from another would be artificial. Mai's withdrawal from the family and her seemingly uncontrollable outbursts of anger could be a manifestation of her physical illness, or these problems could result from her anxieties about an illness she suspects is serious and fears is terminal. The services of several specialists, such as a physician, an X-ray technician, a nutritionist, and a nurse, might well be called upon in the course of the assessment process. A counseling professional could help explore the impact of the recent move to a new and strange society and the lack of a respected male figure in the household. Advice from Vietnamese professionals who could comment on the cultural dimensions of the changes in Mai's life would be particularly helpful. The social worker would also need to understand as much as he or she could about Vietnamese culture and the challenges facing the Vietnamese immigrant. Lappin and Scott (1992), for example, state that all immigrants struggle with the extremely stressful process of acculturation. The authors suggest that the Indochinese, like many non-English speaking immigrants, find language to be a major problem in the acculturation process. Many adults are forced to rely on their children, who frequently learn the language more quickly, to negotiate their new environment and, thus, this reliance may place stress on the family's authority structure. Mai's situation, involving the possibility of a serious illness without clearly and directly being able to articulate her needs, symptoms, and concerns, would cause much additional stress. If services were requested by the family, the social worker in this case would need to gather all the information available from the diverse sources to make an informed assessment and, in consultation with Mai and her family, to develop a supportive and effective plan of action.

SCREENS AND FRAMEWORKS

A screen is a device used to separate the finer elements from the coarser parts of a substance or, to use a more common expression, to separate the wheat from the chaff. Think for a minute of a screen as a kind of sieve through which ideas filter. Some ideas are filtered out, unable to sift through the mesh. Other ideas filter through easily. The health, growth, strengths, and ecological perspectives presented in Chapter 1 can be thought of as screens through which information and data are filtered. The screen in this instance filters information by asking four questions:

1. Does the information or data focus on health, wellness, and competence, or does it emphasize pathology?
2. Does the information emphasize growth and strengths, or illness and deficits?
3. Does the information consider the multiple dimensions of human behavior, or does it stress only one, such as psychological functioning?
4. Does the information lead to understanding that would promote dignity, respect, and self-determination?

Applying this screen to theories of human behavior that will be presented in succeeding chapters will help to identify, through the filtering process, those theories that might be more appropriate for use in social work's persons-in-environment approach. Such a view is congruent with the value base of the profession, which sees supporting strengths and promoting competence as more effective than focusing on deficits (Weick et al., 1989). This is not to say that the theories these screens filter out are wrong. All knowledge adds to our understanding of the universe we live in, and we must be open to all new knowledge, whatever the source.

The framework presented in this chapter also functions as a screen. It sifts information from the biological, social, and behavioral sciences (especially the disciplines of sociology, psychology, biology, and anthropology) to find concepts, theories, and data that help us to understand how the multiple dimensions of human behavior interact. Our goal in using the framework is to understand human behavior in its wholeness. As we shall see, this understanding includes what people are trying to accomplish in their lives (their life goals), as well as the strategies they are using in trying to attain these goals. Figure 2.1 is a diagram that illustrates how the framework functions as a screen.

Biological, psychological, social-structural (i.e., social institutions such as the family, schools, the military, political organizations, and so forth), and cultural factors, affecting a person's identification of life goals and the strategies used to attain those goals, can serve as either resources or obstacles. **Resources** are factors that facilitate a person's ability to define and achieve life goals, whereas **obstacles** are factors that inhibit goal definition and attainment. Because humans have relatively few genetically programmed reflexes, they are heavily dependent on each other for physical care and social learning. Biological and psychological characteristics that facilitate interaction with others—in some cultures, physical attractiveness (itself culturally defined) and an outgoing personality, for example—are likely to be resources as people attempt to identify their life goals and work toward attaining them. On the other hand, social-structural and cultural conditions that lead to alienation and conflict may impede the formation of fulfilling life goals and behavioral strategies. Prejudice and discrimination illustrate how these social-structural and cultural forces can operate to impede, rather than facilitate, attainment of one's aspirations. Prejudice toward those seen as unattractive and not outgoing frequently results in discrimination toward them.

FIGURE 2.1 Identifying elements of holistic behavior

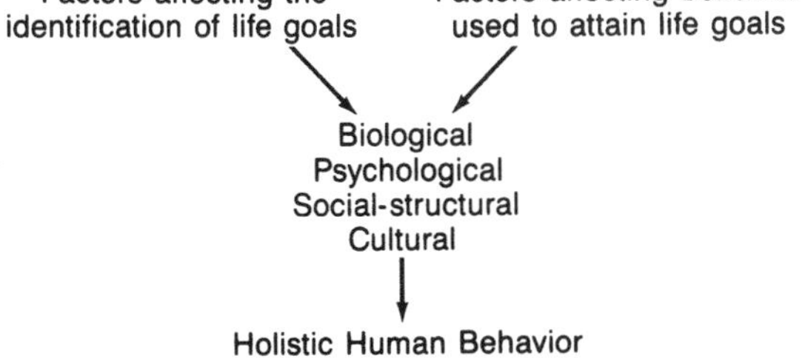

Factors affecting the   Factors affecting behavior
identification of life goals   used to attain life goals

Biological
Psychological
Social-structural
Cultural

Holistic Human Behavior

Keep in mind that the interaction of resources and obstacles is complex and subtle. Anything can be either a resource or an obstacle, depending on the way it is defined and the context in which it occurs. The acquisition of information is usually considered a resource, yet people who have a large amount of information may become frustrated in work situations requiring strict observance of rules and performance of highly routinized activities. However, in another context, the performance of routinized activities, as a means of attaining a higher consciousness, is of great value. Consider that Mohandas Gandhi,[1] in part as a demonstration of his economic beliefs and in part as a source of meditation, spent hours at a spinning wheel, making thread. Physical characteristics, such as blindness, deafness, or quadriplegia, have historically been thought of as obstacles, yet they can also enable a person to find resources of strength, courage, and creativity that would have otherwise been untapped. Indeed, many persons referred to as disabled, handicapped, or challenged resent those labels and point out the many advantages and abilities they possess that others do not.

The framework presented in this chapter requires a careful screening of ideas. The complexity of the interaction of biological, psychological, social-structural, and cultural factors that informs behavior must be approached with sensitivity and without preconceptions about what behavior is "good" or what is "bad." Our task as practitioners is to understand what facilitates or impedes goal definition and attainment. The framework will allow you to sift through resources and obstacles, as long as you do not impose your own biases on the data and thereby limit your ability to analyze the situation. Keep in mind, however, that even as we labor to be aware of and avoid imposing our values, we are often unaware of many of our biases.

THE FRAMEWORK FOR INTEGRATING AND APPLYING KNOWLEDGE

Three parts of the framework will be developed in this chapter to help you view behavior holistically, which means understanding resources and obstacles in biological, psychological, social-structural, and cultural dimensions of behavior. These three parts consist of the following:

1. *Systems.* A systems perspective helps us to maintain a holistic view. It focuses on the whole, and how the parts of the whole interact so that outcomes are affected.
2. *Human diversity.* An understanding of human diversity helps us to see why dimensions of behavior become either resources or obstacles for a person, given his or her characteristics, goals, needs, preferred

---

[1] Mohandas Gandhi sought to free India from English colonialism. He believed that one means to that end was to increase and gain control of the production of indigenous crafts, such as the spinning of thread and the weaving of cloth.

behavior patterns, and environment. How others view diversity is crucial. Being female, African-American, Hispanic, Catholic, or Jewish is merely one aspect of a person's life. How the dominant culture values or devalues him or her determines life chances and choices.

3. *Directionality.* The concept of directionality helps us in our search for purpose and in detecting order and pattern in what sometimes appears to be highly idiosyncratic and even illogical human behavior.

These three components of the framework are illustrated in Figure 2.2.

To illustrate how the framework is applied, try to understand a parent's neglectful or abusive behavior toward his or her children. There are many stresses that lead to the physical or emotional abuse of children. A parent suffering from malnutrition or an illness may lack the energy necessary to perform even minimal parenting tasks. Poverty and unemployment (social-structural factors) may create anxiety and withdrawal that impede the ability to relate to one's own children. These factors may also restrict a parent's access to resources, both physical and emotional, that could provide support in dealing with these highly stressful life experiences. A parent who has high expectations for himself or herself and others may find that a young child's normal behaviors, such as soiling or spilling things are extremely difficult to tolerate. The combination of having high expectations and a lack of understanding of child development and discipline could lead to parental anger and physical punishment. When the parent is overstressed, punishment may become abusive. Cultures differ, however, in

FIGURE 2.2 The three components of the human behavior framework

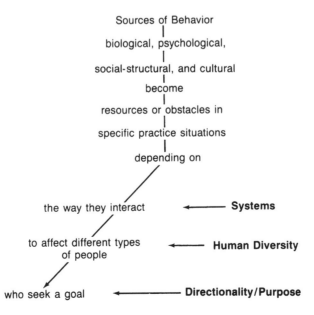

expectations about child development and discipline. What one culture considers abusive, another culture may consider normal parental discipline. Julian, McKenry, and McKelvey found that when socioeconomic status (SES) is controlled, the study of two-parent Caucasian, African-American, Hispanic, and Asian-American families revealed that there were many more cultural similarities than differences in parents' perceptions of childrearing tasks. These researchers found, however, a tendency among the ethnic parents they studied to emphasize self-control and doing well in school as goals for their children. These ethnic parents were stricter—placing greater demands and expectations on their children because of the difficulty they perceived their children would face as they attempt to deal with a bicultural socialization process; in other words, as the children tried to meet the expectations of their own culture and those of the larger society, which is often racially discriminatory. The study suggests that "any assistance must be framed in terms of what these parents perceive as important and must be consistent with the long-term needs of the ethnic family living in a racist society" (1994: 36). These researchers also refer to Slonim (1991), who suggests that Asian-American families in stress may not seek professional assistance because of cultural norms that prohibit discussion of personal feelings or problems. Minorities often report that they do not always feel safe being open with dominant-culture professionals.

The interaction of the above factors (illness, personality, stress, and parental expectations) may exacerbate the effect they have on an individual. Childrearing is a community responsibility in some cultures. Relatives or friends are encouraged to assume child-care responsibilities when parents are having difficulty, lessening the possibility of abuse or neglect. Some cultures prefer to offer struggling parents help by means of a formal social welfare system, leaving the children in the home unless extreme conditions require alternative arrangements. Meeting biological needs, such as adequate nutrition, is also tied to the availability of social-structural resources, such as income assistance or medical care. Psychological problems that impede childrearing may be the result of childhood traumas, current marital or employment difficulties, physical addiction to drugs or alcohol, or even genetic factors. The impact of these problems on the child will be affected by available treatment resources, formal or informal (social-structural), as well as by cultural values that offer possible remedies for such situations.

You can see from this example that human behavior is indeed complex. However, notice how the major elements of the framework are illustrated. The biological, psychological, social-structural, and cultural dimensions of behavior are systematically explored in terms of initiating factors and possible solutions. For example, malnutrition or illness may be a factor in neglectful behavior, because it drains parents of the energy needed to care for children. However, assistance may be available in the form of providing adequate nutrition through increased income, medical care, and so on. Each dimension is viewed as either a possible resource or an obstacle, as we see when cultural values may help stressed parents (by relatives offering child-care assistance) or when they make it more difficult to seek assistance (e.g., when cultural norms do not promote seeking outside help).

In addition, the systemic nature of child maltreatment is illustrated by observing how parenting is affected by such factors as employment, poverty, parental expectations, and psychological functioning. Thus, child maltreatment is itself linked to other behaviors and structures. These linkages will vary for different groups. If parental stress is a major contributing factor, then those families who are experiencing financial difficulties through poverty, unemployment, or underemployment may be at risk for child maltreatment. In another case, parents in a high-income family who have high expectations for their children may find that an underachieving child threatens the parents' self-esteem, a situation which could lead to emotional or physical abuse.

Finally, directionality (purpose) is important. When parents mistreat their children, it is important to determine how this behavior fits into the life goals of the parent. Rarely do parents purposely intend to harm their children. In most cases, they want to be good parents but lack resources or information. This suggests that the use of intervention strategies will help them move toward their goal of competent parenting, rather than the use of punishment for failures that they themselves would like to avoid. In the next chapter, a more detailed discussion of the four sources of behavior—biological, psychological, social-structural, and cultural—will be presented. However, next we will discuss the three components of the framework.

SYSTEMS

A **system** can be defined as a whole made up of mutually interdependent parts. Systems theory states that in any system a change in one part has an impact on the other parts. Systems theory, as it is applied to the social sciences, has strengths and limitations. The language and concepts used in discussing systems theory seem quite mechanical when applied to human interaction. The limitations of systems theory will be discussed later in this section but, for now, however, we will accept that systems theory can be helpful in conceptualizing an ecological or holistic perspective for the social worker.

The idea of systems can be readily grasped by looking at the ecology of our planet. Over the last 15 years, concern has been expressed about the so-called greenhouse effect. Briefly stated, scientists believe that the planet's temperature is rising, a condition that threatens all life on earth. Polar ice caps will melt, causing ocean water levels to rise. Temperature in weather zones will change, thus radically altering earth's fragile ecological balance and threatening all life on the planet.

Rachel Carson (1987), in her book *The Silent Spring,* expresses the concern that the delicate balance of earth's biological life forms is in danger of being lethally altered by pollution and the destruction of natural resources. These life forms can be seen as a system. Cutting down rain forests in South America and

Africa depletes the production of oxygen in the atmosphere and also diminishes the planet's capacity to moderate its temperature, which could thereby negatively affect all life forms. More recently, we have become aware of the hole in our planet's ozone layer, which also threatens our planet's ecology. Scientists suggest that this depletion is caused by the overproduction and overuse of fluorocarbons found in refrigeration systems and the spray cans of various products. Thus, we can see how what happens to one part of a system (for example, destruction of the rain forest or releasing fluorocarbons) affects other parts (the depletion of oxygen and the ozone layer), threatening to extinguish all forms of life.

A system can also be visualized as a series of smaller units nestled inside progressively larger ones. A city that discharges untreated sewage into a river illustrates how one system (the city) affects another system (the ecology of the river), even as both are part of the larger system (planet Earth). Similar relationships can be seen in human systems. Individuals, families, small groups (work, school, and friendship groups), bureaucratic organizations, communities, societies, cultures, and, ultimately, the community of humankind can also be viewed as systems. Each of these entities affects the others, as, for example, when wage decisions made in the workplace affect the income of workers' families. In addition, we can see how larger systems, such as communities, are composed of smaller systems, such as families and other small groups. A systems perspective provides a model that focuses on multiple levels of phenomena simultaneously (families, the workplace, and community life, for example), and it also emphasizes the interaction between behavior units (for example, what happens in families is affected by what occurs in the workplace). The result is that a systems view helps the social work practitioner understand behavior in context and suggests a means by which units of varying size and levels of complexity can mutually influence each other.

CHARACTERISTICS OF SYSTEMS

Boundaries

A system is an organized collection of activities and resources that exists within definable social and physical **boundaries** (Federico, 1984). A person, for example, exists within the physically defined body, whereas a community has both physical (geographical) and social (for example, who interacts with whom) boundaries.

Boundaries regulate the amount of energy (from information, resources, and people) exchanged between a system and its environment. An *open system* allows a constant interchange between the system and its environment. *Closed systems* do not allow the easy exchange of energy, information, and resources across their boundaries. Optimal functioning of systems requires that their boundaries remain flexible. The boundaries of a given system need to be sufficiently open to respond to changing environmental conditions, so that new energy and information can be incorporated, yet be firm enough to maintain the internal integrity of the system.

Meeting the mental health needs of a community provides an example of the role of boundaries. The mental health planner must consider the internal and external pressures, such as economic constraints and political realities, that could make community boundaries more rigid, depending on how they are handled. An illustration of this point is the community reaction to proposed group homes for mentally retarded adults. Often, the prospect of including these homes in a community draws criticism from surrounding residents. In some cases, the community is closed to new information regarding mental retardation, and responses to such homes from community residents are often grounded in fear and prejudice. Other communities are open, accepting of the mentally retarded residents, or are willing to accept new information and resources so that they can welcome these persons into the fabric of community life.

Working with troubled families involves attending to family boundaries. Practice experience tells us, for example, that men who abuse their spouses tend to limit the family's contact with the outside world. In this way they are able to maintain excessive and destructive control over their spouses and children (Jones and Schechter, 1992). Parents with teens may face a very different problem—that of maintaining family boundaries. In some cultures, as teens begin a process of increasing their independence and distance from the family, they begin to alter the established pattern of relationships. Teens may be present less frequently at family gatherings, or the family may have to accommodate their child's new relationships with other teens. In this case, the family has to begin to reconceptualize its view of its boundaries. Conflict may arise when the family attempts to maintain its former boundaries and tries to limit a teen's movement in and out of family life. The adjustment process requires considerable sensitivity on the part of both parent and child; otherwise, both may feel threatened and react with either rejecting or controlling behaviors.

When viewed from a social work perspective, the system seeking help is viewed within its environment. Differentiating a system from its environment is an important part in the assessment phase of the helping process. The concept of boundaries helps in accomplishing this task. In addition to identifying the boundaries of the system itself, any system can also be analyzed in terms of the smaller systems that exist within it. A hospital's social service unit, for instance, may be analyzed as its own system, made up of its own personnel, services, and clients. However, the entire social service unit may itself be part of a larger hospital system that includes many other units—admitting, maintenance, out-patient services, the laboratory, and so on. The hospital is a part of an even larger system—the community's health care system, which includes the hospital, physicians, home health services, and more. The hospital system is also a part of and is affected by the local and national political and economic systems, as evidenced by the ongoing national health care debate. Who will provide care? What care will be available and for whom? How will health care be delivered and financed? Here we see the concept of systems within systems clearly illustrated.

When we analyze systems, the larger system is called the suprasystem, whereas the smaller systems within it are called subsystems. Thus, in the example above, the social service department is a subsystem of the hospital, which, in turn, is a subsystem of the health care suprasystem. This suprasystem has a relationship with the economic and political suprasystems, of which it is a component. This relationship can be both supportive and limiting.

The language of systems helps to clarify the relationship between the boundaries of a system and its component parts and the relationship between the parts themselves. In the case of a hospital social service unit, you might find that tension and stress between the supervisory staff and the direct service workers—that is, between subsystems (parts of the system)—negatively affect its functioning. This situation may have a negative effect on the other systems in the environment of the social service department (such as the nursing department) and, finally, on the quality of service received by individual clients. If poor patient care is prolonged, a hospital's reputation may suffer. Working from the opposite direction—from the suprasystem to the system level—the entire hospital system may be under stress because it lacks adequate resources as a result of activities in the larger political and economic systems.

The concept of boundaries can be readily applied to biological, psychological, cultural, and social-structural systems. The biological structures of cells, organs, and the entire human organism, while interdependent, can be isolated as separate subsystems for independent analysis and treatment by demarcation of their boundaries, such as skin, tissue, and membrane. Such demarcations, however, are always somewhat limiting, because treatment of one bodily system often has side effects on other bodily systems. In the psychological realm, boundaries can be drawn to identify discrete personality traits or the total personality system. Social-structural boundaries can be used to delimit family, political, and economic structures, as well as to identify group, organization, and community variables. Similarly, religious, ideational, and value factors serve to create cultural boundaries.

Purpose

In addition to identifying system boundaries, we are concerned also with system *purposes*. For a system to achieve its goals, balance must be maintained between the components of that system and the environmental forces interacting with it. The concept of *homeostasis* refers to the regulatory process through which the system achieves a state of internal and external balance, or equilibrium. Systems always experience a degree of tension between the need for stability and the desirability of change. For example, the perpetuation of welfare policies that do not adequately meet people's needs ensures the continuation of the welfare bureaucracy but shows little concern for the well-being of those receiving supportive benefits.

Maintaining the integrity of a system is, in and of itself, not enough. Growth and evolution of new and emerging forms are also characteristics of life. The idea of purpose as directing systems to seek change and new experiences, as well as stability, is compatible with social work practice as presented in this text. It is also consistent with the concept of an open system with flexible boundaries. This type of perspective is dramatically illustrated at the biological level by the infinite adaptive arrangements through which the continuation of the species is promoted. Because systems are interrelated (see the earlier discussion of sub-systems and suprasystems), it can be expected that they need to respond to changes in their environment if they are to continue to interact successfully.

Attitudes, ideas, and values related to such fundamental human concerns as family life, sex-role identification, the meaning of work, and the existence (or nonexistence) of a deity form the nucleus around which social and cultural purposes are organized. The excerpt at the end of this chapter from Soshana Zuboff's *In the Age of the Smart Machine* (1988) demonstrates how human behavior is affected adversely when such a fundamental value as the meaning of work is not fully considered. She shows how efforts by management to rectify hazardous situations at a paper mill led to a decline in worker efficiency and satisfaction. When interviewed, employees expressed a feeling of detachment from their work. The workers were no longer as physically involved, using their "hands on" skills and, therefore, felt less pride in their workmanship. Their desire was not to return to unsafe conditions but to incorporate needed improvements in working conditions in a manner that respected their skills and knowledge and that involved them in the reconstruction of their environment. We can see, then, how a sense of purpose is fundamental to human endeavors and that purpose goes well beyond mere homeostasis to include changes in response to changing environments.

Exchange

A third characteristic of systems is **exchange,** the process of interaction between systems through which resources and outcomes are shared. Systems require resources in order to function effectively and achieve their purposes. These resources may be supplied from within the system or from the external environment (other systems). The resources utilized by systems as part of goal attainment are called **inputs.** Conversely, **outputs** refer to the products created by systems after inputs have been used in the system. The biological process of breathing illustrates the relationship between inputs, processing by systems, and outputs. Human beings (biological systems) inhale oxygen (an input) from the atmosphere (an external system). The lungs absorb the oxygen, which is then distributed to the heart and brain through the blood. The system output is energy and life— the ability of the human body to continue to function. A vital aspect of the system is its ability to screen and regulate input. When regulatory processes fail or are overstressed, the system is jeopardized. For example, when hyper-ventilation occurs, breathing becomes too rapid for the body to process all of the oxygen that is inhaled, and serious complications can result. On a psycho-logical level, a person may become overwhelmed emotionally when too many stressful events occur in his or her life. Likewise, a community can become stressed and threatened when too many new residents or businesses move into it at one time.

Inputs can be real or imagined. If people interpret situations as real (that is, accept them as inputs), there will be real behavioral consequences (output). For example, in a culture that glamorizes youth, physical appearance (often culturally defined) and wealth may have an impact on people's behavior. If persons who do not possess these attributes internalize these values (inputs) as valid, they can develop negative self-images (outputs) or engage in a potentially harmful preoccupation with changing their appearance through excessive dieting or cosmetic surgery. Society's failure to meet the needs of those who do not possess these attributes is the result of society's tendency to emphasize appearance over productivity and personhood, and is evidence of a collective denial of the body's fragility.

Another example demonstrates how exchanges occur in larger social-structural systems. The nation's economic system receives inputs in the form of labor contributed by family members; the labor is an output by the family system. This labor is processed to produce items (outputs) that generate income for corporations (inputs for the corporation), from which salaries are paid to working family members (inputs for the family).

Examining exchanges between and across boundaries by biological, psychological, social-structural, and cultural systems aids social work professionals in dynamically interpreting events and phenomena. A wide range of interchanges between different types and sizes of systems becomes more understandable. Understanding the impact of a proposed military base on the economic life of the surrounding community can yield multiple levels of analysis. By looking at such factors as the effect of the base on community housing patterns and the job market, we can see how political and economic systems become part of the environment of family systems. Internal family dynamics are likely to be affected by the availability of jobs and the type of housing that exists. The behavior of family members will, in turn, affect the larger systems—the availability of skilled workers for the base, for example. This type of perspective provides a holistic view in which subsystems and suprasystems are identified. In addition, the exchanges that provide inputs and lead to outputs can be identified, and they become significant resources that affect goal identification and goal attainment in the interacting systems.

Networks

A **network** is the means by which exchange occurs between systems. It is established when patterned relationships develop between systems that permit the regular exchange of inputs and outputs (Hanchett, 1979). The educational system, for example, is comprised of a network of public, private, and religious educational systems, each further divided into preschool, primary, secondary, undergraduate, graduate, and trade or business schools. The regular exchange of inputs and outputs that is made possible by networks of systems uses the concepts of subsystems and suprasystems discussed earlier.

Networks are established because of shared or related purposes among systems to ensure the availability of needed inputs and to coordinate the activities of systems so that they can all survive. Emphasis during the 1960s on the sciences in the educational system was directly related to concerns in the political system that the Soviets were winning the space race. In the early 1990s, during the period of *glasnost* and *perestroika,* such competition was of less concern. However, the political and economic systems of the United States are currently becoming more closely and visibly involved with the educational system to overcome shortage of young workers sufficiently literate and skilled to perform increasingly complex jobs.

People participate in many systems throughout their lives. The pregnant teenager, the unemployed factory worker, the working mother with three children, and the recently retired business executive are all part of systems joined in networks. To understand each is to understand them in this context: Each person is affected by the other systems in which he or she functions, and each system is affected by the other systems in its network. We can see, then, how a systems perspective is multifaceted. It is a tool to help us understand and appreciate individual systems, as well as systems in interaction, and it alerts us to the fact that there are multiple layers of systems, ranging from the individual to large and complex organizations, communities, and societies.

Limitation of Systems Theory: Power and Chaos

Power.   As stated previously, there are many benefits and limitations in the use of systems theory in application to human behavioral theories. One point of criticism centers around the concept of homeostasis, which states that a system will attempt to reorganize itself to maintain its internal balance within the system. On the human behavioral level, this sometimes is translated into the idea that persons, families, groups, and communities will attempt to minimize or negate efforts to change in order to maintain the status quo. General systems theory might then fall into a category of human relations theory sometimes referred to as *structural-functionalism.* This school of thought will be discussed in greater detail later, when the social-structural components of human behavior are explained. However, for our purposes here, we may summarize by stating that structural-functionalists suggest that systems maintain a natural harmony in their relationships. These relationships have been mutually agreed upon as a means of preservation of the whole. An example might be medieval Europe's feudal system, in which feudal lords provided housing and protection to serfs, who in return worked on their lands.

It should be noted, however, that these "harmonious" relationships are neither necessarily equal nor mutually agreed upon. Scholars find within this unequal relationship the basis for criticism of systems theory and its parent theory, structuralism. When utilizing an ecological perspective, we must take into consideration the concept of power. **Power,** as defined by Max Weber, is "the possibility of imposing one's will upon the behavior of others" (1954: 323). In the feudal system, power most surely rested with the lords, and little, if any, with the serf laborers. Consequently, whereas the feudal system may have been mutually beneficial, it was only so because of the lack of other options afforded the serf population. Power within and between social institutions is distributed unequally and is often based upon ethnicity, gender, and socioeconomic status. Golden and Frank (1994) suggest an imbalance of power exists in such situations. Many family intervention models that use systems theory and mediation assume equal power of the parties involved to negotiate changes. Jones and Schechter (1992) point out that unequal power of the women and children in these relationships is supported by patriarchal cultures and the social and legal institutions that encode these gender-based inequalities. The contemporary economist, John Kenneth Galbraith (1983), offers an explanation of how power is exercised. Table 2.1 below presents an outline of Galbraith's analysis, in which he suggests three types of power and three sources of power.

An understanding of the nature of power, its sources, and its methods of implementation is an essential ingredient in the study of human behavior and practice theory. All human interactions contain some exercise of power. All three types of power may be used in any interchange within or between systems. For instance, in the case of the family with an abusing husband, power rests primarily with the husband. He may use all three forms of power in attempting to control his wife. Condign power may be used via physical punishment or through the threat of withdrawal of needed income. Conversely, if the wife is economically dependent upon her husband, he may "reward" her compliance and submission through continued financial support or the temporary cessation of abuse. Finally, as in many abusive relationships, the husband may begin to minimize the wife's own sense of personal worth and power through his constant verbal abuse. In this situation, a form of negative conditioning takes place.

At the suprasystem level, a capitalist economy often functions on the principle of supply and demand. When the supply of laborers is high and the

TABLE 2.1 Outline of Galbraith's analysis of power

Types of Power	Sources of Power
Compensatory power: the power to reward	Property, wealth, needed resources
Condign power: the power to punish	Strength—personal, organizational, the ability to withhold resources
Conditioned power: the ability to win cooperation through persuasion, education	Personal charisma, organizational—influence over members

Adapted from Galbraith, J. K. (1983). *The Anatomy of Power.* Boston: Houghton Mifflin.

demand for labor is low, workers are at a disadvantage in terms of their ability to call for higher wages or better working conditions. They lack equal power with the corporation who employs them. Conversely, when the labor pool is low, or the demand for specialized workers is high, labor may occupy the more powerful position. Organizations usually hold more power than the individuals within those organizations. Organizations may use all three forms of power to influence the behavior of their members. The use of power, whether overt or covert, is a major instrument employed in the process of socializing people and influencing their behavior.

Let us look briefly at the widely used concept of "codependency" as an example of system homeostasis. "Codependency is a pattern of painful dependence on compulsive behaviors and on approval from others in an attempt to find safety, self-worth, and identity" (Treadway, 1990). This definition suggests that the term is most often applied to persons (codependents) who have relationships with alcoholic or abusive partners (dependents). The model also suggests that the codependent person (usually the female) maintains the painful relationship out of pathological necessity. Anderson (1994) criticizes the model of codependency for its disregard of the significance of oppressive (and powerful) social and political structures that shape the behaviors of women. He suggests that these behaviors are coping strategies used to deal with the spouse's abusive behaviors and are not a set of dependent behaviors. He also states that codependency fails to address the unequal distribution of power between men and women. The result, he suggests, leads to defining the woman as codependent and in need of therapeutic intervention. If, however, an assessment of this relationship includes an understanding of differential power based on gender, the nonaddicted spouse is no longer viewed as pathologically dependent but as using various coping and survival strategies. The *target system* (focus of intervention) then shifts to the addicted or abusing spouse and to the oppressive social structures and cultural values that devalue women. Accurate assessment and helping strategies incorporate an understanding of the nature of power in systems interactions.

Chaos.   Systems theory was born in the physical sciences as an attempt to frame the interaction of physical phenomena. Like many models in the physical and social sciences, it can be viewed as an effort toward the development of a **grand theory**. Weinberg, in his book, *Dreams of a Final Theory,* states, "The most extreme hope for science is that we will be able to trace the explanations of all natural phenomena to final laws and historical accidents" (1992: 37). The application of **determinism** in physical science models (the ability to predict cause-and-effect relationships) to social science has come into question. For example, chaos theory, from contemporary mathematics, postulates that within ordered systems, pockets of disorder exist and that within disordered systems, pockets of order exist. Given this phenomenon, direct cause-and-effect relationships within and between systems cannot be predicted with certainty. Therefore, universal models, including some systems theories that attempt to predict human behavior with direct cause-and-effect explanations, are cast into doubt (Young, 1991). Many practice approaches are based upon deterministic thinking. Take, for example, traditional psychoanalytic theory, which posits that a person's present distress is rooted in unresolved early psychosexual conflicts. In some family therapy models, it is considered axiomatic that a child's "acting out" behavior is a result of problems within the marital relationship. Deterministic thinking limits our ability to develop alternative ways of viewing and, therefore, of understanding human behavior, such as illustrated in the "codependency" model discussed earlier.

These critiques, concerning the use of power and the unpredictability within systems, are important considerations when using systems theory in social science, and they have critical implications for the study of human behavior. Having looked at systems theory and its limitations in some detail, we will now examine the other parts of our analytical framework.

DIRECTIONALITY AND MOTIVATION

People do not generally act in a random manner. Milton Erickson (see Bandler and Grinder, 1975) discovered that even the seemingly incoherent verbalizations and actions of schizophrenic patients whom he treated contained elusive but meaningful content. All behavior is directed toward the attainment of some purpose. The goals people seek may be biological, psychological, social, or cultural in nature. People eat to maintain health, a biological goal, yet what they eat may reflect cultural or religious beliefs about what is healthy, sacred or profane, or fashionable. People sob as a means of expressing emotion, a psychological goal, although crying is in part biologically determined. To some degree crying is also affected by social and cultural dictates about when such an emotional display is appropriate. Employment is sought to meet various goals: biological (the body's need to grow through activity), psychological (the quest for a feeling of competence), social (the need for money to purchase the necessities of life), and cultural (expectations that adults will work and be financially independent).

Personal goals and choices are influenced by multiple factors. People do not formulate their goals independently, nor do they seek only to attain their own personal goals. Persons come together to attain the goals of the groups to which they belong. Unions became a powerful force during the late nineteenth and early twentieth centuries in this country when workers began to seek improved economic benefits for themselves. When a group of today's workers refuses to cross the picket line set up by another group, they are reaffirming the goals of the larger collective of workers, rather than their own immediate goals. Communities that participate in Block Watch or Child Safe Place programs work together to provide safe neighborhoods for themselves and their children.

White (1963) and Montessori (1963) both concluded, after extensive observation of children, that humans possess an innate need to interact and master their environment through meaningful interaction. Competence itself provides intrinsic value to the individual. (Refer again to Exhibit 2.1 at the end of this chapter and reflect on the needs expressed by the workers in the paper mill.) It is clear that the quality of the work experience is meaningful to people, a point that we see in the accounts of those who leave high-paying or prestigious jobs for less well-paid jobs that offer more rewards.

Although individuals make the decisions that guide their behavior, these decisions are strongly affected by their access to resources and the obstacles each person faces. Therefore, when trying to understand an individual's actions, social work practitioners should assess the systems involved in his or her decision making, including the resources and obstacles they offer and the person's perception of them. One person who does not receive a promotion may view it as a disastrous personal setback, whereas to another it is only a disappointment and motivation to work harder.

Some goals provide clear-cut strategies for action. In order to purchase a home, a young couple must save, cut back on purchasing nonessentials, establish good credit, and so forth. To compete in sports, athletes must eat properly, rest, and exercise in prescribed ways. In both of these examples, the social environment can either support or inhibit people's achievement of their goals. For example, a young couple's parents can offer to babysit for them to enable them to save the cost of hiring a sitter. On the other hand, racist policies of a bank may work to deny the approval of an African-American couple's mortgage application (a practice called redlining, in which certain areas of the city are marked as high-risk loan areas). Sexist policies may deny women the opportunity to compete in sports or fail to provide the same support as their male counterparts.

Strategies for attaining other types of purposes may be less clear-cut. To receive love and acceptance from another person requires balancing personal needs with the needs of the other individual. Problems in relationships may arise when this balance is not achieved. Issues of personal privacy, intimacy, careers, and children all call for negotiation between the people involved (Jordan et al., 1989). Negotiation is a sensitive and delicate process that requires much trial and error, quite different from the relatively straightforward tasks of saving money or maintaining a healthy diet. Here, too, the social environment, including cultural values, plays an important role. The availability of social welfare agencies to provide counseling is a resource for some people attempting to establish or preserve relationships. For other couples, family and friends provide such emotional support, especially in cultures that do not view professional help as an option. On the other hand, cultural values that devalue nontraditional relationships, such as those between homosexual couples or unmarried hetero-sexual couples, are obstacles that may deny needed emotional and financial support (Gutis, 1989).

Personal choices can lead to behaviors that appear self-destructive. For example, adolescents may begin to abuse drugs and alcohol in an effort to find acceptance with peers. Negative consequences, such as failure in school, family problems, injuries, and failing health, may result. In such situations the link between purpose and behavior can seem weak. It is hard to believe that people are acting purposefully when what they are doing is hurting themselves. Yet, this can be the case. Trying to attain one goal sometimes leads to behavior that interferes with other goals.

It would be a mistake to assume that people were acting randomly just because what they were doing was, at least in part, self-defeating. When we understand all of the goals that are being sought, we can attempt to determine what behaviors are consistent with achieving them. It is then easier to assist people in developing less-adverse strategies to meet their goals. In the above illustration, for example, drug abuse may be motivated by a need for peer acceptance, rather than by personal weakness or intentional self-destructive behavior. However, using drugs will often have negative consequences for the attainment of other goals, such as remaining healthy and completing one's education in preparation for future employment. When providing service to such adolescents, the social worker explores with the client the relationship between their drug use and the pursuit of their goals. If the young person is interested in stopping his or her drug use, the social worker and the client, together, can then begin the work of developing other means of goal attainment.

Because people share many basic **common human needs**, they create or structure environments to help meet those needs. Social decisions about ways to meet common human needs interact with biological and other natural factors. The infant's need for physical touch from caregivers is universal. Different cultures, however, vary in the ways in which infant care is provided. While all people share the biological need for food, persons, as well as cultures, differ in what, when, and how they eat.

The idea of common human needs serves to link knowledge of systems and directionality (purposeful behavior). Each type of system has its own particular basic needs that must be met if it is to survive. Because some systems are individual and others collective (subsystems and suprasystems), a holistic approach requires not only understanding of the characteristics of the systems experienced by the person but also of the person's *interpretation of their experience*. The reasons why common human needs are experienced and interpreted differently leads to the last part of the analytical framework: human diversity.

HUMAN DIVERSITY

When social workers look at different strategies utilized by different persons, groups, communities, and cultures to meet their common human needs and the shared purposes resulting from them, they are not evaluating one as better or worse than another. To do so would be to adopt an ethnocentric point of view that does not value the expression of **human diversity**. Diversity refers to the biological, psychological, social-structural, and cultural ways in which people differ. The genetic inheritance of people makes them different in many ways. As they grow (biological) and have life experiences (social and cultural), their individual characteristics emerge. People become characterized as outgoing or reserved, calm or anxious, carefree or serious, for example. They bring their biological and psychological characteristics into their social world, making friends easily or with difficulty, working steadily or moving from job to job, getting married or remaining single.

The separate characteristics and life histories that individuals carry with them interact with the needs and characteristics of the systems in which they function. Sometimes, this interaction occurs smoothly, but many times it does not. To understand this interaction, a **dual perspective** is helpful. This type of perspective suggests that all behavior may be viewed in two ways. The first is how people see their own behavior, and the second is how others view the same behavior (Norton, 1978: 3–12). People with physical limitations often focus on their abilities, rather than on their limiting condition, but they are often viewed by others primarily in terms of their "disabilities". When seeking employment, these persons may focus on the contributions they can make to an organization, whereas employers may instead emphasize the costs incurred by employing them. To understand what happens as these two systems interact (that of the individual worker and the organization), we must be aware of both points of view. The dual perspective is especially helpful for social workers who are called upon to mediate conflicting system viewpoints.

The Experience of Diversity

The dual perspective allows social workers to see that people are constantly managing two views of themselves. As people (individual systems), they develop a sense of identity based on their biological characteristics (often culturally defined as handsome or unattractive, smart or average, disabled or able-bodied) and their psychological attributes (outgoing or aloof, passive or assertive, adventuresome or cautious). In addition, people develop social identities based, at least in part, within the context of their ethnicity, gender, sexual orientation, and socioeconomic position. Taylor suggests that persons are involved in a dialogic process with their social environment:

> We become full human agents, capable of understanding ourselves, and hence of defining our identity, through our acquisition of rich human languages of expression. For my purposes here, I want to take language in a broad sense, covering not only the words we speak, but also other modes of expression whereby we define ourselves, including the "languages" of art, of gesture, of love, and the like. But we learn these modes of expression through exchanges with others. People do not acquire the languages needed for self-definition on their own. (Taylor, 1994: 32)

Identities become important in two ways. They strongly influence the goals that people (and larger systems, such as ethnic groups) consider appropriate and attainable. When societies value particular personal characteristics (ethnicity, gender, sexual orientation, intelligence, and so forth), persons with those characteristics usually find support and encouragement. When these characteristics are seen negatively by society, persons often find themselves devalued. Members of minority groups often experience discrimination and attempts to devalue them as persons. Aaron Fricke's (1981) account of growing up as a gay man is a good example. He describes how, after a childhood that included spontaneous and highly enjoyable sexual and nonsexual encounters with other boys, he became labeled as a "queer" in his adolescence. As a result, Fricke changed from a happy child to a troubled and very unhappy teenager. It was only when he started to make contact with other homosexual men, who were able to reinforce his sense of himself as a decent person, that he was able to emerge as an adult with a secure sense of self. During the period when his self-identity was being attacked, however, he withdrew from his former activities and became very isolated. This is quite common for people who believe that they are not valued. The consequences, however, can be much more serious than social withdrawal. Proctor and Groze (1994) conclude from their data that gay, lesbian, and bisexual youths are two to three times more likely to commit suicide than other youths and that 30 percent of all completed youth suicides are related to issues of sexual identity. In their own research, Proctor and Groze found that gay, lesbian, and bisexual adolescents were at high risk for suicide. They also found that family support (especially from parents) and the presence of a supportive peer group were important factors that reduced suicide risk. These resources are necessary to combat the negative self-image created by an oppressive social environment that is hostile and sometimes openly violent toward such an individual. In the case of devalued minorities, the "language" (Taylor's dialogic language) provided them by their social environment is often negative and hostile. The supportive "language" of family and significant others is of even more importance if socially devalued persons are to define themselves in positive ways.

The second way in which personal or group identity is important can be seen in the effect it has on members of other groups. The dual perspective alerts us to the fact that people are constantly reacting to the behavior of members of other groups of which they are not a part. In other words, some portion of their own identity is formed in relation to those other groups. For instance, some men who believe that women are too "emotional" reinforce their own sense of identity as being "strong" by acting unemotionally, or by showing only angry, hostile, or tightly controlled emotions. In this way masculine behavior becomes defined as actions that favor control over sharing and dominance over mediation. In the case of relationships between men and women, the actions and attitudes adopted by men to separate themselves from stereotypes of the "feminine" role also lead to their oppression of women. This process of stereotyping and emphasizing differences is not an uncommon way for groups to establish their own identities, and it often leads to oppression of some groups by others. Identity, then, develops in each system in part through its interaction with other systems. Those persons or groups who are defined as different or inferior because of their ethnicity, gender, sexual orientation, age, socioeconomic status, physical traits, or mental characteristics are often targets of discrimination. When the power (condign, compensatory, and conditioned) of these oppressive groups is sufficiently strong, members of the minority (devalued) group may become "socialized" into perceiving themselves as inferior. These oppressive groups may also develop social-structural obstacles that prevent members of minority groups from enjoying opportunities for growth.

Implications of Diversity in Human Behavior

Life on this planet is possible only because of the diversity of life forms that has developed over millions of years through the evolutionary process. Diversity is not only natural, it is essential for the continuation of life as we know it. Diversity within the human species is also essential for the continuation of the human race. At this stage of our evolutionary process, the biological difference of gender is necessary for the propagation of the human race. Of course, gender is not the only difference among members of the human race. We differ in ethnicity, sexual orientation, age, physical abilities, values and beliefs, and preferences. However, these characteristics are just a few of the many ways persons differ from each other. The many ways that people meet their needs accounts for the phenomenon of human diversity. A basic value in social work practice is respect for the dignity of the individual. By implication, social workers must respect what is unique about each individual. Individual persons develop their identities through the dialogic process with significant others (Taylor, 1994). Our contact with others is not limited to family and friends. Persons exist and, therefore, develop within larger systems (groups, communities, institutions, economies, societies, and so on). Each person, then, experiences the world from his or her distinctive position within the world. Whereas each person is formed by a unique combination of life experiences, one may share similar experiences with others. A person may attend school with a number of friends. All of these people share the same classes, teachers, and extracurricular activities. They may, however, experience these activities differently, depending on their particular interests, their ethnic backgrounds, and their genders. On the other hand, persons with similar characteristics, though very different as individuals, may share similar experiences by the nature of these characteristics. For example, for many years in American high schools, girls were discouraged from taking math and science courses, which was based on a societal expectation that such courses were beyond their capabilities, as well as the belief that these subjects were unnecessary in terms of helping women play their role in society as a "homemaker." Persons with physical disabilities, though unique as individuals, may experience the world in ways very different from those of persons who do not have physical disabilities. We have already discussed how our sense of ourselves as persons is developed in the context of our social experience. Our experience of the world is made up of the experiences we have and the meaning we give to them. The experiences we have in the world can be supportive or harmful to our development as persons. The nature of those experiences often depends on whether particular individual and group characteristics are valued or devalued by those who make up the social environment in which we live, especially by those persons who hold power over us.

When persons are not viewed as unique individuals but instead in terms of certain characteristics, they become victims of stereotyping. **Stereotyping** is a process by which persons are assumed to possess certain attributes by virtue of their membership within a particular group. Members of a group share the characteristics that define membership in that group. Women share a gender, Puerto Ricans share an ethnicity, the elderly share a chronological age range, and those with physical limitations share barriers to their full physical activity. However, within each group there is also considerable diversity. Women, Puerto Ricans, the elderly, and persons with disabilities vary in terms of their ethnicity, age, sexual orientation, education, job status, economic situation, religious experiences, and a multitude of other variables. Therefore, whatever stereotypes are developed about a group will inevitably be inaccurate because of the variations within that group. As a result, people who are treated according to a stereotype will endure treatment that is often disrespectful and sometimes dehumanizing.

Any system that stereotypes people or groups, especially for the purpose of disadvantaging them, treats people as categories, rather than as individuals. Seen in sociological terms, people occupy many positions simultaneously—mother, wife, Cuban-American, physician, middle-aged adult, and so on. This richness of human biological, psychological, social, and cultural wholeness is violated when people are viewed according to only one of the dimensions. Why, then, do stereotypes develop? They serve the function of distancing people from each other. This sense of distance is often captured by such labels as "queer," "nigger," "bitch," "kike," "spic," "retard," and "cripple," which are negative and dehumanizing. The targets of these terms are no longer individual people with hopes, needs, abilities, and self-worth. Therefore, it no longer matters to the perpetrator of the stereotype how these people are treated, because they have been defined as unimportant and faceless. They are seen as different and inferior. Keen (1986) suggests that this process of dehumanizing others is an essential ingredient in personal and organized violence. Keen's study of propaganda tools (literature, posters, and film) explores how those mediums are used to characterize persons in negative and even inhuman ways. He suggests that this dehumanization makes violence toward those being attacked more acceptable on a personal and social basis.

One result of stereotyping and labeling is **oppression**, the systematic restriction of people's **life chances** based on personal or institutionalized prejudice and discrimination. In terms of access to all the major categories of life-sustaining and life-enriching resources, members of oppressed groups are disadvantaged. Not only is poverty growing in the United States but also it is very unequally distributed, with families headed by single women, African-Americans, and Hispanics more at risk (Day, 1989; *American Family,* 1989a). A recent study of the homeless in Ohio shows that members of minority groups, the severely mentally limited, chronic substance abusers, and those with physical limitations are most affected by poverty (Roth, et al. 1988). Blacks of both sexes and women of any ethnicity are paid less than white men, a fact that is correlated to the incidence of poverty noted above (*American Family,* 1989b). Low income also correlates with high rates of premature births, low birth weights, poor health, and high infant mortality rates (Children's Defense Fund, 1992). The reality of these data can be seen daily in the neighborhoods populated by members of minority groups who are forced to live in substandard housing or who are denied housing altogether. These people go to inadequate and sometimes segregated schools, endure crime as a part of their daily lives, are denied sufficient health care, and are excluded from stable employment that pays a living wage.

Stereotyping based on human diversity characteristics becomes even more insidious when it becomes a tool for maintaining existing oppressive social structures. A common tactic of business throughout this century was to pit one ethnic group against another in order to stave off unionism. This process can also be seen in the present-day rhetoric from politicians and business groups who attempt to lay blame for America's economic woes on the high cost of social programs. In November 1994, California passed a statewide referendum, banning access to educational and health care services to all illegal immigrants. The proponents of the initiative suggested that "native" Californians were being harmed by the influx of illegal immigrants. Great numbers of these illegal immigrants are, however, a large source of cheap labor, especially for agricultural enterprises. An argument was made that an alternative to eliminating services to illegal immigrants and their children, as a means of stemming illegal entry into the United States, would have been to mount a more aggressive enforcement effort at fining employers who hire "illegals" as laborers. Instead of focusing legal sanctions against the business community, voters chose to eliminate access to educational and health care services for this mainly impoverished Hispanic population.

Oppression is not just an intellectual concept. It describes day-to-day life that offers illness, danger, discomfort, and hopelessness. This is not something that just happens, but instead is a result of social-structural arrangements that systematically create an **underclass**, a group of people who are excluded from the mainstream of America's social institutions (Auletta, 1982). When a powerful ethnocentric group devalues other less powerful groups, it uses its power in oppressive ways. Even though people share common human needs, the fact that their styles of living vary allows groups to focus on differences rather than on shared humanity. Rather than viewing these differences as resources rich with opportunities for societal development, they are used to categorize, stereotype, and discriminate against people. Efforts of majority groups to oppress minority groups set the stage for conflict. As noted above, some groups have entered into the struggle to improve their collective position. Many have been successful in terms of a more positive self-identity and greater, but still limited, access to basic resources. For the poor, however, regardless of race or ethnic background, the situation has worsened. Since 1979, the bottom one-fifth of the population of this country has experienced an 18 percent decrease in available income, while the top one-fifth of the population has increased its income by 16 percent (Phillips, 1990). As long as oppression continues, conflict will be an ever-present possibility.

Quality of life is also a dimension of human experience that needs to be addressed. Oppression may make even survival difficult. However, the whole idea of diversity as both natural and a potential resource goes far beyond survival. Underlying the idea of cultural pluralism is the belief that different groups have distinctive contributions to make to the whole of society. In other words, these groups have resources to offer. Oppression blocks these resources, turning them instead into obstacles for members of the oppressed groups. When persons are discriminated against because of their differences, the unique contributions they can make are wasted, and both the oppressed persons as well as society suffer.

Social Work Commitment to Diversity

To conclude this section on human diversity, a brief look at the impact of the concepts discussed in this chapter on the role of social workers is appropriate. In Chapter 1, the purpose of professional social work was defined as helping people to function more effectively by facilitating transactions between them and their environments. Maluccio (1981: 10) suggests that insights from systems theory, the ecological perspective, and strengths or competency-based practice provide themes for practice. These themes include:

1. the view of human organisms as engaged in ongoing, dynamic transactions with their environment and in a continuous process of growth and adaptation;
2. the conception of people as "open systems" that are spontaneously and essentially motivated to achieve competence in coping with life demands and environmental challenges;
3. the premise that varied environmental opportunities and social supports are necessary to sustain and to promote people's efforts to grow, to achieve self-fulfillment, and to contribute to others; and
4. the conviction that appropriate supports should be matched to people's changing qualities and needs so as to maximize the development of individual competence, identity, autonomy, and self-fulfillment.

Social workers utilize a holistic approach to identify the resources and obstacles present in their work with client situations. A holistic assessment that includes biological, psychological, social-structural, and cultural dimensions helps to identify targets of intervention at various levels of systems.

A holistic view of people in their environment includes the distinctiveness of people as well as the shared tasks faced by all human beings. It also means that social workers endeavor to understand tasks shared by particular sets of people and the manner in which particular groups are discriminated against. From biological beginnings that create the limits and potential for individual development, people move into larger systems that increasingly shape their behavior. Unfortunately, this development includes various forms of oppression against members of diverse groups. The social and personal problems created by oppression and neglect have become pandemic. Until the environmental systems that deprive people of the life-sustaining and life-enriching resources they need are changed, individuals and groups will continue to suffer and die needlessly (Brown, 1984). Social work seeks to eradicate the sources of oppression, to remove obstacles, and to support inherent resources.

To do this, social workers:

1. seek to understand and appreciate diversity through continued acquisition of knowledge;
2. seek to understand the nature and utilization of power as a tool of oppression;
3. seek to assist oppressed people as they identify their own power and support their acts of empowerment;
4. work to eliminate personal, group, ethnic, and cultural prejudice, as well as the forms of institutionalized discrimination that encodes and sanctions them; and
5. work for social justice.

Figueira-McDonough (1993) suggests that social justice means a commitment to ensuring equal access for all persons to basic social goods, and, therefore, a significant focus in social work practice should be the modification of social policy. Labonté's empowerment continuum (see Chapter 1) suggests that social work practice with disenfranchised persons include intervention efforts from personal support to political action as an effective plan to combat oppression.

SUMMARY

This chapter has attempted to develop a framework for viewing human behavior. This framework includes systems theory, directionality, motivation, and human diversity.

Systems theory helps to conceptualize persons in interaction with their environment. It views persons as dynamically interacting with other systems. One significant limitation of systems theory is that it does not adequately incorporate the different amounts of power held by persons or groups within the system. The battered wife does not have equal power with her abusing husband, and the Hispanic immigrant does not have the same power as the California business community. A second limitation is that systems theory cannot be utilized as a universal model for predicting human behavior because of the randomness that occurs within any system.

The concept of directionality addresses the issue of human purpose. It suggests that people's behavior is directed toward goals they have established.

It also attempts to explain that seemingly idiosyncratic or self-destructive behaviors can be understood in terms of conflict *between* personal goals.

Lastly, human diversity seeks to develop an understanding and appreciation for the myriad ways in which people seek to fulfill their goals. Discrimination and oppression are factors in a person's growth that limit his or her life chances. The elements of this framework, in conjunction with the social work perspectives discussed in Chapter 1, will assist the social worker in screening the theories of human behavior that will be discussed throughout the following chapters.

STUDY QUESTIONS

1. Examine the four practice examples that introduce this chapter. How can the integrating framework of systems, directionality, and human diversity help you to understand the common base and the differences among the various examples?

2. Analyze Exhibit 2.1 at the end of the chapter from a systems perspective. Does such a perspective help or hinder your understanding of human diversity and/or directionality? Explain how it does or does not help.

3. According to the systems approach, change introduced into one part of the system affects changes in other parts of the system and even other systems. What is the implication of this for social work intervention at the individual level, the family level, and the community level?

4. Systems perspectives lend themselves to graphic representations. Make a diagram in which your class is viewed as a social system. Illustrate its boundaries and chart the inputs and outputs exchanged between it and the subsystems and suprasystems that relate to it. Then discuss the level of power held by entities within that system. What types of power are utilized by entities within the system?

5. Societal resources are allocated through social arrangements encompassing political, economic, and ideational systems. In what ways are ethnic minorities, women, the elderly, gay and lesbian individuals, and persons with physical and mental disabilities discriminated against politically and economically? In what ways is power utilized in this process? How is stereotyping utilized to oppress these populations?

6. Social workers need to keep in mind that a great deal of diversity exists within groups of people. What are some of the variables that account for this diversity?

7. When social workers interact with clients or client systems (the elderly, persons with AIDS, AFDC recipients, and others), they become a part of a particular person's system. When considering the element of power in interactions between persons within a system, what implications are raised concerning the relationship between the social worker and the client?

KEY TERMS

Boundaries. Those barriers that separate a system from its environment. The identifiable limits of a system.

Common human needs. Needs shared by all human beings, which are basic for survival in a healthy state.

Determinism. The doctrine that every event is the inevitable result of previous conditions.

Discrimination. Acts that disadvantage those who are considered less worthy.

Dual perspective. Understanding the self-view of a population, as well as the view of other groups that evaluate its behavior.

Ethnocentrism. A state in which cultures or subcultures evaluate each other on the basis of their own cultural elements.

Exchange. The process of interaction between a system and its environment.

Grand theory. A theory that seeks to trace the explanation of all natural phenomena to final laws and historical accidents.

Homeostasis. A process of maintenance of a relatively steady state of a system.

Human diversity. Differences between individuals and groups based on biological, cultural, social, and psychological variables.

Inputs. Internal or external resources of a system.

Life chances. Access to basic life-sustaining and life-enriching resources.

Model. A way of organizing related concepts and theories.

Network. Aggregations of connecting lines, links, or channels among systems.

Obstacles. Factors that inhibit the definition and the attainment of one's goals.

Oppression. Systematic restriction of people's life chances based on institutional prejudice and discrimination.

Outputs. Resources that have been processed by a system and transformed into a system product.

Power. Ability of a person or group to enforce its will on others.

Resources. Factors that facilitate people's ability to define and achieve life goals.

Stereotyping. A process by which a generalized and biased conventional expression, mental image, and so on is applied to a group of persons based on characteristics (usually inaccurate and negative) of that group.

Subsystem. A component of a larger system.

Suprasystem. A larger system that incorporates smaller systems.

System. A whole that is composed of interrelated and interdependent parts.

Underclass. People who are excluded from the mainstream of the dominant culture's social institutions.

REFERENCES

American Family (1989a). Hispanic Poverty Remains at Near-Recession Levels, and Economic Disparity Gap between Blacks and Whites Widens. Vol. 12, No. 1 (January), pp. 21-22.

American Family (1989b). Equality between the Sexes: New Studies Create a Stir. Vol. 12, No. 5 (May), pp. 1-3.

Anderson, S. (1994). A Critical Analysis of the Concept of Codependency. *Social Work,* Vol 39, No. 6 (November), pp. 677-684.

Auletta, K. (1982). *The Underclass.* New York: Random House.

Bandler, R. and J. Grinder (1975). *Patterns of the Hypnotic Techniques of Milton H. Erickson, M.D.,* Vol. 1. Cupertino, CA: Meta Publications.

Brown, C. (1984). Manchild in Harlem. *New York Times Magazine,* September 16, pp. 36ff.

Carson, R. (1987). *The Silent Spring: 25th Anniversary Edition.* Boston: Houghton Mifflin.

Children's Defense Fund (1992). *Vanishing Dreams: The Economic Plight of America's Young Families.* Washington, D.C.: Children's Defense Fund and Northeastern University's Center for Labor Market Studies.

Day, P. (1989). The New Poor in America: Isolation in an International Political Economy. *Social Work,* Vol. 34, No. 3, pp. 227-233.

Federico, R. (1984). *The Social Welfare Institution,* 4th edition. Lexington, MA: D. C. Heath.

Figueira-McDonough, J. (1993). Policy Practice: The Neglected Side of Social Work Intervention. *Social Work,* Vol. 38, No. 2 (March), pp. 179-187.

Fricke, A. (1981). *Reflections on a Rock Lobster.* Boston: Alyson Publishing Co.

Galbraith, J. K. (1983). *The Anatomy of Power.* Boston: Houghton Mifflin.

Golden, G. and P. Frank (1994). When 50-50 Isn't Fair: The Case against Couple Counseling in Domestic Abuse. *Social Work,* Vol. 39, No. 6 (November), pp. 636-637.

Gutis, P. (1989). What is a Family? Traditional Limits Are Being Redrawn. *New York Times,* August 31, pp. C1ff.

Hanchett, E. (1979). *Community Health Assessment: A Conceptual Tool.* New York: Wiley.

Jones, A., and S. Schechter (1992). *When Love Goes Wrong.* New York: Harper Collins.

Jordan, C. with N. Cobb and R. McCully (1989). Clinical Issues of the Dual-Career Couple. *Social Work,* Vol. 34, No. 1, pp. 29-32.

Julian, T., P. McKenry, and M. McKelvey (1994). Cultural Variation In Parenting: Perceptions of Caucasian, African-American, Hispanic, and Asian-American Parents. *Family Relations,* Vol. 43, January, pp. 30-37.

Keen, S. (1986). *Faces of the Enemy: Reflections of the Hostile Imagination.* San Francisco, CA: Harper and Row.

Lappin, J., and S. Scott (1992). Intervention in a Vietnamese Refugee Family. In *Ethnicity and Family Therapy,* edited by M. McGoldrick, J. Pearce, and J. Giordano, pp. 483-491. New York: The Guilford Press.

Maluccio, A. (1981). *Promoting Competence in Clients.* New York: Free Press.

Montessori, M. (1963). *Education for a New World.* Madras, India: Kalakshetra Publishers.

Norton, D. (1978). *The Dual Perspective.* New York: Council on Social Work Education.

Phillips, K. (1990). *The Politics of Rich and Poor: Wealth and the American Electorate in the Reagan Aftermath.* New York: Random House.

Proctor, C. and V. Groze (1994). Risk Factors for Suicide among Gay, Lesbian, and Bisexual Youths. *Social Work,* Vol. 39, No. 5 (September), pp. 504-513.

Roth, D. et al. (1988). *Homelessness in Ohio: A Study of People in Need.* Columbus: Ohio Department of Mental Health, Office of Program Evaluation and Research.

Slonim, M. B. (1991). *Children, Culture, and Ethnicity: Evaluating and Understanding the Impact.* New York: Garland.

Taylor, C. (1994). The Politics of Recognition. In *Multiculturalism,* edited by A. Gutman, pp. 25-73. Princeton, NJ: Princeton University Press.

Treadway, D. (1990). Codependence: Disease, Metaphor, or Fad? *Family Therapy Networker,* Vol. 14, No. 1, pp. 39-42.

Weber, M. (1954). *Max Weber on Law in Economy and Society.* Cambridge: Harvard University Press, p. 323. See Bendix, R. (1960). *Max Weber: An Intellectual Portrait.* Garden City, N.Y.: Doubleday, pp. 294-300.

Weick, A. et al. (1989). A Strengths Perspective for Social Work Practice. *Social Work,* Vol. 34, No. 4, pp. 350-354.

Weinberg, S. (1992). *Dreams of a Final Theory.* New York: Pantheon Books.

White, R. (1963). *Ego and Reality in Psychoanalytic Theory.* New York: International Universities Press.

Young, T. R. (1991). Chaos and Social Change: Metaphysics of the Postmodern. *The Social Science Journal,* Vol. 28, No. 3, pp. 289-305.

Zuboff, S. (1984). *In the Age of the Smart Machine.* New York: Basic Books.

exhibit 2.1

The Work System

The following is taken from In the Age of the Smart Machine: The Future of Work and Power, *by Shoshana Zuboff. Copyright © 1988 by Basic Books, Inc. Reprinted by permission of BasicBooks, a division of HarperCollins Publishers, Inc. It uses the workplace as an example of a system, and provides particular insight into how human values affect the use of technology.*

> We had pleased ourselves with the delectable visions of the spiritualization of labor. . . . Each stroke of the hoe was to uncover some aromatic root of wisdom. . . . But . . . the clods of earth, which we so constantly belabored and turned over and over, were never etherealized into thought. Out thoughts, on the contrary, were fast becoming cloddish. Our labor symbolized nothing and left us mentally sluggish in the dusk of the evening. (Nathaniel Hawthorne, *The Blithedale Romance*)

THE AUTOMATIC DOORS

The bleach plant is one of the most complex and treacherous areas of a pulp mill. In Piney Wood, a large pulp plant built in the mid-1940s, railroad tank cars filled with chemicals used in the bleaching process pull up alongside the four-story structure in which dirty brown digested pulp is turned gleaming white. Each minute, 4,000 gallons of this brown mash flow through a labyrinth of pipes into a series of cylindrical vats, where they are washed, treated with chlorine-related chemicals, and bleached white. No natural light finds its way into this part of the mill. The fluorescent tubes overhead cast a greenish yellow pall, and the air is laced with enough chemical flavor that as you breathe it, some involuntary wisdom built deep into the human body registers an assault. The floors are generally wet, particularly in the areas right around the base of one of the large vats that loom like raised craters on a moonscape. Sometimes a washer runs over, spilling soggy cellulose knee-deep across the floor. When this happens, the men put on their high rubber boots and shovel up the mess.

The five stages of the bleaching process include hundreds of operating variables. The bleach operator must monitor and control the flow of stock, chemicals, and water, judge color and viscosity, attend to time, temperature, tank levels, and surge rates—the list goes on. Before computer monitoring and control, an operator in this part of the mill would make continual rounds, checking dials and graph charts located on the equipment, opening and shutting valves, keeping an eye on vat levels, snatching a bit of pulp from a vat to check its color, sniff it, or squeeze it between his fingers ("Is it slick? Is it sticky?") to determine its density or to judge the chemical mix.

In 1981 a central control room was constructed in the bleach plant. A science fiction writer's fantasy, it is a gleaming glass bubble that seems to have erupted like a mushroom in the dark, moist, toxic atmosphere of the plant. The control room reflects a new technological era for continuous-process production, one in which microprocessor-based sensors linked to computers allow remote monitoring and control of the key process variables. In fact, the entire pulp mill was involved in this conversion from the pneumatic control technology of the 1940s to the microprocessor-based information and control technology of the 1980s.

Inside the control room, the air is filtered and hums with the sound of the air-conditioning unit built into the wall between the control room and a small snack area. Workers sit on orthopedically designed swivel chairs covered with a royal blue fabric, facing video display terminals. The terminals, which display process information for the purposes of monitoring and control, are built into polished oak cabinets. Their screens glow with numbers, letters, and graphics in vivid red, green, and blue. The floor here is covered with slate-gray carpeting; the angled countertops on which the terminals sit are rust brown and edged in black. The walls are covered with a wheat-colored fabric and the molding repeats the polished oak of the cabinetry. The dropped ceiling is of a bronzed metal, and from it is suspended a three-dimensional structure into which lights have been recessed and angled to provide the right amount of illumination without creating glare on the screens. The color scheme is repeated on the ceiling—soft tones of beige, rust, brown, and gray in a geometric design.

The terminals each face toward the front of the room—a windowed wall that opens onto the bleach plant. The steel beams, metal tanks, and maze of thick pipes visible through those windows appear to be a world away in a perpetual twilight of steam and fumes, like a city street on a misty night, silent and dimly lit. What is most striking about the juxtaposition of these two worlds, is how a man (and there were only men working in this part of the mill) traverses the boundary between them.

The control room is entered through an automatic sliding-glass door. At the push of a button, the two panels of the door part, and when you step forward, they quickly close behind you. You then find yourself facing two more automatic doors at right angles to one another. The door on the right leads to a narrow snack area with booths, cabinets, a coffee machine, and a refrigerator. The door to the left leads into the control room. It will not open until the first door has shut. This ensures that the filtered air within the control room is protected from the fumes and heat of the bleach plant. The same routine holds in reverse. When a man leaves the control room, he presses a button next to the frame on the inner door, which opens electronically. He then steps through it into the tiny chamber where he must wait for the door to seal behind him so that he can push a second button on the outer door and finally exit into the plant.

This is not what most men do when they move from the control room out into the bleach plant. They step through the inner door, but they do not wait for that door to seal behind them before opening the second door. Instead, they force their fingertips through the rubber seal down the middle of the outer door and, with a mighty heft of their shoulders, pry open the seam and wrench the door apart. Hour after hour, shift after shift, week after week, too many men pit the strength in their arms and shoulders against the electronic mechanism that controls the door. Three years after the construction of the sleek, glittering glass bubble, the outer door no longer closes tightly. A gap of several inches, running down the center between the two panels of glass, looks like a battle wound. The door is crippled.

"The door is broke now because the men pushed it too hard comin' in and out," says one operator. In talking to the men about this occurrence, so mundane as almost to defy reflection, I hear not only a simple impatience and frustration but also something deeper: a forward momentum of their bodies, whose physical power seems trivialized by the new circumstances of their work; a boyish energy that wants to break free; a subtle rebellion against the preprogrammed design that orders their environment and always knows best. Yet these are the men who also complained, "The fumes in the bleach plant will kill you. You can't take that chlorine no matter how big and bad you are. It will bleach your brains and no one (in management) gives a damn."

Technology represents intelligence systematically applied to the problem of the body. It functions to amplify and surpass the organic limits of the body; it compensates for the body's fragility and vulnerability. Industrial technology has substituted for the human body in many of the processes associated with production and so has redefined the limits of production formerly imposed by the body. As a result, society's capacity to produce things has been extended in a way that is unprecedented in human history. This achievement has not been without its costs, however. In diminishing the role of the worker's body in the labor process, industrial technology has also tended to diminish the importance of the worker. In creating jobs that require less human effort, industrial technology has also been used to create jobs that require less human talent. In creating jobs that demand less of the body, industrial production has also tended to create jobs that give less to the body, in terms of opportunities to accrue knowledge in the production process. These two-sided consequences have been fundamental for the growth and development of the industrial bureaucracy, which has depended upon the rationalization and centralization of knowledge as the basis of control.

These consequences also help explain the worker's historical ambivalence toward automation. It is an ambivalence that draws upon the loathing as well as the commitment that human beings can experience toward their work. Throughout most of human history, work has inescapably meant the exertion and often the depletion of the worker's body. Yet only in the context of such exertion was it possible to learn a trade and to master skills. Since the industrial revolution, the accelerated progress of automation has generally meant a reduction in the amount of effort required of the human body in the labor process. It has also tended to reduce the quality of skills that a worker must bring to the activity of making something. Industrial technology has been developed in a manner that increases its capacity to spare the human body, while at the same time it has usurped opportunities for the development and performance of skills that only the body can learn and remember. In their treatment of the automatic doors, the bleach plant workers have created a living metaphor that reflects this ambivalence toward automation. They want to be protected from toxic fumes, but they simultaneously feel a stubborn rebellion against a structure that no longer requires either the strength or the know-how lodged in their bodies.

The progress of automation has been associated with both a general decline in the degree of know-how required of the worker and a decline in the degree of physical punishment to which he or she must be subjected. Information technology, however, does have the potential to redirect the historical trajectory of automation. The intrinsic power of its informating capacity can change the basis upon which knowledge is developed and applied in the industrial production process by lifting knowledge entirely out of the body's domain. The new technology signals the transposition of work activities to the abstract domain of information. Toil no longer implies physical depletion. "Work" becomes the manipulation of symbols, and when this occurs, the nature of skill is redefined. The application of technology that preserves the body may no longer imply the destruction of knowledge; instead, it may imply the reconstruction of knowledge of a different sort.

The significance of this transposition is impossible to grasp without reference to the grounds of knowledge for workers in the past. In the factory, knowledge was intimately bound up with the efforts of the laboring body. The development of industrial technology can be read as a chronicle of attempts to grapple with the body's role in production as a source of both effort and skill and with the specific responses these attempts have evoked from workers and managers. The centrality of the body's historical meaning for production has informed the self-understanding of managers and workers and the relationship between them. It has also been a salient force guiding the development and application of manufacturing technology. A better understanding of what the body has meant for industrial work and how it has been linked to the logic of automation will sharpen an appreciation of the character of the current transformation and its capacity to provoke comprehensive change in the relationships that structure the workplace. Before deciphering the present or imagining the future, it is first necessary to take ourselves out of the twentieth century and return, if only briefly, to a time when the nature of work was both simpler and more miserable, a time when work was above all the problem of the laboring body.

chapter **3**

The Dimensions of Human Behavior

There are more things in heaven and earth, Horatio, than will ever be dreamed of in your philosophy.

Shakespeare*

Man is an organism with certain desires existing in an environment which fails to satisfy them fully. His theories about the universe are attempts, whether religious, scientific, philosophical, or political, to explain or overcome his tension. If we regard the environment as static, then the problem is one of modifying our desires; if we take the organism as static, one of modifying the environment. Religion and psychology begin with the first; science and politics with the second.

W. H. Auden**

OVERVIEW

Shakespeare and Auden indicate the breadth of factors that influence human behavior, as well as the creative thinking needed to comprehend the complexity of people's lives. In this chapter we will try systematically to review major concepts from the biological, behavioral, and social sciences that help practitioners to identify the parameters of the human behavior they work with each day.

---

* Shakespeare, W. (1947). *Hamlet*, act 1, scene 5, lines 165-166. In *Yale Shakespeare*, edited by J. R. Crawford. New Haven, CT: Yale University Press.
** Auden, W. H. (1986). *The English Auden: Poems, Essays, and Dramatic Writings 1927-1939*, edited by E. Mendelson, p. 342. Trowbridge, Great Britain: Redwood Burn, Ltd.

The existing body of knowledge in the many disciplines from which social work draws seems at times frightfully incomplete and inconsistent. This makes the task of selecting relevant material a difficult and confusing one. Informed intervention based on data supported by scientific research has been the ideal condition in social work. As stated in Chapter 2, new methods of inquiry and sources of knowledge are being developed and legitimized in social work practice. The urgency of the professional task, however, presents the practitioner with a dilemma. Withholding action until all of the research or the development of new methodologies is completed may suggest "fiddling while Rome burns," whereas planning an intervention without conceptual clarity may be professionally irresponsible. Caught in this less-than-ideal situation, practitioners must make the best use of the information available. The vast amounts of new information in a variety of fields requires an ever-increasing collaboration between social workers and professionals from other disciplines. Likewise, a diversity- and strengths-based approach mandates that social workers also view the persons we serve as legitimate providers of information and collaborators in service planning and implementation.

The previous chapters provided both screens and a framework for filtering and utilizing knowledge pertinent to social work practice. The screens are based on social work values and practice principles, and they can guide practitioners in selecting theories of human behavior that are appropriate for specific types of intervention. The framework, built upon systems, diversity, and directionality, flows from those values and principles and helps integrate sources of knowledge regarding human behavior.

This chapter will focus on current knowledge that we believe will help in conceptualizing the complexities of human behavior. It will present a brief overview of the concepts from the biological, behavioral, and social sciences. An extended essay called "Helping and Hating the Homeless," at the end of the chapter, illustrates further multiple sources from which human behavior springs and serves as a stimulus for further discussion.

UNDERSTANDING THE FOUR SOURCES OF BEHAVIOR: BASIC CONCEPTS

The previous chapter introduced the biological, psychological, social-structural, and cultural sources of behavior. This chapter will examine these dimensions in further detail. An understanding of the four sources of behavior depends on aquiring a working knowledge of their basic concepts. These concepts are generated and codified in the major social, biological, and behavioral science disciplines, most importantly in human biology, psychology, sociology, anthropology, political science, economics, and the fine arts and humanities. You may have already studied some or all of these disciplines and may have been introduced to their most important concepts, or you may be in the process of doing so. Studying the concepts in the context of their respective disciplines provides the historical and methodological perspectives needed to understand them fully in all their richness.

The remainder of this chapter reviews many of the major concepts needed to understand the four sources of behavior. This review is to ensure your knowledge of individual concepts so that you can use them in various combinations dictated by the need to view helping situations in a holistic way. Later chapters will help you to combine concepts. Although the following summary of concepts will provide a useful common base for the rest of the text, three cautions should be observed:

1. There is no substitute for the level of understanding gained from studying these concepts in their respective disciplines.
2. This summary is selective. The concepts presented here are only a representation of those that are potentially useful in professional practice. You should constantly be alert to others that may be useful.
3. Resist fragmentation of concepts, and remember that human life is a complex whole. The concepts discussed in one area, such as the biological source of behavior, frequently have applicability in other areas as well.

To avoid a random listing, concepts will be organized under the familiar headings of biological, psychological, social-structural, and cultural. We believe that this four-part framework will prove to be convenient and manageable. Before beginning, remember that this is only a selection of very briefly summarized concepts.

BIOLOGICAL CONCEPTS

We begin our study of the four sources of behavior with human biology, because of its importance to our basic understanding of our physical existence. The age-old question as to what predominantly influences human behavior—our biological processes (nature) or our physical environment (nurture)—has not, and perhaps never will, be completely answered. Throughout human history, and especially within the last century, the debate has raged between and among the biological and social sciences as to the influence of biological and social dynamics on human behavior. This debate is not merely academic musing; it has also had significant political ramifications. As stated in Chapter 1, the racist policies of Nazi Germany were reported as having a basis, in scientific evidence, of Jewish inferiority. In this country, during the middle of the twentieth century, our courts upheld decisions to sterilize mentally retarded mothers because of the then-scientific belief that genetics had proved that mental retardation would definitely be passed on to their children.

The question of biological influence on behavior is greater today than it has ever been, as a result of our increasing knowledge and research methodologies in genetics. Steve Jones, a geneticist, states:

> Most modern geneticists find queries about the relative importance of
> nature and nurture in controlling the normal range of human behavior
> dull, for two reasons. First, they scarcely understand the inheritance
> of complex characters (those like height, weight, or behavior which is
> measured rather than counted) even in simple creatures like flies or
> mice and even when studying traits like size or weight which are easy
> to define. Second, and more important, geneticists know that the
> perpetual interrogation—nature or nurture?—is largely meaningless. Its
> only answer is usually that there is no valid question. . . . It is impossible
> to sort them into convenient compartments. An attribute such as
> intelligence is often seen as a cake which can be sliced into so much
> "gene" and so much "environment." In fact, the two are so closely
> blended that trying to separate them is more like trying to unbake a
> cake. Failure to understand this simple biological fact leads to confusion
> and worse. (Jones, 1993: 183)

That is not to say, however, that the study of human biology and genetics as a
specific area of knowledge is not important. Much of human behavior is biologically determined, deriving from the genetic inheritance that establishes both
potentials and limits on a person's behavior. Let us look, for example, at the
behavior of an infant. It will automatically grasp and move its limbs because of
a species **reflex** (reflexes are genetically programmed predispositions). The
sucking reflex, however, may not be present in an infant who has a genetic
disorder that causes brain damage. In some cases these innate deficits can be
compensated for through learning whereas, in others, the possibilities for remedy
may be limited. Potentials for behavior are biologically created, but in humans
certain social conditions are usually needed to realize them. Whereas a brain-
damaged child may be able to coordinate eye-hand movements only rarely
because of an organic deficit, a child who is not brain damaged may not possess
eye-hand coordination because of a lack of stimulation from caregivers. Although
the behavioral results are similar in both cases, the cause is biological in one
child and social in the other. As stated in the chapter overview, the interaction
of all four sources of human behavior are intertwined.

The previous example underlines the importance of the interaction of biological and social dimensions. Throughout this text we will stress the importance
of the interaction of these sources of behavior as evidence of system interaction,
diversity, and directionality. Next, we will focus on genetics, human physical
development, and illness as factors in human behavior.

Genetics

The most fundamental concept of human biology is **life** itself. The physiological
process of life is the management of complex chemical processes mediated by
the brain through an elaborate series of neurobiological impulses. The brain
serves as a center that activates (or fails to activate) chemical substances and

their interactions that begin at conception. At conception, a female egg is fertilized by a male sperm. The union combines genetic information from the two parents in the form of 46 chromosomes, which then chart the newly conceived individual's biological potential. Each combination of genetic information is multigenerational, as well as unique; it is multigenerational in that the parents carry genetic information from their parents, which *may* in turn be passed on to their offspring. This is also true for genetic information that is not physically evident in the parent as, for example, when red-haired children are born to parents, neither of whom have red hair.

Genetic combinations are unique in that a mixing process occurs during fertilization so that only some genetic elements of each parent become part of the fetus. Recent discoveries have modified earlier thinking about genetics. Human cells contain 23 chromosome pairs, with one in each pair thought to come from the mother and the other from the father. However, instances have been found where both chromosomes have come from the same parent. It has been further discovered that genes may behave differently, depending on whether they come from the mother or the father (*Science News,* 1989). These discoveries derive from research seeking to find ways to modify genetic material to prevent or cure physiologically based problems. The modification of genetic material is called **genetic engineering**. Research in this area has led to proposed links between genetic material and behavior, intelligence, health, and illness.

Another influence acting on the usual pattern of gene transmission is **mutation**, a process in which genes are changed from their original form when they are transmitted at conception. Although mutations are relatively rare, they and the natural genetic mixing process that occurs at conception ensure human differences. Thus, a person's genetic inheritance becomes an important basis for his or her social uniqueness, because social development depends on the potential created by genetic inheritance.

Genetic Disorders.   We will first focus our discussion on genetic disorders. Julia Rauch states:

> In its broadest sense, human genetics deals with those qualities that distinguish human beings from other species and with those that differentiate human populations, families, and individuals. (Rauch, 1988: 389)

Social workers practicing in medical, counseling, and adoption services inevitably find themselves in practice situations in which genetic disorders are a factor. A basic understanding of the role of genetics in disease and developmental disorders is essential in such practice situations. Rauch discusses four types of genetic disorders: those associated with (1) single-gene inheritance, (2) multifactorial inheritance, (3) chromosome aberrations, and (4) exposure to harmful environmental agents. All humans carry abnormal or mutant genes, which are considered hidden or recessive. When two persons with the same recessive gene produce children, the chances are 1 in 4 that the gene will be passed on to the child. Cystic fibrosis, sickle-cell anemia, Tay-Sachs disease, Huntington's disease, hemophilia, and a form of muscular dystrophy are all examples of diseases related to single-gene inheritance. Rauch further states that multifactorial inheritance involves interaction between genes and environment, citing the effects of health and nutrition on differences in height, weight, and intelligence. Asthma, cleft lip, cleft palate, congenital scoliosis, diabetes mellitus, spina bifida, and some forms of mental retardation are a result of genetic and environmental factors. Chromosomal aberrations are caused by too many or too few chromosomes with abnormal chromosomal structures. Down syndrome is an example of this genetic disorder. Finally, Rauch discusses noninherited, environmentally induced genetic disorders. Exposure to alcohol, prescription and nonprescription drugs, radiation, carcinogens, sexually transmitted diseases, and poor nutrition can disrupt normal genetic processes and lead to a variety of diseases and disabilities. Studies have also demonstrated the existence of a genetic factor in Parkinson's disease, hypertension, rheumatoid arthritis, and peptic ulcers.

Genetic disorders of the type mentioned earlier have significant affects on the lives of those persons with such disorders, on their families, and on society at large. Certainly, persons with such disorders, as well as their families, are faced with significant challenges and decisions. Science now has the capability of predicting the chances of parents passing on genetic disorders to their children. The parents who undergo genetic screening are then faced with a choice as to whether or not to conceive. Social policy issues regarding the amount of social and financial support that society will bear are also important factors that affect a person and his or her family's life choices and life chances. Social workers provide a holistic perspective in both micro- and macrolevels of such practice situations.

Genetic Influence and Mental and Behavioral Disorders.   Plomin, et al. (1994) summarize studies that focus on genetic influence on mental and behavioral disorders. They suggest that genetic influence is substantial for schizophrenia, Alzheimer's disease, autism, major affective disorder, and reading disability. They also report that specific language disorders, panic disorder, eating disorders, and antisocial disorder are subject to some genetic influence. Initial studies reporting a genetic predisposition to alcoholism have since been retracted. Genetic linkages to depression and schizophrenia have also been called into question. Studies on these conclusions, however, are not without criticism. Critics suggest that genetics-based research does not adequately factor in environmental influences. These studies also have political implications. For example, John Horgan reports in 1992 that:

> Frederick Goodwin, the then director of the Alcohol, Drug Abuse and Mental Health Administration cited research on monkey violence and sexuality and commented that "maybe it isn't just the careless use of

the word when people call certain areas of certain cities 'jungles'."
(Horgan, 1993: 24)

Horgan also notes that soon afterward, a conference entitled "Genetic Factors
in Crime: Findings, Uses, and Implications" was scheduled to be held at the
University of Maryland. The conference brochure noted "the apparent failure of
environmental approaches to crime" and suggested that genetic research might
lead to methods of identifying and pharmaceutically treating potential criminals
at an early age (Horgan, 1993: 26). Because of statistics which indicate that
African-Americans are disproportionately represented in homicide and crime
rates, the concern over racist "preventative" measures was raised and the
conference was cancelled. Critics of the "crime gene" theorists point to studies
that have found no genetic relationship to crime. Again, as in the case of genetics-
based diseases, studies of mental and behavioral disorders have social and
political implications in the study of human behavior.

Genetics and Basic Human Characteristics.   Philosophers, theologians, and
scientists have long pondered the question: What is the nature of human beings?
The answers provided have significant influence on how societies organize
themselves. Theologians may wonder whether human beings are basically good
or evil. Economists may conjecture as to whether we are basically greedy or
generous. Anthropologists may seek to discover whether human beings are
naturally social or solitary. Sociologists and psychologists may question whether
humans are basically aggressive or cooperative. Many theories of human behavior
in these disciplines begin with questions or suppositions regarding basic human
nature. As stated in Chapter 1, social work has adopted a basic philosophical
stance that human beings are oriented toward health. A continued interest in
the genetic influence of heredity on behavior, then, is an important facet of a
social worker's knowledge base.

Edward O. Wilson, a leading sociobiologist, in his book, *On Human Nature*
(1978), presents his views on the biological (genetic inheritance) and social roots
of basic human behavioral dispositions. One of the perennial questions regarding
human nature is whether human beings are inherently aggressive or cooperative
and altruistic. Sociobiologists look to both human anthropological and biological
studies and to animal and insect behavioral studies to surmise the extent of
inherited traits on human behavior. Wilson suggests that human beings possess,
as part of their genetic inheritance, the capacity for both aggression and altruism.
Wilson and other sociobiologists also suggest that there are inherited influences
on human activities such as sexuality, mate selection, population control,
preferred social groupings, family constellation, housing and habitat, and even
spirituality. Most sociobiologists concede, however, that social and cultural aspects
of the environment greatly influence genetic predispositions in human behavior.

Genetics and Personality.   On a more individual level, Bouchard (1994)
suggests that basic personality structures may also reflect a genetic influence.
Bouchard, reporting on studies of identical (monozygotic) and fraternal (dizygotic)

twins, found that certain personality dispositions, such as extraversion, introversion, anxiety, irritableness, emotional stability, conformity, playfulness, organization, impulsiveness, irresponsibility, agreeableness, friendliness, aggressiveness, curiosity, insightfulness, and superficiality, may be the result, to some degree, of inherit-ability. Using various statistical analytic methods, these studies suggest between 40 and 46 percent genetic influence on studied behavioral traits and only modest (7 percent) environmental influence, including factors traditionally thought of as determinants of human behavior, such as birth order. Bouchard suggests that the influence of environment on personality is largely unknown and that current thinking, however, "holds that each individual picks and chooses from a range of stimuli and events largely on the basis of his or her genotype and creates a unique set of experiences—that is, people help create their own environments" (Bouchard, 1994: 1701).

Genetics, Gender, Sexual Orientation, Race, and Intelligence.   The attri-butes of gender, sexual orientation, race, and intelligence have received much attention from sociobiologists and sociologists in the last two decades. Because these four attributes are often factors in discrimination, they are of special interest when one is examining human behavior.

Gender.   Gender determination is a biological phenomenon. Sex differentiation begins in humans with the influence of chromosomes carried by sperm. Twenty-two of the twenty-three pairs of chromosomes are nonsexual, and copies are carried in either sex. The twenty-third pair determines gender. Females carry a pair of X chromosomes, and males have one X and one Y chromosome. The female egg carries a single X chromosome, and the male sperm contributes either an X or a Y chromosome. After conception, hormonal production begins the development of sex organs. Both sexes secrete estrogen and androgen. The ratio of these "female" and "male" hormones determines the development of male or female physiology. The question is: To what degree does genetics play a role in determining male and female behavior? Fairweather (1976), summarizing research of gender differences, states that, in regard to children, claims have been made that females are more tactile and auditory, emotionally more dependent, more calm, less exploratory, and have greater verbal ability than males. Males have been reported to be more visual, fearless, and independent; better in spatial relationships; more aggressive; and more right hemisphere-oriented than females. However, after a review of all the research, Fairweather found that the only differences that seem to have a strictly genetic basis are a female propensity for precise digital activity and a male propensity for large-muscle activities and certain spatial abilities. Some sociobiologists suggest that women are more biologically suited to nurturing roles (childrearing, homemaker, peacemaker) and that males are more suited biologically to the work world because of their aggressiveness, developed by their original roles as hunters and gatherers. These claims persist, even though anthropology has revealed many societies where these roles were held differentially by both men and women. Lewontin et al. state:

The question is of course not simply whether or not there are hormonal differences between males and females—for clearly there are—nor whether there are small differences, on average, in structure and hormonal interactions between the brains of males and females; clearly this is also the case, though the overlaps are great. The point is the meaning of these differences. For the (biological) determinist these differences are responsible not merely for differences in behavior between individual men and women but also for the maintenance of a patriarchal social system in which status, wealth, and power are unequally distributed between the sexes. (Lewontin et al., 1984: 153-154)

Sexual Orientation.   The nature and origins of homosexuality have been a source of controversy and debate for centuries. Until recently, social workers accepted a psychoanalytical explanation for homosexuality. Male homosexuality, viewed from that perspective, is seen as caused by a dominating mother and/or a weak, absent, or hostile father (Bieber et al., 1988). Female homosexuality is also seen as an aberration of "normal" family relations. Child abuse of female children has also been suggested as a contributing factor in the development of a lesbian sexual orientation. Social theorists suggest that sexual behavior is culturally defined, and they point out that in other cultures, homosexual activities are expected as a part of the normal socialization process (Miller and Waigandt, 1993). More recently, some studies have suggested a biological or genetic link to homosexuality (LeVay, 1991; Bailey et al., 1993; Bailey and Pillard, 1991). These studies have been criticized on both scientific and religious grounds. Reinisch et al. (1990), after reviewing the current biologically and psychologically based theories of homosexuality, suggest that the causes remain elusive and that current theory holds that there are probably many different developmental paths by which a person can come to be homosexual, heterosexual, or bisexual.

The explosion of interest and research in the genetic basis of human behavior will undoubtedly bring more focus on the biological differences between men and women. Sociobiologists state that biologically inherited behavior is the result of past adaptations to the environment and social roles. The question remains unanswered, then, as to whether future biological sex differences will change or diminish as gender roles change.

Race.   In 1758 Carolus Linnaeus provided one of the first classifications of *Homo sapiens.* He divided humankind into four basic varieties based on geog-raphy: Americanus, Europaeus, Asiaticus, and Afer. He characterized these varieties by color, humor, and posture. Linnaeus did not, however, place these varieties in any hierarchical order. In 1795, Johann Friedrich Blumenbach, a student of Linnaeus, developed another schema. Blumenbach divided *Homo sapiens* into five categories, defined by both geography and appearance: Caucasians, referring to light-skinned Europeans and adjacent parts of Asia and Africa; Mongolians, referring to most Asians, including China and Japan; Ethiopians, referring to Africans; Americans, referring to native people of the Americas; and the Malayans, referring to Polynesians, Melanesians, and Australians. Unlike Linnaeus, Blumenbach did provide a pyramidical hierarchy based on his opinion of ideal beauty. Blumenbach saw Caucasians as the most beautiful of all varieties, followed by Americans, Malayans, and, finally, Asians and Africans. Blumenbach did not, however, claim superiority of any variety over another. He believed that *Homo sapiens* began in one region and that the varieties of the species developed as humans spread out over the globe. For Blumenbach, racial diversity was based on adaptation to different topographies. Blumenbach, as do many contemporary biologists and anthropologists, believed that all supposed racial characteristics grade continuously from one people to another, thus making racial grouping irrelevant (Gould, 1994). Shreeve (1994), referencing a 1972 study by geneticist Richard Lewontin, states that "Indeed, despite the obvious physical differences between people from different areas, the vast majority of genetic variation occurs *within* populations, not *between* them, with only some 6 percent accounted for by race. . . . Put another way, most of what separates me genetically from a typical African or Eskimo *also* separates me from the average American of European ancestry" (Shreeve, 1994: 60).

Of course, not all biologists and anthropologists agree with a one-race theory, and they stress the importance of the physiological differences carried within that 6 percent "accounted for by race." Race continues to be a factor in much of what we do. Health data, for example, is often reported by race, as is socioeconomic data. African-American males are reported to have a higher risk of cardiopulmonary disease than Caucasian Americans. Hispanics and African-Americans are more likely than their Caucasian counterparts to live in poverty. The degree of genetic difference or similarity among peoples is of less importance than the fact that race is also a cultural phenomenon and, as such, is subject to positive or negative social valuation. We will discuss the cultural dimension of human behavior later in this chapter. Race is also subject to political manipulation, which will also be discussed later in this chapter.

Intelligence.   Our final discussion of genetics will focus on intelligence. This topic has received new attention with the 1994 publication of *The Bell Curve: Intelligence and Class Structure in American Life,* by Richard Herrnstein and Charles Murray. In their book the authors suggest that an ever-increasing gap between social classes is occurring. They state that, in the future, high-wage and high-prestige jobs will increasingly be filled by persons of higher intelligence. Conversely, low-wage and low-status jobs will be filled by those of lesser intelligence. The controversy stirred by this book, however, concerns the authors' suggestion that intelligence varies on the whole from one ethnic group to another. After a review of current research, the authors state that "cognitive ability is substantially heritable, apparently no less than 40 percent and no more than 80 percent" (Herrnstein and Murray, 1994: 23). They report that East Asians (e.g., Chinese, Japanese), whether in America or Asia, score between a few to ten points higher than Caucasian Americans on intelligence tests. European-Americans score an average of 15 points higher on these tests than African-

Americans. Although Herrnstein and Murray state that, "The debate about whether and how much genes and environment have to do with ethnic differences remains unresolved" (Herrnstein and Murray, 1994: 270), their previous reference to the percentage of genetic contribution to intelligence seems to strongly suggest a genetic link. University of California genetics biologist, Christopher Wills, on the other hand, stated: "We (geneticists) have known for decades that variation in skin color is caused by rather small genetic differences, and it seems highly unlikely that these differences have anything to do with intelligence, personality, or ability" (Wills, 1994: 78). It is not our purpose here to critique Herrnstein and Murray's work but to point out the topical nature of the study of genetics. Nor are we suggesting an answer to the question regarding the contributions of heredity and environment. In every genetic study, whether one is researching biological contributions to a particular illness, gender behavior, or intelligence, the contribution of the environment is always present. Here, we are reminded of Steve Jones' statement that unraveling the genetics-environment issue is like "unbaking a cake."

Research into genetics will increase as technology becomes more sophisticated. As a profession, social work must stay informed of genetic research. The nature of the social work perspective offers a unique opportunity to place such research into a social context and to assist in developing supportive intervention when necessary.

Human Development.   Once created, life must be actively sustained, or it will quickly end. Part of human genetic inheritance is a set of instructions that causes physiological growth and development to occur in an orderly process throughout the **life span**, which is the period of life from conception to death. When the genetic plan is able to unfold because the resources needed to permit growth and development have been provided, we can then talk about **physiological health**. The genetic plan can accommodate extensive variation and adaptation while moving the human organism through the ever-increasing complexity of human growth and development.

In a state of health, there is relatively stable interaction and exchange among the various components of the human body. For example, enough blood is pumped by the heart and adequately oxygenated by the lungs to feed the muscles so that they can contract and relax in the process of use, which leads to their increase in size and strength. This view of the human body is a systemic one, focusing on the way the parts (organs, bones, muscles, blood, nerves, and so on) of a whole (the biological body) work together to enable the whole to maintain itself in its environment. Although the organs of the body operate in a homeostatic state, maintaining an internal balance while accommodating resources from the environment, the body itself is always in a process of growth and change. Our human physiology is always changing. The internal organs and systems of the body, such as the brain, the nervous system, and the sexual organs, develop at varying rates over the first 15 years of life. Children usually develop control over their large muscles before mastering fine motor skills, such as writing. Human development is a continuous, though not always even, process in which persons acquire new abilities and skills that they use to engage their environment. Social workers, therefore, study human growth and development to understand a person's physical, cognitive, and emotional capacities and limitations at various points throughout the life span, while acknowledging individual variation in development.

Because the end of life is part of the life span, **degenerative processes** are also part of the developmental process. As the human body ages, the genetic plan begins to enact the deterioration of cells at a rate and in a pattern unique to each person. Degenerative processes are strongly affected by stressors on the organism. Stress may occur at any point in the life span and is often experienced in a variety of forms: for example, in inadequate **nutrition**, which is the lack of the basic nutrients needed for physiological health; in inadequate **nurturance**, or lack of the basic protection and caring needed for psychological and physical well-being; and in an environment that lacks basic life-sustaining and life-enriching resources. Stress often generates **pain** as a warning that some part of the system is being pushed toward its adaptive limit.

Genetic disorders and illness, as well as physiological trauma, may limit growth and development of some human capabilities. Brain damage, for example, may affect the entire neurological structure and the ability of the brain to manage other physiological processes. These factors often interact with and accelerate the degenerative processes that are a natural part of the life course. Life ends in **death**, the point at which the human body is no longer able to sustain itself. Death is inevitable and is the result of genetically programmed patterns. Death may also be caused by stress to the system, such as an accident, or through illness.

Although conception, growth, and death are fundamentally biological processes, their significance is most often defined by the social context in which they occur. For example, the death of an infant, a middle-aged mother, or an elderly person may have very different effects on other individuals and social groups, such as family members and family units. Survivors may react differently to the death of an individual after a long chronic illness than they would to a sudden accidental death, or to a murder, no matter what the age of the deceased. The meanings of life, health, illness, and death may vary from person to person, as well as from one culture or religious group to another. The beliefs people have regarding these experiences often affect their reactions to them: Some persons may approach these experiences with calm acceptance, whereas others may feel anger and distress.

Now let us turn to some examples of how biological processes affect human behavior and discuss their implications for social work practice. Genetic research continues to stress the influence of heredity factors on human behavior (Snyderman and Rothman, 1987). Specific cognitive processes, including verbal and spatial abilities and styles of learning, have been linked to genetic factors. An individual, for instance, may possess skill in mastering foreign languages, yet encounter difficulty in geometry because of problems in conceptualizing spatial relationships. Manual dexterity and fine motor coordination have also been found to be linked to genetic factors. Someone with unusual sensitivity, combined with manual dexterity, may find art, drafting, or architecture congruent with his or her innate abilities. Conversely, someone lacking these skills may find attempts at mastering the same areas a frustrating experience. Howard Gardner (1993) suggests a human capacity for seven "intelligences": musical intelligence; body-kinesthetic intelligence; logical-mathematical intelligence; linguistic intelligence; spatial intelligence; interpersonal intelligence (the ability to understand mood, temperament, motivation, and the intentions of others); and intrapersonal intelligence (knowledge of the internal aspects of oneself, including feelings, cognition, and behavior). Gardner's schema is particularly helpful to social workers as they seek to understand and appreciate each individual's unique capabilities. The holistic perspective in social work also provides an understanding that social resources and psychological support, combined with an individual's innate capacities, are essential elements people use in realizing human potential.

Social workers need to be familiar with other biological processes that influence human behavior. For example, nutritional disorders, such as failure-to-thrive syndrome in infants and malnutrition, are more likely to occur in the context of poverty. Research supports strong linkage between these disorders and impairment in cognitive and physical development (Lozoff, 1989). A disproportionate number of students from inner-city schools are diagnosed as suffering from ADD (attention deficit disorder). These children are described as unable to attend to various tasks as a result of an inability to block out extraneous stimuli. The provision of economic resources, improved health care, and supportive educational programs may minimize the impact of this disorder.

Social workers find it helpful, when attempting to understand the impact of biological factors on behavior, to consider the life style changes that are often necessitated by illnesses like AIDS, arthritis, asthma, diabetes, and hypertension. Individuals react differently to each of these illnesses, in part depending on the severity of the symptoms and on the prognosis, and in part because of individual coping styles and interpretation of a particular situation. Yet, each life style change may affect a person's functioning ability and needs to be carefully addressed when one makes an assessment for intervention purposes. The social worker's own beliefs, cognitions, and emotions regarding life, health, illness, and death also become a factor when he or she is interacting with clients, and also need to be carefully monitored. (Exhibit 5.4, in Chapter 5, will demonstrate this principle.) Saleebey stated: "A person's body is in the most essential way his or her fate. How he or she understands that body, how he or she imagines it will be in the world, and how the world accommodates that body has everything to do with life chances and a lot to do with life style" (Saleebey, 1992: 113–114).

This discussion points to some of the ways that biological factors influence human behavior. Beginning social workers may find themselves in practice settings that require more specialized knowledge. A social worker in a child protective agency may need to know much more about early childhood development, parent-child bonding, physical indicators of abuse and neglect, and, in some cases, special childhood illnesses and disorders, as well as adult mental disorders, such as depression and schizophrenia. A worker in a multiservice center serving older adults, on the other hand, will need more specialized knowledge about the impact of physical changes on the behavior of the aging person. In all cases, the social work profession seeks to maximize biological potential, promote growth and development, and eliminate the disabling effects of illness through programs, policies, and services that support and encourage the development of all people.

Saleebey suggests that social work has generally neglected to cultivate an understanding and appreciation of human biology as the primary source of human behavior. He indicates that the profession has undervalued the biological contribution to understanding mental health and mental illness, as well as its role as a source of restorative and recuperative power. Saleebey states:

> . . . helpers cannot be enablers without knowledge, and if in some subtle and complex way autonomy proceeds from bodily awareness and sensuous vitality, and if social workers are to be as loyal to the ecological view as they claim to be, then they must fashion a knowledge base out of the reality that biology and society exist in a continuing interaction in everyone; that individuals have unique properties because of their social life and biological inheritance; and that the character of individuals' social lives is, in part, a result of the kind of physical beings they are. The biological revolution is, for social work, a unique opportunity once again, to realize a biopsychosocial approach to helping. (Saleebey, 1992: 113)

Gerontologist, Mildred Seltzer, in an article in which she combines personal and professional reflections on the aging process, provides a poignant illustration of how the biological process of aging is influenced by cultural, psychological, and social factors:

> Whose body does not speak to her or him? We may not always listen, but the clues are there. With age we begin to listen, sometimes restlessly, sometimes with interest. We need no mirror to reflect an image. Instead, the arms/eye ratio changes resulting in the need for glasses. The sound barrier is greater. The thresholds for fatigue, taste, and recuperation change. The data are reinforced by our daily experiences. Research and reality match. We have achieved, for the moment, reliability and validity. Our concepts are grounded by the lives of daily experience.
>
>   These clues result in changes in self-perception. We cannot do what we used to. Is our occasional disinterest in doing what we used to do an effort to reduce cognitive dissonance? To avoid embarrassment? Are we accepting of the changes? We begin to redefine ourselves as more vulnerable and our increasing vulnerability, in turn, results in anxiety.

One is reminded of the song "Sunrise, Sunset" in (sic) "Fiddler on the Roof." The days have flown swiftly, and the body that housed that earlier "me" is heavier, more demanding, changing in how it responds to stimuli, food, and the general environment. It tells the person "I am not what I used to be" and thus forces acknowledgement at some level that "What I was is not what I am." There are benchmarks, signs, and evidence of aging, and while one is not sure when or where the process occurred which caused these cues, signs, and evidence, it is obvious that they necessitate reappraisal of what these changes mean. Being and becoming, as Allport noted so long ago, dictate an unending process of negotiation; one waged within as well as without. (Seltzer, 1989: 4–5)

PSYCHOLOGICAL PROCESSES

A second source of behavior is psychological, resulting from people's perception, cognition, and emotional development. The human species is unique in that the amount of our behavior controlled by reflexes is limited. Much of what we can do we have learned through the use of biological-psychological potential. Human behavior is made operational through the development of perceptual, cognitive, and motor capacities, as well as through the development of personality structures that mediate between individual and societal needs. The development of psychological components is heavily dependent on human interaction—the process of individuals relating to each other in supportive, competitive, or even destructive ways. Once psychological capacities have been developed, they become important determinants of the behavior of individuals and groups.

Psychological growth and development, like biological functioning, do not exist in a vacuum. It is responsive to the cultural and social context in which it occurs. Developing a positive self-image, for example, is supported by an environment that encourages the accomplishment of one's goals. The social environment, however, could just as easily present obstacles to building a positive self-concept, as demonstrated in Aaron Fricke's remembrances of growing up gay (Chapter 2). Ageism, racism, sexism, classism, and homophobia are examples of some of the powerful ways in which the cultural matrix impacts on one's sense of self-worth.

Using aging, for example, one can see how social-structural forces have a direct impact on life changes. Some elderly people, for example, have a seriously compromised self-concept as a result of having internalized society's negative stereotypes about old age. Societal supports often crumble and a series of losses ensue—less income, reduced capacity for physical functioning, and restricted social roles. The congregate meal program (a social arrangement that brings elderly people together for shared meals), acknowledges the interrelationship between the necessity for programs that provide nutritional (biological) needs and the need to provide opportunities for socializing with others (psychological).

This service attempts to reduce both nutritional deficiency and social isolation, thereby recognizing how closely intertwined these sources of behavior are.

Let us move now to an examination of some psychological concepts that are fundamental to our understanding of human behavior. People's responses to their environment depend on their understanding of it, which, in turn, is the result of psychological processes combined with biological and social factors. The term "understanding" usually refers to a person's comprehension of an object, event, or text. However, infants and young children also have an understanding of external events at a subcognitive level. An infant is aware of external stimuli and reacts to them. Infants withdraw from stimuli that they perceive as frightening or uncomfortable, such as loud noises or rough handling by a caretaker. Conversely, infants often respond favorably to other stimuli, such as soft repetitive speech, a smiling caregiver, and rocking. In terms of understanding the environment, three biologically based capacities are of particular importance. **Perception** is the ability to see, smell, feel, and touch, and to develop organized responses to the sensory characteristics of the environment. The multiple stimuli that fill the natural and social environment require the capacity to perceive selectively to avoid becoming confused and overwhelmed. Residents of large cities may be accustomed to the loud noises and fast-paced movements found there, and they may find ways to block out extraneous stimuli. Note the number of runners wearing headphones in their attempt to block out unwanted noise. Visitors to those same cities, however, confronted with the same stimuli, may experience tension and confusion, until they learn adaptive strategies. Through their sensory mechanisms, people receive stimuli that enable them to react to their environment for specific (often, survival) purposes. Children who have been physically abused often develop heightened sensitivity to visual (fast movements) and auditory (loud voices) stimuli as a result of their constant need to monitor their environment for possible physical aggression. This adaptive strategy is often referred to in the literature as "hypersensitivity." War veterans often report that they needed to be acutely aware of danger signs provided by sight, sound, and smell to survive in the hostile war environment.

Cognition is the ability to process and organize information so as to utilize the environment to achieve one's goals. It involves remembering, understanding, and evaluating information from the environment. Cognitive processes are highly individualized, which partly explains why the same events are experienced by each person in a unique manner. Reactions to sensory information and events are, therefore, determined not only by the events themselves but also by the various meanings the person assigns to the events (Newberger and DeVos, 1988). Stated in another way, objective realities are sifted through the person's subjective interpretation of those realities. In the examples of the child-abuse survivor and the war veteran cited earlier, sensory data have been processed cognitively to strengthen adaptation and coping. Situations in which persons develop maladaptive coping strategies will be discussed later in the chapter.

Watzlawick et al. (1974) provide the following exercise to demonstrate how cognitive structures influence one's perception. Using four straight lines, connect all nine dots without lifting your pencil or pen from the paper or retracing any line. The solution can be found at the end of this chapter.

As you do this exercise, keep in mind what it teaches about cognition. If you encountered difficulty in completing the exercise, the reason is probably that you limited yourself to unstated, yet assumed, rules regarding its completion. (People often see the nine-dot configuration as a limited space in which all possible solutions must be contained.) Memories, past experiences, similar or related tasks, and previous learning all influence how you approached the task. Our cognitive structures, in other words, have an effect on our ability to perceive spatial relationships, thereby limiting our possible solutions.

We can see, then, that the world is both an objective and a subjective reality. Our behavior is sometimes affected more by what we perceive and understand about our environment than by what actually exists. Although we all inhabit and share much of the same physical world, we do not all perceive and organize data in the same way. Therefore, our behavior differs according to our cognitive processing of our environment.

Affect refers to the feelings and emotions that become attached to information derived from our sensory and cognitive processes. Affect involves feelings, temperament, and emotions.

Think back to the last examination you took. What emotions did you experience prior to the test? Did you feel anxiety? Tension? Excitement? (Just kidding.) If you did well on the exam, did you feel some sense of pride and accomplishment? If you did not do as well as you would have liked, did you feel disappointment, more anxiety, fear? Feelings are a result of the meanings we attach to our cognition. Behavior, as expressed through action, is partially determined by these feelings.

Perception, cognition, and affect all have physiological roots. The workings of our sensory organs, functioning of the brain, hormonal responses, and visceral responses to a threatening situation are all examples of this principle. However, the social environment is obviously a powerful influence on the ways these biologically based capacities are developed and used, demonstrating once again the close interaction of biological and social roots of behavior.

The flexibility that comes with being human, because of genetic inheritance, adds another dimension to perception, cognition, and affect. The social environments in which people live attribute particular meanings to certain events and objects. These meanings are learned through the process of **socialization**, through which people acquire the beliefs, customs, values, and attitudes of their culture. Through socialization we learn what we are expected to do and how we are to accomplish it. Socialization is at work when we use our cognitive capacity to learn to do some things and are relatively unconcerned about learning to do others. For example, Europeans consider it valuable to learn several languages because of the close geographical proximity of other countries, but the relative geographical isolation of the United States has tended to make this ability less of a perceived concern.

Socialization influences our perceptions, which in turn influence the way we react to others and to situations, including the amount and type of affect (emotional investment or response) we accord to people, events, or objects. People we perceive as important to us often evoke feelings of affection and respect. Conversely, people we perceive as powerful and threatening often evoke feelings of fear and anger. Situations that we have learned are threatening or confusing become associated with feelings of apprehension or inadequacy. We can see how our behavior is often determined by our subjective interpretation of events, rather than by their objective reality. Misperceptions are often an aspect of the socialization process. Our perceptions, developed through socialization, often stereotype persons, based on misinformation about them. These stereotypes frequently form the basis for racism, sexism, ageism, and homophobia.

The physiological potentials for perception, cognition, and emotion become part of an individual's response to the environment. **Personality** is the integrating psychological structure that develops to help the individual function in the environment. Personality is composed of fairly consistent, but not fixed, patterns of response to situations, patterns that are relatively consistent within an individual but differ from one individual to the next. Whereas some people may respond to threatening situations by avoiding them, others respond to them because of the excitement they provide. Some people (and cultures) express anger very directly, whereas others find it difficult to let people know when they are angry. Cultural norms are an important factor in the socialization of behavior. Consequently, as social workers, we need to acquire knowledge of the cultural norms, customs, and life expectations of the persons with whom we work. In these and countless other ways, people differ in their responses to situations, according to their personality characteristics.

Efforts to better understand personality development have been going on for centuries. The ancient study of astrology is based on the belief that the forces of the moon, sun, and planets converge to affect human personality. Also, ancient myths from many cultures speak of the natural and supernatural forces and events that affect human development. Previously, we discussed the research that reported genetic influence on human behavior, including emotional dispositions. The view that personality is linked to biological functions dates back to the early

Roman physician, Galen, who proposed the idea of four humors. Galen believed an imbalance in the four primary fluids—blood, yellow bile, black bile, and phlegm—to be responsible for the four basic personality types. These types were the sanguine, the angry, the sad, and the lethargic or empathetic personalities. The disciplines of psychology and sociology have presented us with several theoretical perspectives on personality development. Ideas from learning, cognitive, psychoanalytic, and humanistic theories will be discussed in succeeding sections.

Learning Theories of Personality

Learning theories assume that all human behavior is learned and reactive, meaning that specific acts have specific antecedents. The behavior or learning theorist you are probably most familiar with is B. F. Skinner (1904-1990). Personality theories based on conjectures about the workings of the inner mind were of little use to Skinner, who believed psychologists should only study that which could be measured. Skinner believed that persons are more a product of their environment than of their nature. He did, however, believe in the uniqueness of each individual, because the exact nature of the external environment that affects each person is unique. All behavior, according to Skinner, is controlled by the consequences it engenders.

Human behavior, according to behavior or learning theorists, involves constant transactions between individuals and their environment. Behavior is linked to a chain of units consisting of stimulus (S) and response (R). Skinner distinguished between what he called *respondent behavior,* or that which is merely reflexive, such as removing one's hand from a source of heat, and *operant behavior,* which is learned. The learning process involved is termed *operant conditioning.* Skinner believed that all behavior is shaped by the distribution of either positive or negative responses from the environment. From our earliest experiences as infants, Skinner suggests, we display behaviors that, when positively reinforced, are repeated and if ignored or negatively reinforced are likely to become *extinct.* Using this basic theory, Skinner studied the methods by which behavior can be influenced and/or modified. His approach to the study and intervention of human behavior consisted of what he called a *functional analysis.* This analysis asked three questions: What is the frequency of the behavior? (How often does it occur, or what is the baseline?) When and where does it occur? What reinforcement is given to continue the behavior? Despite his somewhat deterministic explanation of behavior, Skinner believed that people have some measure of control over their environment. This control is exercised through avoiding stimuli that are likely to produce specific responses. For example, the child who has failed an exam may suffer many negative consequences. She or he may feel embarrassment, receive punishment from adults, or encounter negative remarks from peers. The child may be able to recognize factors that contribute to failing the exam, such as, staying up late the night before or lack of preparation. In this case, she or he may try alternative strategies, which may bring more success on the next exam. However, a child may also decide to avoid all test taking in the future, because of the negative events associated with this activity. In this case the child develops *avoidant behaviors,* which may have longer negative consequences. Because these consequences have not yet been felt or experienced, the child may continue to avoid unpleasant situations that she or he now experiences. These types of stimulus-response (S-R) reactions are, according to learning theories, at the root of all learning and behavior.

Another learning theorist, Albert Bandura (1977), agreed with Skinner that behavior is learned, but he expanded the simple stimulus-response patterns of traditional learning theories to include complex issues of social interaction. Bandura believed that behavior is shaped by the interaction between person and environment and then by cognitive evaluation of the events in that environment. He termed this phenomenon *reciprocal determinism.* Behavior, according to Bandura, involves a person monitoring the behavior and consequences of his or her own actions so as to behave in a way that will produce desired outcomes. Bandura believed that learning can take place not only through our own experiences but also through *observational learning,* that is, by watching and learning from other people's behaviors. Unlike Skinner, who believed that all learning had to be through direct experience, Bandura suggested that by observation persons learn through *vicarious reinforcement.* This process of learning through observation is called *imitation* or *modeling.* We choose to replicate or model behavior based on a cognitive decision about the benefits of that behavior. Cognition plays an important role in Bandura's social learning theory. Unlike Skinner, Bandura suggested the presence of a mediating *self,* or a process of thought and perception. Bandura suggested that persons not only respond to external rewards and sanctions but also have internal expectations or standards of behavior. The internal process of monitoring our behavior in accordance with these standards is called *self-reinforcement.* A violation of these standards can produce negative self-sanctions, such as feelings of guilt. Adherence to these standards can result in a tangible self-reward or a feeling of *self-efficacy* or feelings of competency. Bandura suggested that self-efficacy could be promoted by exposing people to situations in which they could succeed, rather than fail, and by exposing them to successful persons on whom they can model their behavior. Therefore, for Bandura, the assessment process should include not only the behavioral aspects of a Skinnerian evaluation but also a person's cognitions (thoughts and beliefs) about goals, motivation, and meanings of events.

Behavioral and learning theories are widely used in schools and social agencies. The emphasis placed on evaluation and measurement grounded in solid research, as well as on the role of environmental factors in shaping behavior, partly accounts for the popularity of this group of theories with practitioners. Gambrill (1987) reports successful application of behavior modification in child welfare, family services, corrections, and working with the elderly. However, the successful use of these techniques requires the ability to specify stimuli to which people will respond and the rewards or reinforcements that will be effective.

Being able to do so depends on knowledge of social-structural and cultural variables that influence people's behavior.

Learning theories have received some measure of criticism. The use of behavior modification techniques has ethical implications, especially with vulnerable populations, such as children, the mentally impaired, or others who may not be able to understand or consent to intervention strategies. The principle of informed consent, in which full understanding and consent of the client(s) is sought, needs to be applied when one uses such techniques in classroom situations, for example, when they are used to change the behavior of certain children. The benefits of certain behavior modification techniques involving more complicated learning situations, other than simple behavioral change, has also come into question. John Condry, summarizing research on the application of extrinsic rewards to learning in school, states:

> . . . subjects offered an extrinsic incentive choose easier tasks, are less efficient in using the information available to solve novel problems, and tend to be answer oriented and more illogical in their problem-solving strategies. They seem to work harder and produce more activity, but the activity is of a lower quality, contains more errors, and is more stereotyped and less creative than the work of comparable nonrewarded subjects working on the same problems. (Condry, 1977: 471–472)

A social work-ecology perspective would favor Bandura's social-learning theory over a strict Skinnerian approach, because of its emphasis on the interaction of personal cognition and external environment as contributors to human behavior. Skinner's approach does not address the issue of personal growth or goal-directed behavior. Bandura, however, suggests the intervention of cognition as a mediating factor in evaluating the value of particular behavior and suggests the development of goals that are socially learned. Both Skinner and Bandura believe the uniqueness of the individual experience and, therefore, allow for the diversity of human behavior.

Cognitive Theories of Personality

Cognitive theorists believe that human behavior is shaped by the manner in which a person processes information from the environment. Whereas behavioral approaches emphasize stimulus-response and reward and reinforcement as determinants of behavior, the cognitive perspective stresses intelligence, thought, imagination, conceptualization, creativity, emotionality, symbolization, classification, and the development of values as contributors to human action. In this respect, Bandura's emphasis on cognition as a mediating factor in behavior also falls into a cognitive approach.

Jean Piaget (1936), one of the most frequently cited of the cognitive theorists, explains how the child, progressing through sequentially based stages of increasing complexity, learns to respond to the environment. From birth to about 2 years of age, the infant processes information primarily through the senses and body movements. Through interaction with the environment the child develops basic concepts that are necessary for further development. Among these are *object permanence* (objects exist even when not seen), *intentionality* (goal-directed activity), and *causality* (actions cause reactions). Piaget called this period the *sensorimotor stage.*

The *preoperational stage* begins at about 2 years of age and extends until approximately age 7. Children in this age range process information through their own perceptions and actions. Children's thinking is considered *prelogical,* and they are unable to generalize classes of objects and events. The world, therefore, is experienced in a literal way. Children during this time develop the capacity for *symbolic representation* and, therefore, are able to develop language and engage in symbolic play. From age 7 through 11, children begin to use logic in assigning meaning to experience. During this stage of *concrete operations,* they develop the ability to classify information into categories and can begin to form simple generalizations about the world. Piaget's last developmental stage is termed *formal operations* and begins around 12 years of age. Thinking at this stage can involve imagination and complex problem solving.

From a cognitive perspective, a person sifts information from the environment through preexisting cognitive structures called *schemas.* These schemas develop in complexity over time and are sequentially configured. Maria Montessori used such cognitive concepts in her theory of education and designed educational materials consistent with the child's developing capacities to interact with the environment. Piaget saw this process as innate but able to be enhanced or thwarted both by biological impairments and by the environment.

Another important developmental theorist is the Russian psychologist, Lev Vygotsky (1978). Vygotsky is mentioned here because much of what he proposed bridges the gap between the development of cognitive structures and the social and cultural origins of personality. He suggested that a child's exterior dialogues with others are a precursor to his or her inner speech and development of thought processes. He also suggested, as did Piaget, that play is an essential part of a child's ability to develop symbols and metaphors. By implication, the richer the child's environment, that is, opportunities for play, creativity, fantasy, as well as for positive dialogue with children and adults, the more positive the child's perceptions and cognitive stances will be, when interacting with his or her world. Failure to provide these positive interactions depletes a child's ability to trust her or his world and problem-solving abilities.

Piaget hypothesized sequential progression of moral development from a *heteronomous morality,* which is based on egocentric fixed rules of behavior, to an *autonomous morality,* which allows for development of mutually agreed-upon rules of behavior. Lawrence Kohlberg (1981) pursued Piaget's idea further and constructed a six-stage theory of moral development. Like Piaget's cognitive structures, these stages, Kohlberg believed, were innate and sequential. The *preconventional stage* begins at around age 4 and continues on to age 10. During this stage, a child's behavior is based first upon fear of punishment. As the child matures through this stage, he or she modifies behavior, based on the distribution of rewards. The *conventional moral development stage* begins at around age 10. At this stage, the child begins to understand that social norms exist and is motivated to follow them to win social approval. Later in this stage, Kohlberg suggests, people become aware of the need for rules for the maintenance of social order. The last stage, *postconventional moral development,* also consists of two levels. At the first level, he suggests, people are motivated by a sense of moral obligation and mutual commitment. The concept of a mutually agreed-upon "common good" is the basis of a moral contract regulating individual behavior. Kohlberg's last stage is marked by the development of a personal code of ethics based on principles of fairness, justice, and respect for all persons.

It is important to note that stage theories, in general, have been criticized for their emphasis on fixed and sequential stages of moral, cognitive, or emotional development. Carol Gilligan (1982), for example, criticizes Kohlberg's theory as representative of male moral development. She suggests that men and women have different developmental progressions. For example, Gilligan points out that Kohlberg's highest stage is one of individual autonomy. She asserts that women define themselves in relationship to others in nurturing and caring ways and would, therefore, be considered less morally developed, according to Kohlberg's schema.

It is important, as social workers, when viewing theories of human development, to seek out the basis on which these theories were founded, especially when claims of universality are made. In Kohlberg's case, Gilligan points out that his original study, upon which his theory was built, was about eighty-four boys studied over a period of 20 years. Studies need to be examined on the basis of the inclusion of gender, age, ethnicity, and other variables, to determine the universality of the findings.

Weiner's *attribution theory* (1974) is an important contribution to the body of cognitive theory. Attributions are cognitive beliefs about the cause and effects of events; they determine a person's response to those events. In other words, the meaning of reality is interpreted through personal beliefs about causality. For example, a child who attributes his success at playing a video game to his own skill when engaged in such activities is more likely to play more difficult games than a child who believes that his success at playing the game was beginner's luck or that the game was particularly easy. Attribution theory contributes a great deal to our understanding of what motivates people to engage in new activities or behaviors. Attribution theory gives added insight into the need to understand personal views of reality. Important questions that stem from attribution theory in regard to understanding human behavior are: (1) Does a person view events in his or her life as within their control or as determined by outside forces? (2) To what factors does a person attribute his or her present situation?

The concept of *learned helplessness* (Abramson et al., 1978) is rooted in attribution theory. These researchers suggest that when a person encounters a series of failures that he or she attributes to factors beyond his or her control, that individual will eventually "learn" a sense of helplessness, accompanied by feelings of despair, frustration, and hopelessness. Factors that are perceived to be beyond one's control may be internal (personal capabilities) or external (unpredictable forces). In either case, one will withdraw from similar situations. Conversely, persons who believe they have control and experience success will be more likely to repeat situations or to attempt new and challenging situations.

The cognitive theories briefly reviewed earlier provide us with insight into the role that beliefs, feelings, thoughts, and perceptions play in human behavior. Whereas some cognitive theories, such as those of Piaget, claim universality, others, like Weiner's, suggest that human behavior does not follow universal patterns but is based on a unique set of life events and a person's individual interpretation of those events.

Cognitive approaches are used by practitioners to explain human behavior and design intervention strategies. Behavior, according to cognitive theories, is determined by an individual's thoughts, emotions, and conscious judgments, based on existing information or schema. We attribute meaning to events and experiences, and we behave accordingly. The anxiety generated by an upcoming quiz will not often generate the same discomfort as a college entrance exam. The events themselves, in other words, are not as significant in determining behavior as the meaning that we attribute to them.

Cognitive restructuring is the process of applying cognitive theory to intervention and involves a conscious restructuring of the thoughts underlying behavior. Cognitive theorists suggest that thoughts or perceptions create emotional responses and, therefore, a cognitive shift in meaning or perception will cause a change in emotional response and behavior. Social workers often combine cognitive and behavioral approaches in the process of planning change. For example, psychosocial assessments from a cognitive perspective require identifying the thought patterns and beliefs that underlie problematic behaviors. Traditional social work techniques, such as clarification, presentation of incongruity, and interpretation, are frequently used in cognitively based intervention (Sherman, 1987).

Psychoanalytic and Neopsychoanalytic Theories of Personality

Freud believed that human behavior was heavily influenced by unconscious processes. The unsocialized person is motivated primarily by instinctual drives, according to psychoanalytic theory, and it is only through successful resolution of innate conflicts between these instinctual drives and societal constraints that passion yields to reason as the determinant of behavior (Langer, 1969: 13–23).

The struggle between satisfying one's own instinctual drives and the demands of others was seen by Freud as occurring through the interaction of the id, ego, and superego, the major components of the personality structure. The *id* is the part of the personality that operates from the *pleasure principle,* seeking to gratify instinctual drives or increase pleasure and reduce pain. The *superego* is the part of the personality that incorporates the demands of society. Freud (1938) suggested that the development of the *conscience* stems from the adult punishment of unwanted behaviors. Freud also suggests that the punishment of the child's id impulses can result in *neurotic anxiety,* which then surrounds behaviors or thoughts associated with that particular id impulse. The child also develops an *ego-ideal,* which represents the good behaviors that have been praised. The *ego* mediates between the id and the superego, attempting to find ways in which the needs of both can be met. *Defense mechanisms* are used by the ego as part of the mediating process, and healthy personalities, according to Freud, result from the flexible and adaptive use of these tools. One of the major defense mechanisms Freud suggested was *repression.* Repression is the mechanism in which the unconscious denies the existence of anxiety-producing situations. According to Freud, repression of thoughts, feelings, and events plays an important part in the development of neurotic behaviors.

The development of a strong and functional adaptive ego occurs through a series of stages. Each stage corresponds to a specific bodily zone in which instinctual patterns are activated. In the *oral stage,* the mouth is the primary source of stimulation and pleasure and is of most significance from birth to about 1 year of age. During the *anal stage*, attention shifts to the anus, and bowel movements become the prime source of gratification or frustration (1–3 years of age). At about 3 years of age, the child enters the *phallic stage,* in which the genital area becomes the focus of instinctual drives. This lasts until about age 5. Freud believed that the child's sexual drive then becomes dormant and that socialization takes precedence during the *latency stage* (6–12 years of age). Sexual needs arise again during puberty.

Freudian theory asserts that when a child experiences too much gratification or becomes excessively frustrated in dealing with instinctual drives during a particular stage, she or he will become fixated at that developmental level. Each stage needs to be successfully negotiated before one moves on to the next one. Fixation in particular stages leads to development of neurosis or complexes, which Freud described as fixed patterns of response of a person to the environment. Freud's view of human nature was one of constant internal struggle being waged between our innate basic drives and the demands of our environment. A person's primary goal is to reduce anxiety or tension. Freud's primary method of treatment for a person in distress was psychoanalysis. Analysis is the process in which repressed memories, fears, thoughts, and actions are recovered from the unconscious and reevaluated through a more mature ego.

Another school of personality theorists who broke from traditional Freudian theory are termed *neopsychoanalysts*. They include Carl Jung, Alfred Adler, Melanie Klein, and Karen Horney. For an introduction to the general approach, we will only discuss Karen Horney. Generally, the neopsychoanalytic approaches stress the social influences of human behavior and place less emphasis on innate, biologically based drives. These approaches are also less deterministic and tend to be more growth oriented than Freudian theory. Karen Horney (1950) states, for example:

> . . . the human individual, given a chance, tends to develop his parti-
> cular human potentialities. He will develop then the unique forces of
> his real self: the clarity and depth of his own feelings, thoughts, wishes,
> interests; the ability to tap his own resources, the strength of his will
> power; the special capacities or gifts he may have; the faculty to express
> himself, and to relate himself to others with his spontaneous feelings.
> All of this will enable him to find his set of values and his aims in life.
> In short, he will grow, substantially undiverted, toward self-realization.
> (Horney, 1950: 17)

Horney also believed that children need a safe and supportive environment
in which to grow and to meet their potential. The importance of nurturing
parents or caregivers is, therefore, essential for the development of a healthy
personality. Horney believed that the overindulgence of caregivers can lead to
helpless behaviors in children. Hostile, abusive, or neglectful behavior of
caregivers leads to fearfulness in the child. In both cases, however, the child
turns these feelings of fear or helplessness into repressed hostility toward the
caregiver. This change occurs because the child's developmental needs are being
thwarted. This repressed hostility turns into a *basic anxiety* or sense of aloneness
and helplessness. Horney suggested that, to deal with this anxiety, one develops
certain neurotic stances within the personality structure. She postulated
four basic neurotic stances in response to this anxiety: (1) seeking love and
approval at any cost; (2) seeking power over others and feelings of superiority;
(3) becoming submissive as a means of preventing criticism; and (4) avoiding
significant contact with others. These stances are considered neurotic tendencies,
because they are mainly seeking the avoidance of pain, rather than self-
realization. Although Horney did develop some basic neurotic personality types,
she still believed in the uniqueness of each individual. She also believed in the
ability of persons to reshape their personality as they become more aware of
themselves. The neopsychoanalytic theories of Carl Jung (1947), Alfred Adler
(1963), Harry Stack Sullivan (1953), Melanie Klein (1975), and Karen Horney
are a further development of Freudian theory. In varying degrees and methods,
they are more inclusive of environmental factors in the formation of personality
and human behavior.

Freud did not extend his developmental model beyond puberty. However,
a disciple of Freud, Erik Erikson, did extend the Freudian developmental model
throughout the life span through the use of the social and cultural matrix.

Erikson proposed eight developmental stages, each characterized by a
psychosocial crisis involving the interaction of biological, psychological, social,
and cultural variables. He presented psychosocial tasks accompanying each
developmental stage in terms of polar opposites. Because you have probably
already studied Erikson in a basic psychology course, we will only review the
basic tenets of his theory here. Table 3.1 summarizes Erikson's developmental
stages. The psychosocial tasks are presented on a continuum, reflecting the

TABLE 3.1 Erikson's developmental stages

Stage	Psychosocial Task	Successful Resolution
1. Infancy	Trust-mistrust	Hope
2. Early childhood	Autonomy-shame/doubt	Will
3. Middle childhood	Initiative-guilt	Purpose
4. Late childhood	Industry-inferiority	Competence
5. Adolescence	Identity-identity confusion	Fidelity
6. Young adulthood	Intimacy-isolation	Love
7. Maturity	Generativity-self-absorption	Care
8. Old age	Integrity-despair	Wisdom

Adapted from Erikson, E. (1976). *Adulthood*. New York: W. W. Norton.

opinion that individuals function somewhere between the polarities possible for each.

In Erikson's schema, personality is formed through the successful or unsuccessful resolution of sequential developmental psychosocial tasks. For example, infants, although born with many innate capacities to learn and interact with their environment, are unable to care for themselves. Food, warmth, touch, and stimulation are all essential ingredients for the survival of the infant and for successful bonding with the caregiver. Lack of any of these "nutrients" can result in serious emotional or physical harm, including death. Resolution of this developmental stage leads to the infant developing a sense of trust that basic needs will be met. In his latest work, which focuses on the culmination of the impact of each of these stages in old age, Erikson states that the successful completion of the infancy stage results in appreciation of interdependence and relatedness (Goleman, 1988). Old age is Erikson's last stage. Erikson believes that the central task of old age is making sense of one's life and believing that one's having lived matters in a significant way. Successful aging involves a sense of pride in one's accomplishments and an acceptance of one's own life, as well as a willingness to face one's mortality. When these late-life tasks are not resolved, despair and depression characterize old age. When they have been successfully accomplished, old age culminates in existential identity, with a sense of integrity strong enough to withstand physical disintegration.

Those who use the psychoanalytic approach in social work practice generally emphasize therapeutic techniques to focus the client's attention on his or her childhood experiences, thoughts, and emotions. These aspects of life are confronted and worked through so that their effect on current behavior is reduced. Many social workers who practice with individuals emphasize ego functioning, attempting to strengthen the ego's ability to mediate id and superego forces. Focusing on the ego generally involves current behavior, with less emphasis on the past. Social workers also use psychoanalytic developmental theories to emphasize the need for caring, supportive, and creative environments for children, adolescents, and adults. Social workers use these principles, for example, when providing caregivers with information about childrearing. Such principles are also put to work when one is devising early intervention programs, such as Head Start.

One of the issues, however, in psychoanalytic theories that postulate development through stages is *cultural variation* in development. Research shows that there are great differences in the way people are reared, the way they are socialized, and the kinds of problems that characterize people in different societies (Goleman, 1989). This research suggests that personality development must be understood within its cultural context, rather than being seen as an invariant process, based in set developmental stages. This understanding is, of course, what we would expect from our effort in this book to integrate biological, psychological, social-structural, and cultural functioning.

Another concern with the psychoanalytic approach is its gender bias, as noted by Gilligan (1982, 1990), Chodorow (1989), Chafetz (1988), and others. The developmental models of Freud and Erikson consider the male experience to be the norm. By implication, if not by definition, variations are considered deviant. Psychological characteristics, such as emotionalism, dependence, and passivity, for instance, have been attributed to women and interpreted as manifestations of psychopathology. However, Gilligan suggests a young girl's relationship with her mother in infancy and early childhood establishes the base for her adult identity rooted in nurturance, care, and responsibility. Men, on the other hand, having separated from their mothers during their early developmental stages, define themselves in adulthood in terms of abstract qualities such as justice, rather than through interpersonal relationships (Gilligan, 1982: 160–161). Thus, while men and women develop different psychological characteristics, neither is "better" than the other. Men and women simply stem from different life experiences and life needs.

Chodorow (1989), a sociologist, also challenges traditional psychoanalytic theory for its treatment of women as defective or inferior. Chodorow, like Gilligan, believes the mother-daughter relationship is the prototype of the adult capacity to relate in a caring way to others. Males, having to separate from the opposite-sex parent in order to establish identity, often experience difficulty in maintaining intimate relations in adult life. Social learning theories stressing the role of socialization in gender identity and gender roles are more congruent with feminist thought than are traditional psychoanalytic theories (Valentich, 1986: 571).

Humanistic Theories of Personality

Humanistic approaches to explaining behavior view the human person as co-creator of one's own personhood. Directed by an innate thrust toward self-actualization, the person engages with and acts upon the environment in a mutually fulfilling way. Humanistic theories differ significantly from behavioral and psychoanalytic explanations of human behavior but are quite compatible with cognitive theories. Both types of theory emphasize the role of will and choice in human action and underline the importance the individual assigns to the meaning of events and experiences.

Humanistic perspectives on behavior are rooted in philosophical constructs and are illuminated as much through literature and the arts as through the social and behavioral sciences. The assumptions regarding the dignity and worth of the human person and the individual's direction toward growth, inherent in these approaches, are not only congruent with social work values but can be seen as their embodiment. Humanists often find stage theories of development too linear and simplistic to explain human behavior in all its complexity. They also consider psychoanalytical and behavioral theories as too focused on abnormal or deviant behavior, rather than on the positive and growth-oriented nature of persons. Although their criticism may be overstated, it is important to note what contributes to healthy growth and development. Like some of the cognitive and neopsychoanalytic theorists, humanistic psychologists place a great deal of emphasis on environmental factors as contributors to personality development and human behavior.

Abraham Maslow's need theory of human behavior is based on humanistic principles. He sees needs as organized into a hierarchy, with the lower needs having to be fulfilled before higher needs can be met. Figure 3.1 illustrates the needs that Maslow believes are essential for full human development.

According to Maslow, physiological needs must be met before security needs can be addressed. Needs for belonging and esteem follow, and at the apex of the hierarchy are self-actualization needs. The self-actualized human being closely resembles the person who has successfully resolved Erikson's last developmental stage and is thus subject to the same criticisms regarding male bias that were levied at Erikson. Maslow's framework of human needs has obvious implications for social workers. Lack of resources like food, clothing, and shelter leaves basic physiological needs unmet and creates almost insurmountable obstacles to meeting other kinds of needs. Difficulties in providing services to homeless families and individuals may support Maslow's assertion that basic physiological needs must be met before people can find the energy to meet other needs. It should be noted, however, that many people around the world suffer from the

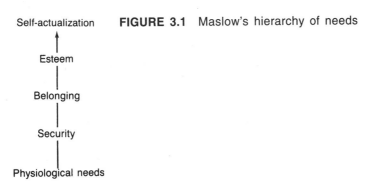

Self-actualization   **FIGURE 3.1** Maslow's hierarchy of needs

↑

Esteem

Belonging

Security

Physiological needs

ravages of poverty and deprivation, yet they are still able to sustain emotional relatedness and maintain a sense of self-esteem. In this sense, Maslow's hierarchy becomes an ideal structure that suggests an optimal environment for growth and development. It should not be viewed as a predictive instrument, which suggests, for example, that when one does not enjoy a safe and secure environment, he or she will not be able to achieve meaningful relationships. Indeed, history demonstrates that in times of disasters, people form close and supportive community.

BASIC SOCIAL-STRUCTURAL CONCEPTS

Social structure, or *social organization,* refers to the ways in which social behavior becomes patterned and predictable. Underlying the concept of social structure is the belief that social behavior (how we act in social situations) is, for the most part, organized and nonrandom. Several kinds of patterning occur. **Social institutions** organize activities around particular social purposes or functions and are especially important parts of the social structure. For example, the family (a social institution) organizes people—father, mother, husbands, wives, sons, daughters, lovers, cousins, in-laws, and so forth—around the performance of functions essential to the survival of society. Reproduction, care for the young, education, primary group relationships, and decision making about economic resources are examples of these functions. Other social institutions include education, religion, politics, economics, organizations, and social welfare. Each of these institutions organizes the behavior of large numbers of people around social functions and thus serves to introduce order and predictability into social relationships. The process by which social institutions form and organize human behavior is called **socialization**. The types of behavior in social institutions are called roles. A **role** refers to the expected behavior of categories of people within social institutions: the role of mothers, sons, group members, couples, religious community members, workers, managers, and so on. Most people participate in many social institutions and occupy many roles at the same time. While the concept of role explains the predictability of much social behavior, occupying multiple roles simultaneously (mother, executive, wife) often produces **role conflict**, wherein the effective performance of one role may be in direct conflict with the effective performance of other roles. Another problem is **role strain**, which occurs when the behavioral expectations associated with a specific role are inconsistent. An example is when parents are expected to provide nurturing and discipline, yet experience these activities as inconsistent. As mentioned in Chapter 1, social workers often experience role strain when placed in practice situations in which they play both a social helping and a social control function, such as in child protective services.

Social institutions are developed to serve social purposes or functions. There are both **manifest functions** and **latent functions of social institutions**. Manifest functions are publicly stated and are assumed to be for the good of society as a whole. Latent functions are less publicly visible and more beneficial for some groups in society than for others. For example, the manifest function of social welfare as a social institution is to provide basic resources for those who lack them. However, the point is often made that the latent function may be to control people, especially minority groups and the poor. Social welfare from this perspective is a means of allocation of wealth for the purpose of maintaining a hierarchical income structure (Piven and Cloward, 1971). In part, this relates to the nature of the interaction among people and groups in a social structure. **Cooperative interaction**, **competitive interaction**, and **conflict** are three ways in which social interaction occurs. Each of these ways of interaction is viewed as positive or negative, according to different theorists. By looking at the economic system we may see how these three methods have been conceptualized by various social theorists. Sociologist Talcott Parsons (1951), for example, viewed cooperation, or the principle of *complementarity,* as essential to social order. According to Parsons, social order exists because of a harmonious relationship between the person, the culture, and the society. The relationships between social institutions, as well as between members of those institutions, functions as a result of the complementarity of their various roles. The roles of the laborer, the manager, and the owner, for example, complement each other for the benefit of all. Social or institutional change is seen as deviant. If necessary, however, change should occur through the cooperation of all members and without major disruption of the social order. Role socialization is essential in this process. Common cultural values influence the establishment of **norms**, or common expectations of behavior within social institutions, which become *institutionalized*. Persons are socialized into normative behavior through the *internalization* of these values and norms. Parsons suggested that if the socialization process were effective, the power of shame and guilt would act as personal factors in role compliance. Conflict, as viewed by Parsons, results from inconsistent rules within the social institution.

Parsons was intrigued by philosopher Thomas Hobbes' view of human nature as the "war of all against all." Parsons' view on the functionality of cooperation for the preservation of the social order was an attempt to suggest an alternative to Hobbes' perspective. One can see how the contemporary "trickle-down" theory of some economists would be compatible with Parsons' view. The theory states that the more wealth available to those at the top of the economic structure, the more wealth will "trickle down" to the lower levels. However, capitalism is also based upon competition and is, therefore, similar to Hobbes' view of human relations. Capitalism, as an economic institution, is based on competition between individuals, groups, and societies for a limited number of resources. Daly and Cobb state:

> Capitalism consists of private ownership of the means of production along with allocation and distribution provided by the market. Individual maximization of profit by firms and maximization of satisfaction (utility) by consumers provides the motive force, while competition, the existence of many buyers and sellers in the market, provides the famous invisible

hand that leads private interest to serve the public welfare. (Daly and Cobb, 1989: 13)

Competition is often seen as the natural state of nature. Many of our social institutions are structured around competition. In capitalist countries, competition is part of the normative behavior that becomes a part of our socialization. Kohn (1986: 70) states that "capitalism can be thought of as the heart of competitiveness in American society." Social reproduction theorists, such as Karl Marx (1969) and Peter Bourdieu (1977), propose that societies tend to reproduce themselves through the structure and content of their formal and informal educational institutions. Marx focused primarily on the reproduction of economic systems, whereas Bourdieu stressed cultural reproduction or transmission of cultural values. Both Marx and Bourdieu stated that the values of the dominant or most powerful are those that are most inculcated into the major social institutions of a society. As an example, we may look at the present American educational system for an analysis of these theories. Bourdieu would suggest that the educational system is the main vehicle of distribution of dominant culture values, including the acceptance of a class-structured society. Education becomes a means of entrance into the higher classes. Participation in the formal educational system guarantees socialization into the dominant culture's values. Marx, however, looked at the educational system as a mirror of the economic system. Grading, private versus public education, testing, teacher and administrative authority, departmentalization of subject matter, and tracking (separating students by ability) would all be seen by Marx as reflecting the values and structures of capitalism and class separation. Whereas the functionalist (Parsons and Durkheim) saw conflict as an aberration of normal relations, Marx saw it as an inevitable consequence of inequality. Yet another view of the equation of competition, cooperation, and conflict is provided by **social exchange theory**. Social exchange theory suggests that any relationship is based on a mutually agreed-upon exchange in which benefits and losses are evaluated and balanced. In the case of capitalism, social exchange theory resembles Parsons' functionalist perspective. The relationship between labor, management, and owners is based, in social exchange theory, on an exchange of commodities (labor, activity coordination, and capital) in which all parties derive equitable benefits. This theory proposes that enlightened self-interest drives cooperation between parties within a system. According to classic capitalistic economic theory, competition between markets is itself a form of cooperation that supports a healthy economy. Conflict, according to social exchange theory, would occur only if the relationships were unbalanced or unfair to one of the parties. Balance can be restored by a renegotiation of the relationship or by one party strengthening its bargaining position. Conflict is seen as a temporary maladjustment in the natural order of things. These are just a few examples of how various theorists have looked at cooperation, competition, and conflict.

Social structures rarely treat everyone equally. Usually, there is some type of social differentiation in which criteria are used to distinguish between groups of people. Commonly used criteria are age, sex, race, ethnicity, religion, sexual orientation, and physical characteristics, such as size, color of hair, and physical abilities. Although such differentiation can be used simply to suggest group membership, it may also be used to stratify people. For example, children are not allowed to drive automobiles, because they lack the ability to do so, but certain ethnic groups or members of the gay community may be denied housing or employment simply because of their skin color or sexual orientation. Only within the last decade were women allowed active-duty status in fire and police departments. **Social stratification** creates a hierarchy, a vertical arrangement of people on the basis of their possession of certain characteristics. This results in **social differentiation**.

In a stratified system, some people are considered more important than others. This lays the foundation for discrimination and prejudice. **Discrimination** involves actions that disadvantage people who are considered less worthy. Those actions are based on **prejudice**, beliefs that attribute negative characteristics to people without any concrete evidence to support those beliefs. Social stratification often guarantees unequal access to societal resources for the less-favored members of society. The result is the development of distinct **social classes**.

Those with access to resources usually have power. As you recall from Chapter 1, **power** is the ability of a person or group to enforce its will on others, and it may be based on **authority**, which is legitimate power, or **coercion**, the use of illegitimate force. The importance of power is the control it provides over necessary or desirable resources—food, shelter, reputation, land, weapons, money, education. The use of condign (punishment) and compensatory (rewards) forms of power in the form of **social sanctions**, and conditioned (influence) power in the form of social indoctrination, are all utilized in role socialization and social control. Those in power control the decision making that establishes the policies that determine the production and distribution of many socially desirable resources.

Most resources needed for survival and personal development are produced through the economic institution. Its social functions are to extract natural resources from the environment, produce goods from them, distribute these goods, and provide needed services. These functions are performed through the use of land, labor, capital, entrepreneurship, and technology. Those with power control economic resources. This control gives them access to more goods and services, as well as to the decision-making ability that enables them to protect their privileged position. As a result, inequalities between groups develop, based on the amount of power they have. Miles (1989) suggested that the development of racist ideology is based on the categorization of social groups according to natural divisions between people and the assignment of false traits. He then states:

> Racism was not simply a legitimation of class exploitation (although it was that) but, more important, it constructed the social world in a way that identified a certain population as a laboring class. The problem that remained was to organize the social world in such a way that forced

the population into its 'natural' class position: in other words, reality had to be brought into line with that representation in order to ensure the material objective of production. (Miles, 1989: 105)

The use of discriminatory language and ideology as a means of social control is not limited to race. In the United States, majority groups include males, those from Western European backgrounds, Caucasians, the wealthy, and heterosexuals, whereas women, other racial and ethnic groups, the poor, the elderly, children, those with physical disabilities, and homosexuals are minorities. Each of these minority groups are subjected to discriminatory ideology and language. Membership in a minority group increases the likelihood that one's resources will be limited. For example, women and minorities have less income than Caucasian males. Women and children of all races account for most of the poverty in America.

We have discussed some of the concepts related to social institutions and their relationship to the socialization process. By way of example, we have also discussed the economic system and, to a lesser degree, the educational system. Let us now look briefly at some of the other social institutions that affect human behavior: the family, the community, and the organization. Each of these subjects is worthy of in-depth study but, again, for our purpose here, we will briefly discuss some of the major concepts.

The Family

The family is the most basic unit of society. In Chapter 2 we referred to the family as a system. As such, it embodies a set of relationships among the members of that system. The family system also relates to other systems. We will discuss both of these internal relationships of the family as they relate to influence on human behavior. We will begin by discussing the variety of family structures present in today's society.

For the purpose of discussion, we will consider couples with and without children as a family constellation. No distinction between heterosexual and homosexual adult couples is made, although a unique set of problems and discriminatory practices face homosexual couples and families with homosexual adult parental figures (Pies, 1988). Some basic family structures are:

1. Two-parent families with both parents in their first marriage.
2. Single-parent families headed either by the divorced or never-married mother or father.
3. Two-parent stepfamilies with children from one or both previous marriages.
4. Couples without children of their own.
5. Extended families in which many related adults and children live in the same household.

6. Communal families in which unrelated adults and children live in the same household.
7. Foster and adoptive families.
8. Subfamilies—young families (married or single-parent) living in their parental home.

The family unit is the initial source of a child's development and socialization. It is usually through the family that the child receives the care and nurturance necessary to sustain life during its early years of life. In the past, and in other cultures, children may have received a great amount of care from surrogates. During the period of slavery in the United States, for example, Caucasian children often were cared for by African-American slave women. In some cultures, childrearing is considered a community responsibility, shared not only by the parents but by all adults within the community.

The number of children in America being raised in traditional two-parent families is declining. In 1960, 87.7 percent of all children under 18 were living in two-parent families. In America today, however, the number has dropped to 70.7 percent. The most dramatic increase is in the number of children being raised solely by the mother. In 1960, 8 percent were living in single-female-headed households, whereas in 1992 the number climbed to 23.3 percent. Table 3.2 demonstrates the changes in the living arrangements of children under 18 years of age in 1960 and 1992. The economic plight of families, especially young families (parents under age 30), is especially difficult. The Children's Defense Fund (1992) reports that between 1973 and 1990, young families' income decreased 32.1 percent. Family income for those headed by adults between the ages 30 and 64 decreased by only 6.4 percent, whereas families without children experienced a 11.2 percent increase in their income. The loss of income may explain why, of the 6 million young families in America today, 1.5 million, with 2.3 million children, are living in their parents' homes. As a result, the poverty rate for children in young families has increased from 20 percent in 1973 to 40 percent in 1990. The poverty rates are significantly correlated to race (African-American families 68 percent, Latino families 51 percent), education (families headed by high school drop outs, 64 percent), and single-female-headed households (77 percent).

The Children's Defense Fund (1992) attributes most of the decline in income to:

> . . . a devastating combination of changes in the American economy, government's inadequate response to families in trouble, and in changes in composition of young families themselves. . . . The growth in young female-headed families with children is in part a reflection of changing values. But the economic hardships associated with falling earnings and persistent joblessness among young adults also have contributed significantly to falling marriage rates and the increasing rates of out-of-wedlock childbearing. (CDF, 1992: 3)

TABLE 3.2 Living arrangements of children under 18, by race and Hispanic origin: 1960 and 1992

Living Arrangement	1960	1992
All Races		
% Living with two parents	87.7	70.7
% Living with one parent	9.1	26.6
% Mother only	8.9	23.3
% Father only	1.1	3.3
% Other relatives	2.5	2.0
% Nonrelatives	0.7	0.6
White		
% Living with two parents	90.9	77.4
% Mother only	6.1	17.6
% Father only	1.0	3.3
% All others	1.9	1.7
Black*		
% Living with two parents	67.0	35.6
% Mother only	19.9	53.8
% Father only	2.0	3.1
% All others	11.1	7.5
Hispanic**		
% Living with two parents	na	64.8
% Mother only	na	28.5
% Father only	na	3.7
% All others	na	3.1

* Blacks include all nonwhites in 1960.
** Persons of Hispanic origin may be of any race.
From: U.S. Bureau of the Census, "Marital Status and Living Arrangements," *Current Populations Reports,* Series P-20. March 1988, No. 433, Table A-4; and March 1992, No. 468, Table G. Excludes persons under 18 years of age who were maintaining households or families.

Social and economic stressors have a significant impact on the family. From a systems perspective, the family plays an important function in society. The family is the primary social and economic component of the social structure. The family is the primary institution for the socialization of children. The family teaches the child the values and the behavioral expectations of the larger society. It also serves an economic function as the primary unit of consumption and labor. Economic conditions over the last two decades have made it increasingly necessary for both parents to work. This in turn has affected the internal function, especially childrearing. When both parents, or in some cases single parents, are required to work outside the home, alternative child-care arrangements are necessary. When stressors, such as worsening economic conditions, occur, the ability of the family unit to perform its roles is weakened, and both the family and society suffer.

Studies by Acock and Demo (1994) regarding family structure and well-being provide interesting data:

1. Mothers' well-being was related less to the type of family structure than to positive internal family process (lack of marital and child-parent conflict) and to their children's well-being.
2. Childrens' well-being was also correlated to positive family relations, regardless of family structure.
3. The well-being of children of divorced parents and who were living with the single mother was less than that of children in any other family arrangement.

Functional and social-exchange theories provide ways to view family functioning. Functional theory would suggest that the family is composed of persons who play various roles (father: income production; mother: childrearing, home-making, emotional nurturance). These roles, according to functional theory, are defined by both biology and culture and represent a natural order. Social exchange theory would postulate that these roles are defined within the family and represent a balance of self-interest. Both of these approaches are criticized from some feminist perspectives. Feminist writers (Baber and Allen, 1992; Goodrich et al., 1988; Walters et al., 1988; Wainrib, 1992; and Gilligan et al., 1991) have suggested that power is not equally distributed within families. Men maintain both social and economic power within the family and are generally supported by a patriarchal social structure. Women are primarily responsible for the majority of the daily activities related to family maintenance, as well as securing additional family income.

Baber and Allen (1992) suggest that "the family is one of the most powerful socializing institutions. It is within the family that people construct beliefs about the sexual division of labor, learn about the regulation of sexuality, and experience the effects of gender, class, and race hierarchies in personal and intimate ways." This position is congruent with economic and cultural reproduction theories, which see the family as a vehicle for the recapitulation of dominant social and cultural values. One final framework in which to view the family is a family development or family life-course model. Such models (Germain, 1991; Duvall and Miller, 1985) seek to frame family life in terms of changing family relationships and related psychosocial tasks over time. These models usually distinguish particular periods throughout the life course: couple formation, various stages of childrearing (according to children's ages), middle-age couple reformulation, caring for aging parents, and old age (retirement and death). Such models provide a framework for viewing family life. However, as noted earlier, stage models need to account for the vast diversity in cultural family arrangements, as well as for the incorporation of nonnormative events. Exhibit 4.1 ("AIDS Toll on Elderly: Dying Grandchildren") at the end of Chapter 4 is one example of a family's struggle to deal with a tragic and unexpected event.

There are many ways in which to view families: via structural arrangements, communication patterns, internal roles, relationships to other systems, to name just a few. It is important in social work to continue to learn more about these issues regarding families from macro (policy), mezzo (program), and micro (individual family intervention) level perspectives.

Weick and Saleebey (1995) suggest that family theory has been influenced by developmental, psychodynamic, systems, and strategic (organizational) theory. Many of these theories have added to the belief that a normative family experience exists and can be quantified through the use of family functioning scales. These authors state:

> The obverse of this theme, however, is apparent in the imagery, symbols, and lexicon by which we describe and discuss families that seek help. Professional discourse about family life and treatment are often articulated in the language of pathology, deficit, disorder, and disorganization. Although our search for the "normal" family continues clinical theory, practice, and education tend to focus on the problem family and family problems. To the extent that this lexicon prevails, we inadvertently perpetuate some of the myths about families that exist at the policy level. (Weick and Saleebey, 1995: 146)

Operating from a strengths and holistic perspective, the individual family should be viewed as goal-directed and possesing resources and competencies. Although problems may exist within the family, it is the strengths and resources that will be used to cope, function, change, and grow. From a social perspective, the family is viewed as an integral part of community and national life. Policies that support families at national, state, and local levels are the subjects of social work advocacy.

Clearly, much of who we are is a result of our family experience. Social work utilizes practice models and empirical research studies (explanatory and intervention) to inform practice. It is equally important, however, to view each family as unique and to strive to understand each family's view of the various aspects of their life together. Although models provide a beginning frame of reference, they should not shadow our perceptions of reality. The family itself is the single most important source of information about itself, and every effort should be made by the social worker to understand its perspective. It is also important, from a social work perspective, to review family theory models as to their emphasis on strengths and their orientation to health and growth.

Economic conditions provide a major stressor on families and family functioning. Social work support for legislation and policies that provide resources to families, either through viable employment and child-care assistance or through adequate support benefits, is needed. Another example in which social work can provide advocacy is to strive to eliminate laws that restrict parental rights due to sexual orientation. Health-care policies that allow for the dignified care of the elderly, regardless of family income, are yet another example of possible social work intervention. These are but a few of the myriad of ways social work can provide support to families so as to improve family health and welfare.

The Community

Communities are another social-structural arrangement that effects human behavior. The German scholar, Ferdinand Toennies (1965), made the distinction between *gemeinschaft* (community) and *gesellschaft* (society). Toennies stated that communities were natural groupings of people based on kinship, neighborhood, or shared cultural values and marked by informal, yet cohesive, relationships. He contrasted community with society, which is marked by formal and legal relationships. The community may be viewed as a larger system that is composed of smaller systems. For example, a *geographical community* is defined by its geographical boundaries. A neighborhood is sometimes called a community. It is comprised of families, individuals, businesses, churches, and service organizations. All of these entities could be referred to as subsystems of the larger community system. This type of community, however, is also a subsystem of the larger societal system. Another form of community is an *ideational community*, which is comprised of persons who share common goals and values. Examples of these types of communities might be groups of professionals from a particular field. (We sometimes refer to ourselves as "the social work community.") Persons who belong to a religious denomination are sometimes called members of the religious community. Artists belong to the arts community. *Affiliational communities* are comprised of persons sharing some common characteristic. Persons belong to various ethnic communities, gay and lesbian communities, the deaf community, etc. Whether involvement is by choice or circumstance, communities play a role in the socialization process of persons. Communities often have a unique culture. Communities, like families, have values and norms that regulate the behavior of their members. Communities may also have specific symbols and rituals that distinguish membership. Street gang members often refer to themselves as part of a community of brothers and sisters. They have a code of behavior, which includes expectations of loyalty, unity, and commitment. Gangs usually have distinguishing symbols, such as their "colors" or a special tattoo that marks membership. The strengths of the relationship between members may be somewhat fluid and social, as in the case of the arts community. They may be very strong, when self-preservation is a factor, as in the case of street gangs. Communities are very important social structures that provide support to their members. In the assessment process, social workers attempt to understand the nature and strength of these relationships for the person with whom they are working. Many persons with whom social workers practice find themselves isolated and without essential support. Single parents, gay and lesbian adolescents, the elderly, and the physically disabled are often in need of a supportive community. Social workers may assist these persons in finding and joining such communities. In cases where no such support communities exist, the social worker may initiate the establishment of supportive communities.

Sometimes, communities may have a negative impact on their members or on other communities. For example, some religious denominations openly condemn homosexuals. In such cases, the homosexual member of that community is either forced to hide his or her sexual orientation or risk losing the support of its membership. When a neighborhood joins together to keep out a proposed group home for the mentally ill, the geographical community acts to the detriment of the mentally disabled community. The social work task in such situations might be to provide education to the people of the neighborhood regarding mental illness or to provide mediation services to the two groups. Conflict and competition models of interaction would view this neighborhood dispute as an inevitable result of a struggle over limited resources—space, property values, safety, etc. (Savage and Warde, 1993). Many models of community work begin with an assessment that focuses on existing or potential problems. McKnight and Kretzman (1993) suggest that such assessments focus on the problems the community has and on the resources it lacks (drugs, crime, poor housing stock). As a result of this perspective, communities begin to see themselves as "needy" and dependent on outside assistance. McKnight and Kretzman suggest, as an alternative, an assessment of community strengths and resources. They call this asset mapping of a community. In this model all entities within the community are seen as assets that can be mobilized in ways that support community life. Figure 3.2 demonstrates McKnight and Kretzman's problem or needs assessment of a community versus a community capacity or strengths-assessment perspective. In this manner it is similar to Collins and Pancoast's (NASW) study of indigenous and informal community support elements they termed *natural helping networks*. This model is especially intriguing from a social work perspective in that it stresses community growth,

FIGURE 3.2   Neighborhood needs map (left) and community assets map (right)

From: McKnight, J. and J. Kretzman (1993). *Building Communities from the Inside Out.* Evanston, IL: Center for Urban Affairs and Policy Research, pp. 3, 7. Reprinted with permission of the authors.

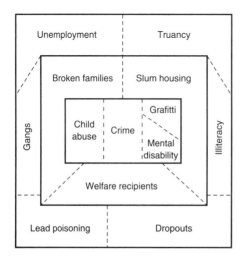
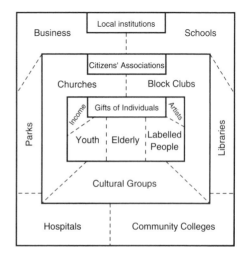

self-determination, health, empowerment, systems interaction, and diversity through the unique gifts of its members.

It is important to view community life in context. Questions of the relationship of the individual to the larger community are found in Plato's *Republic* and Thomas More's *Utopia*. In America, tension has historically existed between two deeply embedded values—individuality and communalism. Bellah et al. (1986) state that this tension can be traced to our earliest traditions. The authors refer to de Tocqueville, who called these traditions "habits of the heart." America has a deep biblical and religious tradition, dating back to its earliest Puritan communities, which suggests an ideal of mutual caring and support of all individuals. It possesses an equally strong tradition valuing individual rights, as suggested in the writings of political economist Adam Smith and businessman and social commentator Benjamin Franklin. The tension between these habits of the heart exists even today. Contemporary issues, such as universal health care or the establishment of "walled communities" (neighborhoods that build physical barriers to limit access to protect against crime), can be viewed in terms of the tension between individualism and communalism. The communal tradition would suggest a societal or communal responsibility for caring for all members of society. This tradition might support universal health care and oppose the segregation of neighborhoods. The individualistic tradition would suggest individual responsibility and oppose universal health care and support the neighborhood's right to protect itself. Cultural values, such as individualism and communalism, have deep historical roots. As such, they affect the development and nature of the social institutions that surround us. These institutions, in turn, socialize human behavior in accordance with cultural values and social expectations.

The Organization

As societies grew from small villages and an agrarian economy (gemeinshaft) to larger cities and an industrial economy (gesellschaft), the relationships that governed social and economic life changed. Agrarian economies are characterized by informal and individualized trade and labor relationships. The industrial revolution and the corresponding development of cities brought about a new form of social and economic relationships—the organization. Organizations are usually referred to as collectives of individuals gathered to serve a particular purpose. Talcott Parsons (1960) suggested that the organization is defined by the primacy of attaining a specific goal. Organizations are formal social structures that are formed to meet the common goals of their members. There are many types of organizations: charitable or service organizations (United Way, Habitat for Humanity, YWCA, Better Business Bureau), civic organizations (League of Women Voters, Rotary Club, The Shriners), professional organizations (National Association of Social Workers, American Psychiatric Association, American Medical Association), and work organizations (businesses, human service agencies). Regardless of type, organizations are distinguished by their relatively formal structural arrangements. These structures are usually developed to maintain effective work towards a defined goal. Structures that define decision making and work coordination are two of the most important within organizations. Much of our daily life is affected by organizations. As social workers we are employed by an organization. The clients we serve are affected by the service organizations with which they have contact, as well as by the work settings in which they may be employed. Sociologists and social psychologists have studied organizations and organizational behavior for many decades. In recent years, renewed interest has been established regarding organizations based on the work of W. Edwards Deming's theories of total quality management. Literally thousands of books and articles have been written over the last 50 years regarding organizational structures, management theory, decision making, work coordination, labor-management relations, and work productivity. Our discussion here will be more modest and focus on a brief overview of bureaucracies, as one type of organization, and on two broad theories of management.

A German sociologist of the structural school, Max Weber (1947), was the first to use the word *bureaucracy*. Weber stated that the bureaucratic organization was marked by several distinguishing principles of operation: a clear and hierarchical decision-making structure; a centralized coordination of work; specialization of labor; formal and impersonal relationships; clear expectations of productivity; and hiring and promotion based on technical knowledge. Weber saw the bureaucracy as an *ideal-type* of organization that embodied rationality, efficiency, and stability. The mass production needs of the industrial revolution gave rise to the bureaucratic arrangement of work. Weber's original interest was in the nature and origins of power and authority. Weber believed that power and authority were bestowed either on the basis of tradition (royalty, patrimony) or charisma (personal influence). He suggested that the bureaucracy was based on a rational or legalistic form of power bestowed on persons based on their technical knowledge and ability to meet organizational goals. The epitome of human behavior with an organization is Merton's (1952) *bureaucratic personality*, which he described as persons who become more concerned with the procedural compliance than with the overall goal of the organization.

Weber's study of organizations gave rise to the development of interventional theories of organizational management. The most noted of these early theories was Frederick Taylor's (1947) *scientific management*. Scientific management closely followed Weber's principles of bureaucratic organization. Taylor's contribution was to postulate that work processes could be studied, analyzed, and streamlined to maximize productivity. Underlying Taylor's management theories was the belief that workers were solely motivated by economic self-interest. As a result, he suggested that the most sensible form of worker motivation would be the piecemeal wage, in which the worker would be paid only for each piece of work completed. This principle is still used today in large-city sweatshops that employ immigrant labor.

The structural or scientific management theorists were followed by the *human relations theorists*, beginning with those of the well-known Hawthorne studies. These theorists believed that workers were motivated as much by individual commitment to organizational goals and responsibility to their peer group as they were by economic self-interest. McGregor (1960) later summarized previous organizational theories into two general categories, which he called *Theory X* and *Theory Y*. Theory X states that workers are primarily motivated by economic incentives, need to be led, and must be coerced to maximize their work output. Theory Y suggests that workers are able to work independently and without coercion, that they are committed to organizational as well as personal goals, and that they should be allowed maximum freedom to use individual creativity. A recent development in organizational and management theory is the concept of *total quality management* (TQM). Based on the work of W. Edwards Deming, Philip Crosby, J. M. Juran, and Armand Feigenbaum, total quality management builds on the scientific management and human relations models. For example, TQM uses the quantitative analysis of the scientific schools to study and improve on the flow of work processes to minimize systems errors. It also resembles the human relations school in its emphasis on the development of work groups or teams. Whereas the human relations theorists studied social groups as a natural phenomenon in the work setting, TQM theorists suggest that the organization use work teams as the most effective means of work organization, decision making, and quality control. Features unique to TQM are its emphasis on consumer satisfaction as the primary driving force of the organization and its focus on the interrelationships of systems within and around the organization.

Lawrence Martin (1993) suggests that TQM principles are very compatible with human service values: efficient and effective service, customer and employee satisfaction and feedback, consumer and worker input in decision making, and prevention over corrective action.

Our discussion of organizations has been limited to a discussion of work organizations. However, most organizations use many of the organizational and management principles discussed. Human behavior is influenced by the nature of the organizations that surround us. Social workers study organizations and organizational behavior to understand better how persons are affected by these social structures. Organizations, including human service organizations, can become both ineffective and impersonal, in regard to their workers and their clients. Social work seeks to enhance resources and minimize obstacles to human growth and development. Effective practice, therefore, requires that social workers strive to improve the organizations that affect their clients.

In conclusion, social structure determines how resources will be made available, and to whom. Looking back to earlier sections, we can see how biology generates potential that is developed through psychological means and enriched or restricted in an environment that is managed by the social structure. Nurturing environments encourage psychological growth and development consistent with biological potentials. Political climates support or inhibit the development of social structures that form the context for human behavior. Family, schools, religious institutions, communities, and economic structures all have supporting or inhibiting effects on our actions. Social work intervention at both the micro- and macrolevels requires an accurate and thorough evaluation of the forces that influence human behavior.

The case material on homelessness at the end of the chapter, "Helping and Hating the Homeless" (Marin, 1987), illustrates the importance of social-structural factors for human behavior. From the perspective of the journalist, the author points out how cultural, psychological, social-structural, and, to some degree, biological factors interact. The issues of physical and mental health and hunger are closely intertwined. Joe Blau, also writing on the nature of homelessness, observes:

> In each historical period, people have made of homelessness what they needed to make of homelessness. In the most tolerant periods, people have admired the homeless from afar for their freedom from the demands of daily life. Even in periods of confidence, however, the existence of the disaffiliated has given rise to apprehension. The apprehension can turn harsh. When it does the Social Darwinist strain in American culture reemerges, and many blame the homeless for their own predicament. The role of progressive human service workers is to combat this view. Without denying the role of psychological factors, there is an economic and political context to which we can attest and that context must be given it's due. (Blau, 1988: 21)

BASIC CULTURAL CONCEPTS

Culture is the repository of the commonly held values, knowledge, and material objects of a particular group or society. Sir Edward Tylor (1958: 1), a social anthropologist, defined culture as ". . . that complex whole which includes knowledge, belief, art, morals, law, custom, and any other capabilities and habits acquired by man as a member of society." Culture is acquired knowledge, that is, it must be learned. Spradley (1994: 25) points out that in this regard it has much in common with the school in sociology known as *symbolic interactionism*. This school hypothesizes that:

1. People act towards things in their environment in a manner based on the meanings they attribute to them.
2. Meaning is derived out of the social interaction between persons.
3. Meaning can change as a result of new interactions.

These aspects of a culture represent a society's way of life and are handed down to each successive generation. However, culture is not static. It evolves from the interactions of the members of a group with one another and with their social and physical environment. As these interactions are influenced by new events, modifications are made to accommodate them. Brunner (1986: 123) states that culture is "a forum for negotiating and re-negotiating meaning . . . it is the forum aspect of culture that gives its participants a role in constantly making and remaking the culture—an active role as participants rather than as performing actors who play out their canonical roles according to rule when the appropriate cues occur." This process is not always a smooth one of assimilation and change, however. Cultures with long and deeply held traditions, values, and beliefs do not always incorporate new influences easily. Cultural anthropologists who study "primitive" societies hold strong convictions about minimizing their intrusion into the lives of the people they seek to study. The reason for these convictions is the stress caused by the incursion of peoples from different cultures. This is especially true for peoples who find themselves a minority in a foreign culture. The case of Mai, the Vietnamese woman discussed in Chapter 2 who migrated to America, would be an example of the difficulties represented in the acculturation process.

Spradley (1994) states that cultural knowledge exists at two levels: the explicit and the tacit. Explicit cultural knowledge is that which we are conscious of and can communicate about with ease, such as rituals, customs, food preferences, etc. However, a large portion of our cultural knowledge remains outside of our awareness. Spradley suggests that how close we stand to strangers, the typical way we arrange furniture around the edge of a room, and when we do and do not touch each other are all examples of tacit cultural knowledge. Culture is composed of several elements, which exist in both levels. *Symbols* exist as a type of cultural shorthand. The use of symbols to represent something requires abstract thinking, because a cognitive leap from the concrete to the abstract is necessary. Numbers, art, artifacts, and language are examples of symbols. Symbols can tell us much about a people. People create symbols to convey meaning, and because of the symbols' abstract nature the creators act to imbue on these symbols the most important traditions of their lives. Symbols exist in many forms. Each religious tradition has its own symbolic expressions of the tenets of its faith. Preliterate and early literate societies used symbols as a means of expression and communication. Language itself is a form of symbolism in its structure (letters, words, sentences, signing) and its content. Language is an important reflection of the society in which it is found. It is through language that society most concretely and directly expresses its ideals, norms, and values. Language mirrors the experience of a society. Societies whose survival depends solely on hunting, fishing, and gathering skills may have hundreds of commonly used words to describe these activities. Their number systems may also be more basic than ours because of the limited need for calculating large numbers. A postindustrial society whose members buy their food in grocery stores will have language and numerical systems radically different from theirs. Consider, for example, how common words related to computer technology are: user-friendly, megabytes, printout, looping, database, and so on.

Language not only reflects but also influences culture. Stop and think for a moment. Does thought form language—or does language form thought—or is the process an interactive one? Persons develop in the context of language (verbal, written, and symbolic). As we encounter our world, we develop perceptions of the reality around us. In doing so, we draw on the language forms available to us. For the child raised in the city, the words available to describe fishing may be quite limited, and, therefore, his perception of the activity would also be limited; however, the child raised in a fishing culture will have a rich vocabulary to describe the multiple activities related to fishing. This example suggests that language forms perception. Yet, the creative and imaginative processes of human beings often require the ability to move beyond what now exists in our reality to create new realities. In such cases, new language follows new thought.

Values are transmitted through symbols and language. **Values** are commonly held beliefs of a society's members. Think of some of the clichés used in the early and middle part of this century that reflected at least male society's view of women: "A woman's place is in the home" or "Women are too emotional to be decision makers." Although these clichés reflect values that are still widely held by many men and women, they are beginning to lose some of their potency. Topics such as free enterprise, school prayer, abortion, affirmative action, stemming illegal immigration, and doctor-assisted suicide all reflect values. These values are sometimes shared by a large number of people, sometimes only by a few. Often, they are in conflict.

English is the dominant language spoken in America. Yet, it is a second language for millions of people living in America. The language structure of English itself may contribute to the intense fractionalization over current issues. English is replete with dichotomous language (such as either-or).

Let us take a word association test. If we say "good," most people will say "bad." If we say "black," most will reply "white." You may continue the exercise: young-old, fat-skinny, high-low, and so on. As stated previously, the structure and content of language can affect how people perceive reality. When the structure of language presents dichotomies, then the ability to see grey areas, areas of compromise, and multiple realities is limited. Such thinking gives rise to social phenomena such as social stratification, labeling, prejudice, and discrimination. Remember, the early biologist Linnaeus, in his system of racial classification, placed Caucasians at the pinnacle based on his assessment that they were the most beautiful. Another example is the frequent use of the term "primitive" when referring to some preliterate societies. Even the terminology *preliterate* conveys the existence of a progression in societal development. Language, as a cultural construct, can be utilized beneficially or as a means of oppression within and between societies.

Values, embedded in language and symbols, influence behavior by acting as guideposts that tell the person which beliefs and corresponding actions will be positively sanctioned (rewarded) or negatively sanctioned (punished). Sanctions are reflected in a society's norms, which are the specific rules for governing behavior based on social values. Society dictates that one does not cut into a line of moviegoers waiting to purchase a ticket. It is considered normative for a widow or widower to observe certain mourning rituals for a given period of time. Behavior that violates norms is sanctioned formally through laws or informally in subtle but effective ways. These norms are usually reflective of the most powerful or dominant persons or classes in society. Men (usually of European ancestry) are often expected to act assertively in business matters to ensure advancement in employment. However, the same behaviors, if displayed by women, are seen as aggressive, and they may be labeled "bitches." Although most norms and subsequent sanctions are means of maintaining appropriate levels of civility in society, they can also be an effective means of oppression for those who are not members of the dominant culture. The major social structures of a society are developed around the values of the dominant culture and serve to sustain the values, beliefs, and social position of that culture.

Remember our discussion of the social welfare system? Piven and Cloward suggest that the system is, on the one hand, an expression of societal responsibility for the underprivileged. On the other hand, they suggest that it serves to maintain the social class structure by preventing social rebellion.

It is clear that variations exist within a culture in the way people think and act because of the existence of a **subculture**, which is a smaller group within the large group that has some unique cultural characteristics. Italian-Americans, for example, may have values and social behaviors with respect to community involvement that are different from those of Native Americans or Asian-Americans. It is important to remember, however, that even within subcultures there is a great deal of intragroup variation. It is unsafe to assume that any individual member of a group will behave in ways consistent with the predominant patterns attributed to the subculture with which he or she identifies. To assume that because someone is a first-generation migrant from Appalachia, she or he will behave in a predictable fashion may be incorrect. Members of cultural groups generally share certain beliefs, values, and behaviors, but each individual combines these factors in unique ways that reflect his or her particular situation.

Subcultures usually coexist in such a way as to preserve the structure of the larger culture of which they are a part. The harmonious coexistence of different subcultural groups is called cultural pluralism. It recognizes the legitimacy of the traditions of diverse subcultures. Cultural diversity is seen as a resource to be encouraged, when viewed from the perspective of cultural pluralism. As a pattern of racial and ethnic relations, cultural pluralism is in contrast to the melting-pot philosophy that has traditionally characterized American society. The melting-pot approach fuses all diverse racial and ethnic subcultures into one "American blend." Cultural pluralism is more accepting of the value of different cultural groups and recognizes the need to preserve as well as blend them.

Cultural pluralism is an ideal made possible when groups are seen as equal and share the power in societal decision making. **Ethnocentrism** refers to cultures or subcultures evaluating each other on the basis of their own cultural elements. Ethnocentric thinking usually leads to one culture dominating another, because each culture believes its own way of doing things is the right way. Practitioners must remember that the cultural integrity of each group is the only appropriate context for understanding its behavior.

Cultural pluralism, or multiculturalism, as it is sometimes referred to, causes special sets of problems for democratic societies such as that in America. Democratic societies attempt to balance the rights of the indvidual with the "common good" of society as a whole. Democracies generally operate on the priciple of majority rule, which is believed to represent the common good. However, even in democracies, the interests of the whole often conflict with those of smaller groups. Conversely, the demands made by subcultures for recognition stress the larger group's capacity to meet those demands. At times, this tension can be mediated through established channels, such as legislation and social policy. At other times, the strain becomes too great and open conflict erupts, as in Los Angeles in April of 1992. Again, language often reveals different perspectives. The events in Los Angeles were referred to as "riots" by some and as "a rebellion" by others, perhaps reflecting varying cultural or racial perspectives.

How do social workers incorporate their understanding of culture into practice? Saleebey (1994: 352) asserts that "culture is the means by which we receive, organize, rationalize, and understand our particular experiences in the world." He further suggests that cultures and individuals carry meaning in the forms of narration and storytelling. He states:

> Interpretation and story are the essence of culture. They are not trivialities unrelated to circumstances. Rather, they are serious and essential creations that grow out of the experiences people have in particular environments. Stories may instruct individuals on how to survive or how to accept—even how to overcome—difficult situations. And at least stories reveal to individuals considerable information and perspective about the nature of their circumstances. (Saleebey, 1994: 353)

Social work practice requires that the practitioner understand, as fully as possible, the perspective of the client. Cultural and personal narratives (that is, a person's revelations about who they are, what they believe in, and the causes of their actions) are an essential part of the dialogue we enter into with our clients. As stated previously, social workers need to be aware that individuals should not be assumed to embody all the beliefs of the culture or subculture to which they may belong. The close attention paid to an individual's narrative will reveal both personal and cultural interpretations of reality. Social workers must view the client's personal knowledge as valid, legitimate, and real and not subjugated to our professional knowledge and constructs of the meaning of human behavior. Social workers seek to enter into the world of our clients, not to draw them into ours.

This perspective is also applicable when social workers move from individual, or micropractice, to other levels of intervention. Social workers seek to ensure that the programs and services offered maintain a high degree of cultural sensitivity. For example, Michielutte et al. (1994) examine the concept of cultural sensitivity in the context of developing cancer control programs for American

Indian populations. First, they offer a three-tiered model for implementing culturally sensitive programs, developed by Rogler et. al. (1987). The tiers are:

Tier 1. If the program does not conflict with important cultural beliefs, increase accessibility.

Tier 2. If incompatibilities exist, choose components from this or other programs that do fit.

Tier 3. If existing programs are definitely incompatible, modify the program to meet cultural values and beliefs.

A strong social work commitment to culturally sensitive practice means that a concerted effort be made to design programs around the client's needs and values, rather than requiring the client's adjustment and accommodation to traditional service delivery systems and services.

Michielutte et al., then, contrast traditional values held in American Indian culture with those of Western culture (see Table 3.3).

The authors then present various methods used in the cancer control program that were respectful of the cultural beliefs of the patients: presenting cancer screening in the context of total health care; hiring American Indians as health educators; and maintaining a flexible schedule of appointments.

Such programs present a level of commitment to culturally sensitive practice. Finally, social workers can advocate for a more just and equitable society. Saleebey reminds us that:

Social work, in a unique way, is a value-driven profession. We cannot ignore, though we might not know how to invoke, our commitments to social and distributive justice, equality, developmental socialization, the uniqueness and value of each individual and culture, and compassion and caring. Neither can we ignore the fact that we work at the

TABLE 3.3 Characteristics of traditional American Indian culture and Western culture

American Indian	Western
Health reflects a balance with nature; illness is a disturbance of that balance, both physical and spiritually.	Illnesses are individual categories of problems that may or may not involve the whole person.
Attitudes towards individuals are based on respect for individual worth.	An individual's worth is measured by roles and status.
Time flows or is flexible and is relative to the task at hand.	Time is discrete; activities take place at specific times.

Adapted from Michielutte, R., P. C. Sharp, M. B. Dignan, et al. (1994). "Cultural Issues in the Development of Cancer Control Programs for American Indian Populations," *Journal of Health Care for the Poor and Underserved*, Vol. 5, No. 4, pp. 280–296. Reprinted with permission of the publisher.

intersection of the self and social environment and the reality that some-
how we have to work both sides of the street. (Saleebey, 1994: 357)

SUMMARY

This chapter has presented an overview of the biological, psychological, social-
structural, and cultural dimensions of human behavior. Selected concepts from
the biological, social, and behavioral sciences that are useful to the social work
professional have been reviewed. The concepts presented are a small sample of
the depth and breadth of knowledge available from the various fields of study.
The goal of professional social work practice is improving transactions between
people and their environments. Knowledge geared toward understanding factors
influencing these transactions comes from several disciplines and demands that
the practitioner possess the ability to select, integrate, and apply information
from diverse sources. Biological sciences tell us about the genetic potential of
human persons; they also inform us about physiological processes and health,
illness, and disability. Psychologoical theories attempt to explain the ways in
which people discover, organize, and interpret the information they receive
through biological (sensorial) and cognitive means. These theories range from
mechanistic models (basic learning theories) to models that incorporate individual and cultural influence (cognitive and neopsychoanalytic). The study of social
institutions reveals one of the ways in which societies structure themselves and
the ways in which persons are socialized by them. It also provides examples of
social institutions, as well as a few theoretical perspectives for viewing the
functions of social institutions. Finally, the meaning and content of culture and
its influences on the development of social structures has been discussed. The
following chapter will present approaches to the study of the life course, that
is, the myriad of ways people grow and develop over the normal life span from
birth to death.

STUDY QUESTIONS

1. Compare and contrast biological, psychological, social-structural, and cultural perspectives on homelessness, using the article "Helping and Hating the Homeless" in
   Exhibit 3.1. Which do you think is/are the most helpful perspectives for understanding
   homelessness? Why?

2. About which of the four sources of behavior do you feel most knowledgeable? Why
   do you know more about some than others? Does this tell you something about
   cultural values and education as a social institution? How committed are you to
   expanding your knowledge in those areas in which you are presently less knowledgeable? How might you do so?

3. When you considered going into social work, you may have had some idea about
   working with certain groups of people—the elderly, children, adolescents, the
   mentally ill, the physically ill or incapacitated. Think about this particular population.

List the biological, psychological, social-structural, and cultural elements you might need to consider when working with this population. Then, think about the same categories and consider how these four elements might combine either resources or obstacles to people's growth and development.

4. At the end of Chapter 1, we asked you to consider how you came to be in this class. Has this chapter helped you begin to see how the four sources of behavior combine to affect individual human behavior? In this chapter we discussed cognitive theories, perception, culture, and symbolic interactionism. How do you think these concepts interrelate? When you think about a population with whom you may wish to work in practice, what perceptions do you presently have about them? What elements in your environment have formed these perceptions? Are these perceptions generally positive or negative? If they are negative, what other possible ways might you use in looking at this population that would be more positive?

5. In Chapter 1, we suggested that theories of human behavior possess five elements: health orientation, growth orientation, ecological perspective, strengths perspective, and an empowerment perspective. On page 36 of Chapter 2, we provide four questions that acted as filters for screening theories of human behavior related to social work perspectives. Choose a theoretical perspective discussed in this chapter relating to any of the four sources of behavior. Use the questions to filter this theoretical perspective. Discuss this perspective with a small group from the class. How does this theory or perspective fare throughout this screening process? What would need to be added to make it more compatible with a social work perspective? Finally, does this theoretical perspective fit within the integrating framework suggested in Chapter 2—one that emphasizes a systemic approach, directionality of human behavior, and an appreciation of diversity?

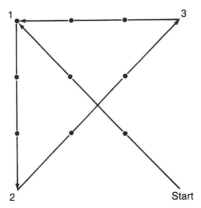

Solution to the nine-dot configuration on page 85

KEY TERMS

Affect. The feelings and emotions that become attached to information derived from our sensory and cognitive processes.

Authority. Legitimate power.

Coercion. The use of illegitimate force.

Cognition. The ability to process and organize information in order to utilize the environment to achieve one's goals.

Competitive interaction. Interaction that encourages people to focus on their own good.

Conflict. Actively destructive behavior by one group towards others.

Cooperative interaction. Interaction that focuses on the good of group members.

Cultural pluralism. The harmonious coexistence of different subcultural groups.

Death. The point at which the human body is no longer able to sustain itself.

Degenerative processes. The genetically determined deterioration of cells as the human body ages at a rate and in a pattern unique to each person.

Discrimination. Actions that disadvantage those who are considered less worthy.

Ethnocentrism. When cultures or subcultures evaluate each other on the basis of their own cultural elements.

Genetic engineering. Purposeful modification of genetic material in the laboratory.

Latent functions of social institutions. Functions that are less publicly visible and more beneficial for some groups in society than for others.

Life. A physiological process that entails the management of complex chemical processes mediated by the brain through an elaborate series of neurological impulses.

Life span. The period from conception to death.

Manifest funcions of social institutions. Functions that are publicly stated and assumed to be for the good of society as a whole.

Mutation. A process in which genes are changed from their original form.

Norms. Specific rules that govern behavior and that are based on social values.

Nurturance. The protection and caring needed for psychological well-being.

Nutrition. Basic nutrients needed for physical health.

Pain. A warning that some part of the physical system is being pushed toward its adaptive limit.

Perception. The ability to see, smell, feel, and touch, and to develop organized responses to the sensory characteristics of the environment.

Personality. The integrating psychological structure that develops to help the individual function in the environment.

Physiological health. When the genetic plan is able to unfold because the resources needed to permit growth and development have been provided.

Power. Ability of a person or group to enforce its will on others.

Prejudice. Beliefs that attribute negative characteristics to people without any concrete evidence to support those beliefs.

Reflex. Genetically programmed predisposition to act.

Role. The expected behavior of categories of people within social institutions.

Role conflict. When the effective performance of one role may be in direct conflict with the effective performance of others.

Role strain. When the behavioral expectations associated with a specific role are inconsistent.

Social classes. Categories in which the stratification process places people, according to their access to life-sustaining and life-enriching resources.

Social differentiation. Categorizing people on the basis of a socially defined criterion.

Social exchange theory. A sociological theory emphasizing mutually agreed upon benefits and losses of interactions.

Social institutions. Social structures that organize activities around particular social purposes or functions, such as the family and religion.

Social sanctions. Socially defined positive or negative responses to behavior.

Social stratification. A vertical ranking of people on the basis of their access to resources or their possession of certain characteristics.

Social structure. Socially created structures, such as the family, the church, schools, and the economic system, that exist to organize and pattern social interaction.

Socialization. The process through which people acquire the beliefs, customs, values, and attitudes of their culture.

Subculture. A small group existing within a larger cultural group that has some unique cultural characteristics.

Values. Commonly held beliefs of a society's members.

REFERENCES

Abramson, L., M. Seligman, and J. Teasdale (1978). Learned Helplessness in Humans: Critique and Reformulation. *Journal of Abnormal Psychology,* Vol. 87, pp. 49–74.

Acock, A. and D. Demo (1994). *Family Diversity and Well-Being.* Vol. 195. Thousand Oaks, CA: Sage Library of Social Research.

Adler, A. (1963). T*he Practice and Theory of Individual Psychology*, translated by P. Radin. Patterson, NJ: Littlefield, Adams. (original work published in 1924).

Baber, K. and K. Allen (1992). *Women and Families: Feminist Reconstructions.* New York: The Guilford Press.

Bailey, M. and R. Pillard (1991). A Genetic Study of Male Sexual Orientation. Arc*hives of General Psychiatry*, Vol. 48, pp.1089–1096.

Bailey, M., R. Pillard, M. Neale, and Y. Agyei (1993). Heritable Factors Influence Sexual Orientation in Women. *Archives of General Psychiatry*, Vol. 50, (March), pp. 217–223.

Bandura, A. (1977). *Social Learning Theory.* Englewood Cliffs, NJ: Prentice-Hall.

Bellah, R., R. Madsen, W. Sullivan, A. Swidler, and S. Tipton (1986). *Habits of the Heart: Individualism and Commitment in American Life.* New York: Harper & Row Publishers, Perennial Library.

Bieber, I., et al. (1988). *Homosexuality: A Psychoanalytic Study*. Northvale, NJ: Jason Aronson Inc.

Blau, J. (1988). On the Uses of Homelessness: A Literature Review. *Catalyst*, Vol. 6, No. 21.

Bouchard, T. (1994). Genes, Environment, and Personality. *Science*, Vol. 264, No. 17 (June), pp. 1700-1701.

Bourdieu, P. and J. Passeron (1977). *Reproduction in Education, Society, and Culture*. Beverly Hills, CA: Sage Publications.

Brunner, J. (1986). *Actual Minds, Possible Worlds*. Cambridge, MA: Harvard University Press.

Chafetz, J. (1988). *Feminist Sociology: An Overview of Contemporary Theories*. Itasca, NY: F. E. Peacock Publishers.

Children's Defense Fund (1992). *Report: Vanishing Dreams: The Economic Plight of America's Young Families*. Washington, D.C.: Children's Defense Fund and Northeastern University's Center for Labor Market Studies.

Chodorow, N. (1989). *Feminism and Psychoanalysis*. New Haven, CT: Yale University Press.

Collins, A. and D. Pancoast (pub. date not listed). *Natural Helping Networks: A Strategy for Prevention*. Washington, D.C.: National Association of Social Workers.

Condry, J. (1977). Enemies of Exploration: Self-initiated Versus Other-initiated Learning. *Journal of Personality and Social Psychology*, Vol. 35, pp. 459-477.

Daly, H., and J. Cobb (1989). *For the Common Good: Redirecting the Economy toward Community, the Environment, and a Sustainable Future*. Boston, MA: Beacon Press, p. 13.

Duvall, E., and B. Miller (1985). *Marriage and Family Development*, 6th edition. New York: Harper & Row.

Erikson, E. (1976). *Adulthood*. New York: W. W. Norton.

Fairweather, H. (1976). Sex Differences in Cognition. *Cognition*, Vol. 4. pp. 31-280.

Freud, S. (1938). *The Basic Writings of Sigmund Freud*, edited by A. Brill. New York: The Modern Library.

Gambrill, E. (1987). Behavior Approach. In *Encyclopedia of Social Work*, 18th edition. Silver Spring, MD: National Association of Social Workers, pp. 184-194.

Gardner, H. (1993). *Multiple Intelligences: The Theory in Practice*. New York: Basic Books.

Germain, C. (1991). *Human Behavior in the Social Environment: An Ecological View*. New York: Columbia University Press.

Gilligan, C. (1982). *In a Different Voice: Psychological Theory and Women's Development*. Cambridge, MA: Harvard University Press.

Gilligan, C. (ed.) (1990). *Making Connections: The Relational World of Adolescent Girls at Emma Willard School*. Cambridge, MA: Harvard University Press.

Gilligan, C., A. Rogers, and D. Tolman, (eds.) (1991). *Women, Girls & Psychotherapy: Reframing Resistance*. New York: Harrington Park Press.

Goleman, D. (1988). Erikson, in His Old Age, Expands His View of Life. *New York Times*, June 14, pp. C1ff.

Goleman, D. (1989). From Tokyo to Tampa, Different Ideas of Self. *New York Times*, March 7, pp. 17ff.

Goodrich, T., C. Rampage, B. Ellman, and K. Halstead (1988). *Feminist Family Therapy*. New York: W. W. Norton.

Gould, S. (1994). The Geometer of Race. *Discover*, November, pp. 65-69.

Herrnstein, R. and C. Murray (1994). *The Bell Curve: Intelligence and Class Structure in American Life*. New York: The Free Press.

Horgan, J. (1993). Genes and Crime. *Scientific American*, February, pp. 24-29.

Horney, K. (1950). *Neurosis and Human Growth*. New York: W. W. Norton.

Jones, S. (1993). *The Language of Genes: Solving the Mysteries of Our Genetic Past, Present and Future*. New York: Anchor Books.

Jung, C. G. (1947). On the Nature of the Psyche. In *Collected Works*. Vol 18. Princeton, NJ: Princeton University Press, pp. 159-234.

Klein, M. (1975). *Love, Guilt and Reparation and Other Works*. New York: Delta.

Kohlberg, L. (1981). The Philosophy of Moral Development, Vol.1. *Moral Stages and the Idea of Justice*. New York: Harper & Row.

Kohn, A. (1986). *No Contest: The Case against Competition*. Boston, MA: Houghton Mifflin Company, p. 70.

Langer, J. (1969). *Theories of Development*. New York: Holt, Rinehart & Winston, pp. 51-73, 107-156.

LeVay, S. (1991). A Difference in Hypothalamic Structure between Heterosexual and Homosexual Men. *Science*, Vol. 258, pp. 1034-1037.

Lewontin, R., S. Rose, and L. Kamin (1984). *Not in Our Genes: Biology, Ideology, and Human Nature*. New York: Pantheon Books.

Lozoff, B. (1989). Environment and Genes. *American Psychologist*, Vol. 44, No. 2, pp. 231-236.

McGregor, D. (1960). *The Human Side of Enterprise*. New York: McGraw-Hill.

McKnight, J., and J. Kretzman (1993). *Building Communities from the Inside Out*. Evanston, IL: Center for Urban Affairs and Policy Research, Neighborhood Innovations Network, Northwestern University.

Marin, P. (1987). Helping and Hating the Homeless: The Struggle at the Margins of America. *Harper's*, January, pp. 39ff.

Martin, L. (1993). *Total Quality Management in Human Service Organizations*. Newbury Park, CA: Sage Publications in cooperation with the University of Michigan School of Social Work.

Marx, K. (1969). *Capital*. Vol. 1. Moscow: Progress Publishers.

Merton, R. (1952). Bureaucratic Structure and Personality. In *Reader in Bureaucracy*, edited by R. K. Merton, A. Gray, B. Hockey, and H. Selvin, pp. 261-372. Glencoe, IL: Free Press.

Michielutte, R., P. Sharp, M. Dignan, et al. (1994). Cultural Issues in the Development of Cancer Control Programs for American Indian Populations. *Journal of Health Care for the Poor and Underserved*, Vol. 5, No. 4, pp. 280-296.

Miles, R. (1989). *Racism*. London: Routledge.

Miller, D. and A. Waigandt (1993). *Coping with Your Sexual Orientation*. New York: The Rosen Publishing Company.

Newberger, C. M. and E. DeVos (1988). Abuse and Victimization: A Life-Span Developmental Perspective. *American Journal of Orthopsychiatry*, Vol. 58, No. 4 (October), pp. 501-511.

Parsons, T. (1951). *The Social System*. New York: Free Press.

Parsons, T. (1960). *Structure and Process in Modern Societies*. Glencoe, IL: Free Press

Piaget, J. (1952, 1936 original ed.). *The Origins of Intelligence in Children*. New York: International Universities Press.

Pies, C. (1988). *Considering Parenthood*. Minneapolis, MN: Spinster Book Company.

Piven, F., and R. Cloward (1971). *Regulating the Poor: The Functions of Public Welfare*. New York: Pantheon Books.

Plomin, R., M. Owen, and P. McGuffin (1994). The Genetic Basis of Complex Human Behaviors. *Science,* Vol. 264 (June), pp. 1733-1739.

Rauch, J. (1988). Social Work and the Genetics Revolution: Genetic Services. *Social Work*, Vol. 33, No. 5, pp. 389-395.

Reinisch, J., R. Beasley, and D. Kent (eds.) (1990). *The Kinsey Institute New Report on Sex*. New York: St. Martin's Press.

Rogler, L., R. Malgady, G. Costantion, et al. (1987) What Do Culturally Sensitive Mental Health Services Mean? *American Psychologist*, Vol. 42, No. 6 (June), pp. 565–570.

Saleebey, D. (1992). Biology's Challenge to Social Work: Embodying the Person-in-Environment Perspective. *Social Work*, Vol. 37, No. 2 (March), pp. 112–117.

Saleebey, D. (1994). Culture, Theory, and Narrative: The Intersection of Meanings in Practice. *Social Work*, Vol. 39, No. 4 (July), pp. 351–359.

Savage, M., and A. Warde (1993). *Urban Sociology, Capitalism and Modernity*. New York: Continuum.

Science News (1989). Modifying Mendel One More Time. Vol. 136, No. 6 (August 5), p. 92.

Seltzer, M. (1989). Random and Not So Random Thoughts on Becoming a Statistic: Professional and Personal Musings. *International Journal of Aging and Human Development*, Vol. 28, No. 1, pp. 4–5.

Sherman, E. (1987). Cognitive Therapy. In *Encyclopedia of Social Work*, 18th edition. Silver Spring, MD: National Association of Social Workers, pp. 288–291.

Shreeve, J. (1994). Terms of estrangement. *Discover*, November, pp. 57–63.

Snyderman, M. and S. Rothman (1987). Survey and Expert Opinions on Intelligence and Aptitude Testing. *American Psychologist*, Vol. 42, pp. 137–144.

Spradley, J. (1994). Ethnography and Culture. In *Conformity and Conflict: Readings in Cultural Anthropology*, 8th edition, edited by J. Spradley and D. McCurdy. New York: Harper Collins College Publications.

Sullivan, H. S. (1953). *The Collected Works of Harry Stack Sullivan*. Vols. 1 and 2. New York: W. W. Norton.

Taylor, F. (1947). *The Principles of Scientific Management*. New York: The Norton Library.

Toennies, F. (1965). *Community and Society*, translated by Charles P. Loomis. New York: Harper & Row.

Tylor, E. (1958). *Primitive Culture*. Vol. 1. New York: Harper & Row (original text, 1871).

Valentich, M. (1986). Feminism and Social Work Practice. In *Social Work Treatment: Interlocking Theoretical Approaches*, 3rd edition, edited by F. Turner, pp. 564–589. New York: Free Press.

Walters, M., B. Carter, P. Papp, and O. Silverstein (1988). *The Invisible Web: Gender Patterns in Family Relations*. New York: The Guilford Press.

Wainrib, B. (ed.) (1992). *Gender Issues across the Life Cycle*. New York: Springer Publishing Company.

Watzlawick, K. P., J. Weakland, and R. Fisch. (1974). *Change: Principles of Problem Formulation and Problem Resolution*. New York: W. W. Norton.

Weber, M. (1947). *The Theory of Social and Economic Organizations*, translated by A. M. Henderson and T. Parsons. New York: Macmillan (first published in 1924).

Weick, A. and D. Saleebey (1995). Supporting Family Strengths: Orienting Policy and Practice Toward the 21st Century. *Families in Society: The Journal of Contemporary Human Services,* Vol. 76, No. 3, pp. 141–149.

Weiner, B. (1974). *Achievement Motivation and Attribution Theory*. Morristown, NJ: General Learning Press.

Wills, C. (1994). The skin we're in. *Discover*, November, pp. 77–81.

Wilson, E. O. (1978). *On Human Nature*. Cambridge, MA: Harvard University Press.

Vygotsky, L. (1978). *Mind in Society*. Cambridge, MA: Harvard University Press.

exhibit 3.1

Helping and Hating the Homeless

The following excerpts are from "Helping and Hating the Homeless" *by Peter Marin,* Harper's, *January 1987, pp. 39ff. Copyright © 1986 by Harper's Magazine. All rights reserved. Reprinted from the January 1987 issue by special permission. In this article, the author describes the homeless, the reality of their lives, and the complexities involved in solving the homeless problem. His analysis illustrates the systemic nature of human behavior and the human diversity inherent in any kind of social activity.*

When I was a child, I had a recurring vision of how I would end as an old man: alone, in a sparsely furnished second-story room I could picture quite precisely, in a walk-up on Fourth Avenue in New York, where the secondhand bookstores then were. It was not a picture which frightened me. I liked it. The idea of anonymity and solitude and marginality must have seemed to me, back then, for reasons I do not care to remember, both inviting and inevitable. Later, out of college, I took to the road, hitchhiking and traveling on freights, doing odd jobs here and there, crisscrossing the country. I liked that too: the anonymity and the absence of constraint and the rough community I sometimes found. I felt at home on the road, perhaps because I felt at home nowhere else, and periodically, for years, I would return to that world, always with a sense of relief and release.

I have been thinking a lot about that these days, now that transience and home-lessness have made their way into the national consciousness, and especially since the town I live in, Santa Barbara, has become well known because of the recent successful campaign to do away with the meanest aspects of its "sleeping ordinances"—a set of foolish laws making it illegal for the homeless to sleep at night in public places. . . .

The trouble begins with the word "homeless." It has become such an abstraction, and is applied to so many different kinds of people, with so many different histories and problems, that it is almost meaningless.

Homelessness, in itself, is nothing more than a condition visited upon men and women (and, increasingly, children) as the final stage of a variety of problems about which the word "homelessness" tells us almost nothing. Or, to put it another way, it is a catch basin into which pour all of the people disenfranchised or marginalized or scared off by processes beyond their control, those which lie close to the heart of American life. Here are the groups packed into the single category of "the homeless":

- Veterans, mainly from the war in Vietnam. In many American cities, vets make up close to 50 percent of all homeless males.
- The mentally ill. In some parts of the country, roughly a quarter of the homeless would, a couple of decades ago, have been institutionalized.
- The physically disabled or chronically ill, who do not receive any benefits or whose benefits do not enable them to afford permanent shelter.
- The elderly on fixed incomes whose funds are no longer sufficient for their needs.
- Men, women, and whole families pauperized by the loss of a job.
- Single parents, usually women, without the resources or skills to establish new lives.

- Runaway children, many of whom have been abused.
- Alcoholics and those in trouble with drugs (whose troubles often begin with one of the other conditions listed here).
- Immigrants, both legal and illegal, who often are not counted among the homeless because they constitute a "problem" in their own right.
- Traditional tramps, hobos, and transients, who have taken to the road or the streets for a variety of reasons and who prefer to be there.

You can quickly learn two things about the homeless from this list. First, you can learn that many of the homeless, before they were homeless, were people more or less like ourselves: members of the working or middle class. And you can learn that the world of the homeless has its roots in various policies, events, and ways of life for which some of us are responsible and from which some of us actually prosper.

We decide, as a people, to go to war, we ask our children to kill and to die, and the result, years later, is grown men homeless on the street.

We change, with the best intentions, the laws pertaining to the mentally ill, and then, without intention, neglect to provide them with services; and the result, in our streets, drives some of us crazy with rage.

We cut taxes and prune budgets, we modernize industry and shift the balance of trade, and the result of all these actions and errors can be read, sleeping form by sleeping form, on our city streets.

The liberals cannot blame the conservatives. The conservatives cannot blame the liberals. Homelessness is the *sum total* of our dreams, policies, intentions, errors, omissions, cruelties, kindnesses, all of it recorded, in flesh, in the life of the streets.

You can also learn from this list one of the most important things there is to know about the homeless—that they can be roughly divided into two groups: those who have had homelessness forced upon them and want nothing more than to escape it; and those who have at least in part *chosen* it for themselves. . . .

The fact is, many of the homeless are not only hapless victims but voluntary exiles, "domestic refugees," people who have turned not against life itself but against *us,* our life, American life. Look for a moment at the vets. The price of returning to America was to forget what they had seen or learned in Vietnam, to "put it behind them." But some could not do that, and the stress of trying showed up as alcoholism, broken marriages, drug addiction, crime. And it showed up too as life on the street, which was for some vets a desperate choice made in the name of life—the best they could manage. It was a way of avoiding what might have occurred had they stayed where they were: suicide, or violence done to others.

We must learn to accept that there may indeed be people, and not only vets, who have seen so much of our world, or seen it so clearly, that to live in it becomes impossible. . . .

It is important to remember this—important to recognize the immensity of the changes that have occurred in the marginal world in the past twenty years. . . .

There began to pour into the marginal world—slowly in the sixties, a bit faster in the seventies, and then faster still in the eighties—more and more people who neither belonged nor knew how to survive there. The sixties brought the counterculture and drugs; the streets filled with young dropouts. Changes in the law loosed upon the streets mentally ill men and women. Inflation took its toll, then recession. Working-class and even middle-class men and women—entire families—began to fall into a world they did not understand.

At the same time the transient world was being inundated by new inhabitants, its landscape, its economy, was shrinking radically. Jobs became harder to find. Modernization had something to do with it; machines took the place of men and women. And the influx of workers from Mexico and points farther south created a class of semipermanent workers who took the place of casual transient labor. More important, perhaps, was the fact that the forgotten parts of many cities began to attract attention. Downtown areas were redeveloped, reclaimed. The skid-row sections of smaller cities were turned into "old townes." The old hotels that once catered to transients were upgraded or torn down or became warehouses for welfare families—an arrangement far more profitable to the owners. The price of housing increased; evictions increased. The mentally ill, who once could afford to house themselves in cheap rooms, the alcoholics, who once would drink themselves to sleep at night in their cheap hotels, were out on the street—exposed to the weather and to danger, and also in plain and public view: "problems" to be dealt with. . . .

The homeless, simply because they are homeless, are strangers, alien—and therefore a threat. Their presence, in itself, comes to constitute a kind of violence; it deprives us of our sense of safety. . . .

What I am getting at here is the *nature* of the desire to help the homeless—what is hidden behind it and why it so often does harm. Every government program, almost every private project, is geared as much to the needs of those giving help as it is to the needs of the homeless. Go to any government agency, or, for that matter, to most private charities, and you will find yourself enmeshed, at once, in a bureaucracy so tangled and oppressive, or confronted with so much moral arrogance and contempt, that you will be driven back out into the streets for relief.

Santa Barbara, where I live, is as good an example as any. There are three main shelters in the city—all of them private. Between them they provide fewer than a hundred beds a night for the homeless. Two of the three shelters are religious in nature. . . .

In the mission, as in most places in the country, there are elaborate and stringent rules. Beds go first to those who have not been there for two months, and you can stay for only two nights in any two-month period. No shelter is given to those who are not sober. Even if you go to the mission only for a meal, you are required to listen to sermons and participate in prayer, and you are regularly proselytized—sometimes overtly, sometimes subtly. There are obligatory, regimented showers. You go to bed precisely at ten: lights out, no reading, no talking. After the lights go out you will find fifteen men in a room with double-decker bunks. As the night progresses the room grows stuffier and hotter. Men toss, turn, cough, and moan. In the morning you are awakened precisely at five forty-five. Then breakfast. At seven-thirty you are back on the street. . . .

It is these attitudes, in various forms and permutations, that you find repeated endlessly in America. We are moved either to "redeem" the homeless or to punish them. Perhaps there is nothing consciously hostile about it. Perhaps it is simply that as the machinery of bureaucracy cranks itself up to deal with these problems, attitudes assert themselves automatically. But whatever the case, the fact remains that almost every one of our strategies for helping the homeless is simply an attempt to rearrange the world *cosmetically,* in terms of how it looks and smells to *us.* Compassion is little more than the passion for control.

The central question emerging from all this is, What does a society owe to its members in trouble, and *how* is that debt to be paid? It is a question which must be answered in two parts: first, in relation to the men and women who have been marginalized against their will, and then, in a slightly different way, in relation to those who have chosen (or accept or even prize) their marginality.

As for those who have been marginalized against their wills, I think the general answer is obvious: A society owes its members whatever it takes for them to regain their places in the social order. And when it comes to specific remedies, one need only read backward the various processes which have created homelessness and then figure out where help is likely to do the most good. But the real point here is not the specific remedies required—affordable housing, say—but the basis upon which they must be offered, the necessary underlying ethical notion we seem in this nation unable to grasp: that those who are the inevitable casualties of modern industrial capitalism and the free-market system are entitled, *by right,* and by the simple virtue of their participation in that system, to whatever help they need. They are entitled to help to find and hold their places in the society whose social contract they have, in effect, signed and observed.

Look at that for just a moment: the notion of a contract. The majority of homeless Americans have kept, insofar as they could, to the terms of that contract. In any shelter these days you can find men and women who have worked ten, twenty, forty years, and whose lives have nonetheless come to nothing. These are people who cannot afford a place in the world they helped create. And in return? Is it life on the street they have earned? Or the cruel charity we so grudgingly grant them?

But those marginalized against their will are only half the problem. There remains, still, the question of whether we owe anything to those who are voluntarily marginal. What about them: the street people, the rebels, and the recalcitrants, those who have torn up their social contracts or returned them unsigned? . . .

We owe them, I think, at least a place to exist, a way to exist. That may not be a *moral* obligation, in the sense that our obligation to the involuntary marginal is clearly a moral one, but it is an obligation nevertheless, one you might call an existential obligation. . . .

I think we as a society need men like these. A society needs its margins as much as it needs art and literature. It needs holes and gaps, *breathing spaces,* let us say, into which men and women can escape and live, when necessary, in ways otherwise denied them. Margins guarantee to society a flexibility, an elasticity, and allow it to accommodate itself to the natures and needs of its members. When margins vanish, society becomes too rigid, too oppressive by far, and therefore inimical to life. . . .

chapter **4**

Human Behavior throughout the Life Course

Life is complex, and my world was destined to change with it.
Loren Eiseley*

OVERVIEW

Each of us comes into the world with a unique genetic makeup. This genetic potential, however, unfolds in a larger social-cultural and historical context. Our individual stories, or autobiographies, as Loren Eiseley suggests, are shaped and formed in interaction with the biographies of others at a given time in history. As you have learned in previous chapters, the study of human behavior does not belong to the exclusive province of any one discipline but involves the interplay of biological, psychological, social-structural, and cultural forces played out in an historical context. Literature and history, especially through the biographical and autobiographical accounts of individuals as they progress through life at any given point, contribute much to our understanding of the richness of human behavior. This interplay of individual biography with social and historical processes is known as the **life course**, defined by Clausen (1986) as "progression through time."

From conception to death, human behavior is shaped by a combination of internal and external factors. Some of these are predictable and are regulated by social norms that give direction and guidance to the individual. As we have discussed previously, social norms can also have a negative influence on individual persons' growth and development. In American society, for example,

---

* Eiseley, L. (1975). *All the Strange Hours: The Excavation of a Life*. New York: Charles Scribner's Sons.

129

chronological age is often accompanied by changes in status and role transitions, reflecting culturally "appropriate" times to begin school, begin dating, drive a car, begin work, start a family, or retire. While there is considerable variability in the timing of these specific life events, individuals internalize "social clocks" and often gauge their progression through the life course accordingly. Some parents express concern, for example, if their 2-year-old hasn't started to talk or if their 23-year-old shows no signs of occupational direction. Questions related to "on-timeness" thereby become charged with emotional intensity. The influence of social norms regarding the timing of certain life events can be especially problematic for oppressed minorities. For example, society usually expects young adult people to obtain some type of employment if they are not in a full-time educational program. In American mainstream culture, employment is an expectation and a means of social status. However, unemployment rates for African-American teenagers and young adult males are significantly higher than for their Caucasian counterparts. Insofar as these unemployment rates reflect the social-structural manifestation of oppression and racism, the African-American male is placed in a double bind, denying a culturally approved avenue for achieving social status.

Social norms define social roles. If these social roles are violated, social ostracism may occur. For example, the social norm in American cultural history was that women were expected to marry in their late teens or early twenties, bear children, and maintain the household. Women who chose careers over marriage and family were viewed with suspicion and, at times, ridiculed as "spinsters."

This chapter will focus on human behavior throughout the life course. It begins by looking at the concept of the life course, followed by an analysis of the interaction of social and historical forces on life-course dynamics. It also discusses some variables influencing life events. From conception to death, behavior is shaped by societal expectations, subcultural values, historical events, and one's individual goals and aspirations. Each factor that shapes behavior does so by means of the resource systems available to the individual. The combination of all of these factors on each person results in their individual narrative.

In the previous chapters we have discussed the influence of biological, psychological, social-structural, and cultural forces on human behavior. It is also important to remember the concepts discussed in the first two chapters when thinking about human behavior in the context of the life course. The first chapter discussed basic professional values and core beliefs that can be utilized when viewing life-course theories. Chapter 2 presented an integrating framework composed of the basic tenets of goal-directed behavior, the interrelatedness of systems, and the understanding of human diversity. Keep these basic values, beliefs, and framework elements in mind while reading this chapter.

DEFINING THE LIFE COURSE

In Chapter 3 we discussed stage theories of individual development (Freud, Erikson, Kohlberg, and Horney). These theories are sometimes referred to as "life cycle" models and are often viewed as fixed, universal, and sequential stages of human development. Also present in the literature are models of family develop-ment. Usually these models include a sequence of life events, such as: courting, marriage or coupling, birth of children, childrearing for independence, children leaving home, couple reformulation, retirement, the death of one spouse, and death of the remaining spouse. Like Erikson's individual developmental stages, these family development theories also suggest psychosocial tasks inherent in each stage of family life. Germain (1994: 259) suggests that these models contain underlying assumptions about what constitutes normative behavior and "do not take into account cultural and historic contexts, variations in sexual orientations, and the influence of poverty and oppression." Germain further states:

> . . . concepts of fixed uniform stages ignore the fact that life-cycle models are rooted in the dominant culture's assumptions, values, and social norms at a particular time in history. Hence, the models are time bound as well as culture bound. . . . Nor are human lives linear; they do not follow a straight path from birth to old age, as conceived in stage models of development. Human life is more aptly conceived as a moving spiral, manifesting predictable and unpredictable twists and turns along its track through physical and social environments. (Germain, 1994: 260)

In contrast to stage models, the concept of life course views life as a series of transitions, events, and processes occurring at any point in the life process. Hagestad and Neugarten (1985: 35) state that a life course perspective shifts one's attention from the biological unfolding of one's potential to a concentration on "age related transitions that are socially created, socially recognized, and shared." Hareven views the life course as "concerned with the timing of life events in relation to the social structures and historical changes effecting them" (1982: xiv).

Rindfuss et al. (1987) point out that life events are not always predictably sequenced. Disruptions and disorders are common occurrences throughout the life course. An unplanned and unwanted pregnancy, the sudden onset of a disease, the loss of a job, or a natural catastrophe all create disorder and disruption in the timing of life events. They induce significant stress and require coping strategies that differ from those needed to meet the demands of pre-dictable and anticipated transitions throughout the life course. The amount of stress often depends upon the resources that individuals and families possess and their interpretation of the events (Moen and Howery: 1988).

In broad terms, the life course of an individual is a combination of personal resources, cultural and subcultural expectations, social resources, and social and personal historical events. The problem for individual and family life course theorists becomes one of finding a framework for discussing individual or family development that allows for the immense diversity of human experience. In addition, discussion of individual growth and development necessitates an understanding of the family life course in specific historical and social time. The following two sections will explain these influences on the life course.

Age-Graded, History-Graded, and Non-Normative Influences on the Life Course

Before examining the life course in detail, let us consider particular influences on human behavior that help explain the complexity of person-environment transactions. Figure 4.1 represents the influence of age-graded, history-graded, and non-normative events throughout the life course (Baltes, 1987).

Included in **age-graded influences** are those aspects of development related to chronological age (i.e., birth, puberty) as well as age-specific societal expectations (i.e., schooling, retirement). The developmental theories of Freud, Erikson, and Piaget, presented earlier in this text, illustrate perspectives on human behavior rooted in age-graded changes throughout the life course. These events are usually anticipated, and as we will point out later in the chapter, although they show some variation, there is enough uniformity throughout a specific culture to agree within that culture on the developmental tasks expected at a given point in the life course. Because of the normative and predictable nature of many of these events, advance preparation through anticipatory socialization is often possible (Hagestad and Neugarten, 1985). Anticipatory socialization refers to the ways in which people are prepared for roles that the culture assumes they will perform. For example, in some cultures, the family practice of assigning chores to children is considered a preparation for developing appropriate values and habits related to later work life. However, in many countries and cultures, children are an integral part of the family's economic life, and their labor is real and vital.

Age-graded influences are culturally and historically defined. In America, for example, until the early part of the twentieth century, child labor was a necessity in poor and middle-class families. This was true for both city and farm families. It was not until the passage of child labor laws in the early 1900s and the

FIGURE 4.1 Influences on the life course

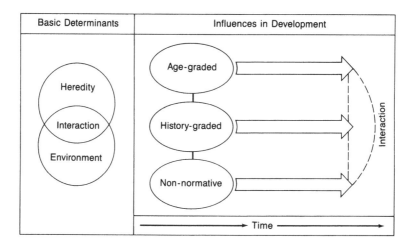

development of compulsory education that these children were freed from the expectation of economic contribution to family life.

History-graded influences involve societal changes brought about by historical events such as demographic shifts, technological changes, and employment rates. People who are born at about the same time and share similar historical experiences are called **cohorts.** The concept of cohort is useful in explaining history-graded influences at various points in the life course. A specific behavioral pattern, therefore, may be heavily influenced by history-graded or cohort variables. The Great Depression in America was a significant historical event that had an impact on the lives of most Americans. Millions of people were unable to find work and suffered great hardships. As a result, many people who lived through that period report that their basic beliefs regarding work, thrift, and economic institutions were altered. Work was no longer regarded as a certainty, and therefore economic thrift became more important. At the same time a suspicion regarding economic institutions, such as banks and the stock market, also resulted from the failing of these entities. Again, however, even such a large-scale historical event did not affect all people in the same manner or to the same degree. For those who were already poor, the depression was experienced merely as "more of the same." For many wealthy persons it was a difficult period but not necessarily catastrophic in nature.

Non-normative influences on behavior include events such as accidents and natural catastrophes (fires, floods, earthquakes), as well as unanticipated and unpredicted occurrences, such as loss of employment, sudden widowhood, or the sudden onset of illness. These events show little correlation with chronological age or historical time (Baltes, 1987: 175) and are often more stressful than life events that occur on schedule.

Each of these influences, age-graded, history-graded, and non-normative, shapes and determines the course of human behavior, and they all facilitate or inhibit the successful resolution of developmental tasks throughout the life course. Consideration of these factors is an essential component of the assessment phase of social work intervention.

Life Events and the Life Course

Danish et al. (1980) have identified a number of events which occur throughout the course of human life that help us to understand human behavior and to plan helping and support strategies. Life events are occasions in a person's existence that signal significant milestones or transition points. Marriage and retirement are two examples. Both are culturally defined, age-related transitions that are accompanied by new role expectations. Life events are not, however, isolated phenonomena. They occur in a larger context and are influenced by other events in the individual's life and in the systems in which people live. An approach to the life course that focuses on **critical life events** is consistent with the health model of social work practice presented in this text. Such a perspective emphasizes continuous growth and change throughout life. It is also consistent with a systems perspective. Critical life events are not viewed as pathological, but rather as occasions that invite growth.

Danish and others (1980) delineate the following properties common to all life events: event-timing, duration, sequencing, cohort specificity, contextual purity, and probability of occurrence. Let us take a brief look at each of these characteristics and examine how they might influence behavior at various points throughout the life course.

Event Timing.   The timing of an event may be more significant than the event itself. Did the event occur at a time consistent with social expectations? Marriage at 25 and retirement at 65 are congruent with social expectations. First marriages at 50 and retirement at 40 are culturally "off time." As pointed out earlier, events that are on time are more likely to gain cultural approval and support than events occurring "off time." Clearly the timing of events is a culturally dependent variable. As culture changes, so do the ideas regarding societal expectations related to "age-appropriate" behavior. Today, for example, more people are choosing to delay marriage until they are firmly rooted in their occupational sphere. Others choose not to marry at all, and in selecting either option they are less likely to incite negative sanctions than might have been expected by previous age cohorts.

Duration.   This refers to the length of time an event is experienced. Danish and others (1980) suggest that it may be helpful to view some events as *processes,* rather than as single occurrences. The duration of the event then includes anticipation of the event, the event itself, and post-event occurrences. The birth of a baby, for instance, involves not only the birth but also the entire course of pregnancy and experiences of early infancy. A career change may involve months of agonizing decision making and often includes consultation with a host of professionals for exploration of career options. In such a scenario the impact of a job change is qualitatively different from the sudden and unplanned loss of employment.

Event Sequencing.   Have the events occurred in the socially expected and sanctioned order? Having a child before marriage is not consistent with the culturally prescribed courtship, marriage, and pattern of family development held by the traditional normative system. The renewed call for welfare reform can be viewed as an attempt to enforce traditional values related to family. Unwed pregnant teenagers violate three traditional normative expectations: children should be born to married couples; adults, not adolescents, should bear children; and the couple should be able to financially support themselves and their children without government support. However, individuals often form their own expectations regarding their personal and/or career paths. The successful completion of life tasks is usually facilitated when the tasks are supported by cultural expectations and when people have planned for them. As with event timing, the past two decades have witnessed considerable changes in event sequencing.

Cohort Specificity.   Events have different meaning for different cohorts. Living together before marriage, or as an alternative to marriage, does not bring the same negative social sanction that it did for young couples in the 1950s.

A phenomenon referred to as the boomerang generation has gained popular attention recently. This refers to young adults choosing to return to their parental home after living independently for some time. This move is often the result of economic necessity, but as it becomes common in the population (i.e., cohort-specific) it is viewed by the larger culture as an adaptive behavior rather than as evidence of personal failure.

Contextual Purity.   **Contextual purity** refers to the degree that one event interferes with other events occurring at the same time. When an event happens at an otherwise uneventful time in one's life, it is considered contextually pure. As indicated above, events also influence the lives of others. For the purpose of helping it is essential to consider how a specific event enhances or inhibits successful resolution of other developmental tasks in a person's life or in the lives of others.

Probability of Occurrence.   This relates to the likelihood that a specific event will be experienced by a large portion of the population. Age-graded normative influences discussed in the previous section have a high probability of occurrence. These are often referred to as *normative life crises* (Ginsberg, 1975). The non-normative influences on development discussed in a preceding section have a low probability of occurrence. To the extent that events have a high probability of occurrence, it is possible to prepare in advance for them. Community support systems and educational programs (preretirement seminars, for example) can be designed to ease the impact of the event itself or the aftereffect of the event.

Events with a low probability of occurrence (discussed earlier in the chapter as non-normative influences) are unplanned and unanticipated. Their impact on the individual or the population affected are qualitatively different and require different coping strategies in response. The San Francisco Earthquake of 1989, for instance, occurred in a community that was demonstrably well prepared for such a disaster. Even so, thousands were left homeless. Such a disaster clearly disrupts the life course of those who are both directly and indirectly affected.

Human beings do not live their lives in isolation. Their lives are entwined with those of their family, their friends, and the larger community. Any setting in which we find ourselves is populated by participants at differing points in their lives. People are also affected by both anticipated and unanticipated life events in terms of their timing, duration, sequencing, cohort specificity, contextual purity, and probability of occurrence. This perspective helps us to view the life course holistically. It is consistent with the person-in-situation perspective and the health model of social work presented in this text.

In the next sections of this chapter, various periods of the life course will be discussed. As stated previously, these are broad and artificially demarcated categories presented for discussion purposes only. Before proceeding, however, stop and read Exhibit 1 at the end of this chapter regarding Kathleen Buete and Geneva Morrison, grandmothers who are raising their HIV-infected grandchildren. In both cases the premature death of an adult child left these women to care for their dying grandchildren. These events represent tragic variations in the life course of three generations. As you reflect on the previous material in this chapter and read further about the tasks of various periods of the life course, think about the disorienting events in these women's stories and the immense strength they bring to coping with these difficult circumstances.

Periods in the Life Course

Dividing the life course into distinct periods, each with its characteristic problems and potentials, has captured the imagination of artists and scientists throughout human history. Shakespeare, in *As You Like It,* presents seven stages of human development that closely parallel Erikson's developmental stages presented in Chapter 3. Others, through the use of metaphor, compare the stages of life with the seasons of the year. Spring is the time of youth and promise; summer the time of adulthood and greatest productivity; autumn the time of harvest and transition to later life; and winter the period of old age and decline (Kimmel, 1980). Recently, however, social scientists have begun to question the validity of viewing the life course as unfolding in a one-directional manner in which each successive stage flows from and builds on the previous stage in a neatly packaged sequential order. Periods of growth and decline are closely intertwined. Germain (1994) believes stage theories reflect a too rigid and linear view of the course of human life and are not congruent with the transactional view of behavior that characterizes contemporary life and scientific thought.

From a biological perspective, human development occurs in a carefully sequenced manner—early childhood, for instance, is a period marked by the development of motor coordination skills; adolescence is a time of rapid hormonal change; and later life witnesses decrements in all five of the senses. These changes occur throughout the species with minimal influence of culture. They are universal and show little variation. Biological development, however, as emphasized throughout this book, occurs in a psychosocial-cultural-historical context. The developmental periods presented in this chapter are merely a way of conceptualizing these multiple sources and influences on behavior in terms of their interaction. As each period is presented, specific developmental tasks accompanying the period will be considered. These tasks are culturally defined and translated through social structures into expected behaviors.

Viewing the life course in terms of periods of growth and transition with specific developmental tasks is simply a tool to help view human life as a totality of biological, psychological, cultural, and social-structural factors. Any attempt to view these periods and their related tasks as occurring in a nonvariant pattern to all members of the population ignores the richness of human diversity. Throughout the discussion that follows we will look at the obstacles and resources related to each period, comment on possible influences (history-graded, non-normative, and life events), and suggest implications for intervention. Table 4.1 graphically presents this framework.

This section of the chapter will focus on the following periods in the life course: conception and birth, infancy and early childhood (birth—about age 4), middle and late childhood (about 4-12), adolescence (about 13-18), young adulthood (18-35), middle adulthood (35-55), later adulthood (55-75), and old age (75 and older).

Conception and Birth as a Life Period

Tasks. Conception and birth result in periods of expansion for individuals, groups, and society. For the individual (the parent), the self becomes the source of life for others. This generally adds to one's sense of competence, continuity, and importance, although it also increases one's responsibilities. For specific groups and for society as a whole, conception and birth ensure the survival of the social unit by replacing members and even increasing the size of the unit. The focus during this **life period** is on decision making and preparation for new life. The decision to have a child is a significant one for the individuals directly involved. It engages a network of interpersonal relationships that will be used to provide emotional and financial support during the pregnancy and after the child is born. Groups impinge on individual decision making through cultural definitions of the desirability of pregnancy and the conditions under which it should occur. Groups also form the support structures that provide the context in which conception and birth occur.

Biological tasks focus on the reproductive act and the physical and emotional conditions needed for a healthy pregnancy and a secure birth. Psychological tasks relate to the readiness of the partners involved to conceive and to carry a child. This includes a sense of well-being about oneself and the baby, knowledge about conception, pregnancy, and birth, and the existence of emotional support systems. Social-structural tasks pertain to creating or finding an environment in which conception can occur by choice and the pregnancy and birth can take place in a safe context. Cultural tasks are those that engage belief and value systems to support the parents and the child. Together, these four task areas attempt to provide the emotional and physical life-sustaining needs of the child

TABLE 4.1 A framework for analyzing the life course

Factors Affecting Life Course Tasks		
Resources and Obstacles	*Influences*	*Variations*
Biological	Age-graded	Gender
Psychological	History-graded	Ethnicity
Social-structural	Non-normative	Physical abilities
Cultural	Life events	Sexual orientation

and its parents. This includes the creation of a receptive social context in which the child will be able to grow and develop.

The life period of conception and birth is unique in that, during it, the person being conceived and born is completely dependent on others. Conception itself is the result of decisions and actions by others that precede the person-to-be. Conditions under which the fetus develops are also strongly influenced by others, particularly the biological parents. The task of the fetus itself—to develop physically and to survive—is engaged through its genetically inherited developmental potential. Thus, for the fetus the task is almost exclusively physiological. The developmental tasks of the fetus, therefore, can be considered as age-graded tasks.

The social, psychological, and cultural factors involved relate to the other people involved in the environment of the fetus. The biological mother is, of course, of particular importance. Consider the contextual purity in which the critical life event of having a child occurs. Is it an otherwise uneventful time for the parent/caregiver? Even the birth process is heavily affected by other factors. The fetus has its own physiological tasks to perform in the birth process, but the environment into which the fetus emerges is determined by others. For example, even if a doctor diagnosed that a cesarean section would be needed for a safe delivery, the parents would have to initiate the decisions and actions to make it possible. Birth complications are examples of non-normative life events.

This life period is a good example of the fact that the tasks faced by individuals at various life periods affect each other. The task of the fetus is to grow and survive, although the likelihood of this happening is strongly influenced by the life period tasks of the biological parents. Are the parents unmarried adolescents or financially secure married adults? In other words, is the timing and the sequencing of this life event congruent with the life course plans of the parents? The readiness of biological parents to see the fetus through pregnancy, birth, and infancy is an important influence on the new person's ability to carry out his or her own life task. These same measures also apply to the person and or couple who wishes to adopt a child. The tasks accompanying conception and birth (or adoption) as a life stage are dependent on both age-graded and non-normative influences. The very decision to have or not to have a child is partly determined by history-graded (cohort) influences. Reproductive technology presents different options to today's parents and potential parents than it did to cohorts a generation ago. This technology, along with changing social attitudes, has allowed, in some limited geographical areas, for lesbian couples to have children through the use of artificial insemination. This was not a medical or social option 20 years ago.

Resources.   Biological resources are those that increase the probability that the mother and child will be healthy. These include the mother's age at conception, her previous pregnancy history, her health, and whether she is addicted to any chemical substances. In general, women between the ages of about 16 and 35 run the least risk of complications during pregnancy. Women who are healthy—

that is, who are disease-free and receive proper nutrition—who have not had pregnancy difficulties in the past and are not dependent on any drugs or chemical substances, are less likely to encounter biological difficulties during pregnancy. The age, nutritional level, and health of the father are also relevant to the biological processes of conception and pregnancy. Finally, the genetic composition of both parents is an important determinant of the course of a pregnancy and birth.

Psychological resources are those that help individuals decide whether they wish to have a child and whether they have the emotional and financial means to do so. This includes knowledge about parenthood, conception, pregnancy, and birth—knowledge basic to informed decision making that will ultimately relate to a sense of readiness for parenthood. Personality variables are also important. A sense of personal well-being and strength and the ability to confront new situations help people adjust to the demands of pregnancy and parenthood. Willingness to share with others and the ability to cope effectively with physical and emotional stress are also beneficial.

Social-structural resources are those factors that provide concrete help for pregnant women and new parents, as well as social-structural conditions that serve to validate their changed identity as parents. Tax benefits for children, health insurance to pay for the medical costs of pregnancy and birth, and company policies that allow women to take leave during pregnancy are all significant resources. Additional social-structural resources include the quality of medical care available, social rituals such as baby showers that allow family and friends to express their support, availability of information about conception and parenthood, and personal and genetic counseling. A direct relationship exists between minority-group membership and the availability of these socioeconomic resources (Harper, 1990). Social-structural resources are generally less available to the poor and to members of minority groups.

Cultural resources are those that allow for group approval for conception and birth and that provide an acknowledged context for these activities. Being the proper age and having appropriate marital status as defined by one's own group places pregnancy in an acceptable value framework that will lead to social praise and support. The culture, in other words, dictates the proper timing and sequencing for the life event of having a child. Using socially acceptable means of prenatal care, following prescribed sex-role behaviors, and adhering to prevailing beliefs and values that support conception, pregnancy, and birth are also important. Of course, each cultural group has its own definitions of whether conception is desirable, and if so, how it should be managed.

Obstacles. Obstacles are those factors that increase the biological and psychological risks of conception and birth and detach people from the usual social-structural and cultural supports at this life stage. Biological obstacles may include a woman being either very young or old at the time of conception or having a history of pregnancy complications. Other biological obstacles might include the presence of venereal disease in either partner, substance abuse or dependency by the mother, or the existence of genetically transmitted conditions in either partner. Psychological obstacles might be having to adjust to an unwanted child or possessing very limited knowledge of conception, pregnancy, and birth. Another psychological obstacle would be feelings of severe inadequacy by either partner related to taking on parenting responsibilities.

Examples of social-structural obstacles might include inadequate financial resources to pay for necessary medical treatment or to provide proper nutrition for the mother or abusive physical conditions that threaten the mother's needs (a factor that is especially important if there is a complication during pregnancy or at birth). Additional social-structural obstacles would include lack of information about conception, pregnancy, and parenthood and the lack of available counseling to help those who are struggling with factors related to conception. As noted earlier, poverty is directly related to physical well-being. Therefore, biological and social-structural resources/obstacles are closely associated because poverty results from economic and political variables. Cultural obstacles are those beliefs and values that devalue conception and birth. A pregnancy occurring "off time" or out of the culturally sanctioned sequence creates obstacles to both parents and child.

Implications for Intervention.   Conceiving a child is a major life event. For many it involves a decision that requires as much information and emotional support as possible. It is often a decision shared with significant others, such as family and friends, who can be critical elements in the decision. For some, conception is not planned; it simply happens. This often reflects lack of information about basic physiological processes. In other cases, conception is considered a natural part of life and accepted whenever it occurs. And for still others, it is a decision made to achieve other goals, such as a sense of intimacy with another, a feeling of personal importance, or a sense of independence. Professionals have to be able to disentangle the many factors that may be involved in conception in order to provide appropriate resources.

Pregnancy is a time of physical and emotional changes and adjustments. The pregnant woman needs as much information as possible about her pregnancy and a great deal of support as she adjusts her activities and emotions to it. Many women also need financial aid, housing, and other supports so that adequate nutrition and physical care are available. Others involved in the pregnancy, especially the father, also need to be supported and informed. When the pregnancy threatens to lead to exclusion from supporting social structures, such as school, family, work, and so on, efforts should be made to strengthen these links or find alternatives. The existence of conditions that threaten the physical well-being of the mother or child—such as drug addiction, disease, illness, or genetic factors—demands a thorough analysis of the implications so that appropriate intervention can be taken.

Professionals can anticipate a host of concerns at this life stage. As we have seen, the need for information, for physical and medical care, for help in decision making, and for solidifying linkages with support systems is especially critical.

In addition, basic life-sustaining resources may be needed, such as money, food, and shelter. The fact that this life stage usually leads to alterations in established life patterns often creates the need for counseling in one or more of the multiple systems that may be involved. For many people, creating new life is a happy, exciting adventure. For others it is quite routine. Still others approach it with fear, anxiety, and a sense of desperation. Professionals must be able to anticipate and respond to all of these possibilities so that newly conceived persons can have the best possible chance of meeting their basic task at this life stage—physical development and survival.

In summary, if both the timing and the sequencing of conception and birth are culturally sanctioned, and if these events occur at a time that is relatively free from serious problems for both parents and family (i.e., contextually pure), professional intervention may not be necessary. The mobilization of the supportive community of family and friends may be all that is indicated.

If, however, conception and birth occur off-time or are out of sequence with either the culturally prescribed pattern or the individual's own life-course plan, professional intervention may be required. In this instance a variety of roles are appropriate for the generalist practitioner. Early identification of at-risk populations requires skills in case finding. After the populations are identified, special referral skills may be needed to get potential users to appropriate resources. Often, however, resources are not available, in which event skills are needed to mobilize new resources.

Another common problem is that resources may be there, but barriers (such as rigid eligibility requirements) may inhibit their use. In this instance professionals need to develop skills in advocacy, both for the benefit of the individual potential user and for the entire population of users. Knowledge about the person-environment transactions at each stage of the life course, therefore, informs not only daily practice interventions but also policy making.

Infancy and Early Childhood as a Life Period

As defined here, infancy and early childhood make up the period from birth to about 4 years of age. Infancy is a period that involves the infant and those around him or her, so the tasks at this stage reflect a range of individuals. For purposes of simplicity, however, we will focus only on the child at this point. The birth and parenting of a child by the adult will be discussed later.

The child is born completely dependent upon the adult caregivers for his or her survival and growth. Adequate food, shelter, and emotional bonding are required if the infant is to mature biologically, mentally, and emotionally. The child gradually matures biologically, gaining increasing mastery over his or her own limbs, bodily functions, perceptual abilities, and communication mechanisms. Provided a secure and loving environment, the child is initially able to develop trusting relationships with caregivers and later extend this trust to larger circles of individuals. Children must begin the long process of moving in the direction of independence and separation from parental figures.

Resources.   The biological resources of the infant are its genetic endowments. Reflexes, neurological mechanisms, skeletal structure, and basic health make it possible for the infant gradually to perceive, organize, and master its environment. The degree of development and mastery will, of course, reflect the nature of the child's genetic equipment. An infant's physical attractiveness, as defined culturally, is also an important biological resource.

Psychological resources in the infant are closely tied to biological endowments. Biological needs in interaction with the social environment produce the psychological resources available to the child. An infant whose needs are met consistently, promptly, and with care will usually develop personality resources that increase the probability of continued growth and strength. Scientists have demonstrated through the study of micromovements of parent and child that many inherited physical and verbal cues are exhibited by both parent and child that stimulate positive feelings, resulting in strong emotional ties between them. Recent research demonstrates that social and physical stimulation is essential for the infant to develop its perceptual and cognitive capacities as well as its ability to relate to others. Parents' resources include their receptivity and feelings toward the infant.

Also considered valuable resources that enhance the child's development are the parents' knowledge of infant and child development, which allows them to provide a nurturing and stimulating environment. Mature parents who can respond to the many changes in their lives demanded by the child's varying needs will also be resources for the child. A sense of competence, closely allied with emotional maturity, provides parents with the confidence to undertake the difficult and uncertain tasks of childrearing.

Social-structural resources for the infant are those that enhance its survival and growth. The family, however defined, is the emotional cradle of the infant. The family constellation provides the infant's first contact with the social world. Stability of the family is, therefore, of great importance in the child's development. The nature of medical care, availability of safe housing, healthful nutrition, and adequate formal and informal child-care arrangements are examples of sound social-structural resources. These factors are also of importance to parents because their availability relieves them of stresses that may interfere with the parent-child relationship. These social-structural resources are necessary throughout childhood, although their form may change as the youngster grows older.

Culturally, the infant benefits from beliefs and values that define children as desirable. Whereas large families are seen as desirable and even necessary in agrarian cultures, industrialization has made the smaller family the norm because it is more adaptable to a wage economy and geographic mobility (a history-graded influence). Culture also defines how we view children and consequently how the infant and child should be reared. Present-day definitions of childhood in the United States are quite different from those during the early part of this century. At that time, at the age of 7 children were expected to join the labor force to assist in the financial stability of the household. Now, childhood is extended well into the teenage years, and full-time work is not generally expected until the age of 18 or beyond. As we might expect, there are sub-cultural differences within these cultural expectations.

Other cultural values also affect childhood. In many cultures, female children were sometimes killed because their economic value to the family was considered minimal. Conversely, male children in those cultures were valued because they could provide labor and income. Similarly, disabled or handicapped offspring were also devalued. While gender, race, and physical ability are viewed today in more positive ways, culture still influences how children are viewed. Cultural norms dictate that male infants wear blue, whereas female infants wear pink. Boys are dressed in miniature football jerseys, while girls wear miniature dresses. Gender-role socialization continues throughout the life course and interacts with social structures such as career availability, subject preferences in school, and role conflicts (being a mother or pursuing a career).

Obstacles.   Obstacles for the infant are those factors that impede growth and development. Given the infant's fragility, genetic and environmental obstacles can easily be life-threatening. For the parents, care for the infant can be blocked by a variety of obstacles (non-normative influences).

Biologically, the infant's genetic equipment may be incomplete or partially nonfunctional, a risk that is especially high for infants born prematurely. This makes it more difficult to perform life-sustaining activities or to interact with the environment so that growth and development can occur. This would be the case for infants born without an organ or limb, or with a defective organ, such as the heart, or with brain damage. An infant who contracted a disease would also be placed at risk. An unusual or undesirable physical appearance can also be an obstacle—for example, a cleft palate, crossed eyes, or a limb deformity. Although these conditions can be surgically corrected in many cases, they may affect the early bonding between the infant and its parents. Parents may also encounter biological obstacles. The blind or deaf parent, for instance, is confronted with different tasks in relating to the child so that its needs are met.

For the child, psychological obstacles are closely related to its biological capacity to perceive and organize the environment and to process information correctly. The development of fearful or rigid personality responses to stimuli can be obstacles to continued growth. These chronic distress responses can also precipitate negative behavior by others, such as abuse or neglect. Parents' personality patterns can be obstacles when they lead to compulsive behavior in childcare that restricts rather than enhances growth.

Social-structural obstacles for the child may include inadequate nurturance, physical care, and nutrition as a result of poverty, dysfunctional family structures, disorganized communities, or adults with poor parenting skills. These factors are also obstacles for parents. Cultural obstacles include beliefs and values that devalue certain types of infants, such as illegitimate, "fussy," or minority children. As noted previously, gender stereotyping can be an obstacle for both male and female children when it inhibits them from developing to their full potential.

Cultural systems can also be considered obstacles when they mandate childcare practices that conflict with biological needs. An example is excessively early or rigid toilet training. Another example of cultural values that interfere with successful parenting is when members of certain groups are discouraged from childrearing. In the United States, this applies to single parents, homosexuals, and the physically or mentally impaired, among others. Members of these groups can and do successfully care for infants and children, but they have to fight dominant cultural values and beliefs that view them as incompetent and unworthy.

While the negative effects of prejudice around race, ethnicity, gender, physical and mental ability, and sexual orientation are not fully manifested until later stages of childhood, their roots take hold in the nature of interactions during infancy.

Implications for Intervention.   Infants need a great deal of care if they are to thrive and develop. This requires many resources, including knowledge, money, energy, love, food, shelter, and time. Many parents lack some of these resources and have few support systems available to help them. Professionals need to be able to assess the resources available, always taking into account the childrearing strategies appropriate to a person's cultural, social, and physical environments.

The infant may also need intervention. A child born with a genetic limitation or who suffers a severe illness needs careful diagnostic and treatment resources. Parents and others may need financial help to pay for these services, as well as knowledge and emotional support to use them most effectively. An infant requiring special care often imposes substantial strains on the entire family system, while relationships between the infant and the parents can also be affected. The social work practitioner must be prepared to address all of these issues.

The prevailing myth in the United States portrays the infant enshrined in a cradle of affluence and acceptance. In reality, babies are sometimes burdens on already strained financial, emotional, or time resources. When they require special care, babies can be even more disruptive. Understanding the joys as well as the heartaches of infancy as a life stage for infants and parents alike requires careful analysis and sensitivity.

The two-parent family is itself becoming the minority, as is the myth that the mother stays home to raise the children while the father is the income producer. Changes in the family and in the roles of family members require that social structures be rethought and restructured so that they enhance rather than detract from the resources that families need to meet children's needs. This suggests that practitioners must address social-policy issues related to strengthening families and the social structures that affect them, in addition to directing service activities on behalf of families and children. These supportive policies apply to all families, stepfamilies, adopting families, and gay and lesbian parents regardless of race, ethnicity, or income level.

Middle and Late Childhood as a Life Period

Tasks.   Middle and late childhood is defined here as the period from approximately age 4 to age 12. It is a period during which biological development continues but comes to be shaped more and more by social interaction in an increasingly wide range of social situations. While basic personality characteristics and gender identification of children are believed to be already established by age 3, they continue to be shaped and modified by their social environment. The child is introverted or extroverted, trustful or distrustful, assertive or passive, but new social contacts and new challenges require emotional adaptability, which serves to test the child's psychological resources.

The beginning of school is an important task during this period. The child begins a period of significant cognitive development along with the need for emotional control. Gradual movement away from parents and family toward peer groups is normative at this stage. The child has to balance the need for independence of thought and action with the ability to follow instructions, rules, and regulations. There is also exposure to formal and informal values regarding gender, race, physical ability, and sexual orientation. Gender-role socialization is especially pronounced, and exposure to individuals from diverse backgrounds is likely to occur—hopefully in a positive way.

Resources.   To face the tasks of childhood, physical health, personality strength and adaptability, and cognitive capacities form the foundation for incorporating the child into society. Since biological resources available to children are similar to those of infants, they need not be discussed here. Sometimes, however, it is only when a child begins school and interacts with a wider range of people than just family members that particular biological resources are noted. This could include unusually well-developed coordination, muscle strength, hearing, and eyesight, and overall resistance to disease.

Psychological resources also continue to develop from infancy, but they are especially important in childhood. Substantial cognitive development occurs in school and through modeling the behavior of peers, family members, and media personalities. The child whose genetic inheritance includes high intelligence, sound perceptual abilities, and general health has important biological-psychological resources to use in confronting the major tasks of childhood. Physical and social stimulation that confronts children with challenging but manageable stresses helps them develop a sense of competence and well-being. Parental nurturance and support also facilitate the development of a stable self-identity that can adapt to increasingly diversified and new life experiences.

Social-structural resources continue to be important through childhood. Family structure, community structures, school systems, and friendship networks are extremely important sources of opportunities for the child to encounter new people and new situations. When these structures support the child's biological growth and psychological development, they become extremely powerful resources. For example, parents who are supportive of exploratory activities by the child and who gently cushion occasional failures help make the world seem a rich and exciting place. Schools that stimulate cognitive and social development by presenting manageable challenges in a structured but supportive context also encourage a sense of security through growth.

Cultural values can be resources when they mandate respect for children's needs and involvement of children in the full range of life activities. For example, in knowing their grandparents, youngsters are exposed to cross-generational learning. Children who participate appropriately in adult activities are better prepared to perform them when they are adults themselves (an example of anticipatory socialization based on predictable normative age-graded events).

Obstacles.   Biological obstacles in infancy often become increasingly limiting as the child grows and is exposed to increased demands. The malnourished child may lack the energy to play with friends or to concentrate in school. Limited physical mobility may increasingly isolate a child from his or her active peers. Sometimes biological obstacles only become apparent in childhood. Hearing or vision impairments are examples of deficits that are sometimes identified for the first time in school.

Biological obstacles become increasingly enmeshed in a web of relationships with social structures, and their ultimate significance in a child's life depends on how these relationships are developed. The child with cerebral palsy who is seen by his or her caretakers as an embarrassment will not receive needed therapy and will gradually become weaker and less mobile. The child with an undetected vision deficit will find school a frustrating and boring experience and may act out as a result. Even a child who has to wear glasses may be ridiculed by peers and gradually withdraw socially. Mitigating these effects of obstacles requires careful medical diagnoses and supportive interpersonal relationships.

Psychological obstacles are frequently tied to biological and social obstacles. The child with cognitive limitations or perceptual deficits may find demands by others difficult to understand and impossible to fulfill. Excessive expectations or harsh demands may generate fear, anxiety, withdrawal, and rigidity that block a child's ability to utilize existing psychological and biological resources. If the world is seen as cruel, unmanageable, and threatening, then the child's psychological development is likely to be restricted. This will lessen the child's ability to understand and adapt flexibly and productively to situations. The reasons the environment seems so hostile may be biological, social, or cultural, but the impact on psychological functioning is similar. Therefore, we can expect that a child of average intelligence who is regularly pushed into educational and social situations beyond his or her abilities will react with hostility, anxiety, and withdrawal. The amount of interpersonal support the child receives will influence the kind of personality that ultimately develops.

Children may encounter many kinds of social-structural obstacles. Poverty brings with it the risk of chronic ill health, hunger, anxiety over physical safety, and an eroded self-esteem. Racism and other forms of prejudice and discrimination may lead to physical assaults, attacks on personal identity and integrity, and social isolation. Extreme stress in families may lead to child abuse or neglect, while unhealthy school structures create a rigid, overly demanding, and nonsupportive learning environment. In addition, accidents, natural disasters, and peer groups that make the child a scapegoat can be significant social-structural obstacles.

Cultural beliefs that lead to gender stereotyping are reinforced in social structures during this time, and they can serve as obstacles to development. Boys play sports, while girls become cheerleaders. Such early gender roles reflect later stereotypes of women as supporters of the male breadwinner. Conversely, culture-bound values give rise to negative male stereotyping. Boys are taught not to cry and to see themselves as protectors of girls. These and similar messages tend to cut off boys from their emotions, making it difficult for them to relate fully to others as they mature. Other cultural beliefs can also be obstacles, such as those that ignore the child's need for privacy, play, protection, and nurturing.

Implications for Intervention.   Opportunities for children to interact with a complex environment are important for growth, but they can easily become overwhelming and restricting. An environment that is too unstructured, unstimulating, and isolating does not provide the challenges necessary for growth. An environment that is too structured and demanding undermines self-development. Professionals need to assess the ways in which existing environments are able to respond to a child's efforts to understand, adapt, and grow. Sometimes environments need to be enriched; other times they need to be simplified. In all cases, the focus is on helping the child find the resources needed in a particular environment—whether these be family activities, life-sustaining resources, school-system supports, or peer interaction.

Considerable agreement exists among theorists that childhood is a time when the basic personality is established. Although personality is subject to modification throughout life, a view of the world as essentially benign or fearsome seems to be established by the end of childhood. At this life stage, then, the interaction between the individual and the environment is especially critical. Adults frequently have enough knowledge and power to modify the child's environment if they feel the need to do so, but the child has relatively little power to achieve this. Thus, it is the job of professionals as well as parents to focus on making the environment as supportive as possible for the child's efforts to grow and develop both biologically and socially.

Again, it is important to keep in mind the concept of contextual purity. Parents, too, may be dealing with their own developmental crises. Some of the child abuse and neglect problems that social workers commonly address may be rooted in the clash between the developmental needs of children and those of their parents. When such problems arise, a variety of social welfare services are available, including such child welfare services as residential child-care recreational programs and such supportive services as daycare centers. However, practitioners must be ever diligent to spot and eliminate those social-structural manifestations of prejudice and discrimination based on race, gender, sexual orientation, and physical or mental abilities in the child welfare system.

Adolescence as a Life Period

Tasks.   The major tasks of adolescence, defined here as approximately age 13–18, revolve around biological development and further integration into social institutions. Adolescence is characterized by selective biological development, building on the basic motor, perceptual, and cognitive maturation that has already occurred during infancy and childhood. During adolescence a substantial increase takes place in physical size, height, and weight. Sexual maturation also occurs, including the emergence of secondary sex characteristics such as breast development, growth of body hair, and so on. The rapid growth in size and sexual maturation is the result of substantial hormonal changes that affect both physical appearance and emotional needs. A large part of the adolescent's task, then, is to adjust to changes in body image, physical capacities, and sexual needs.

These biological changes take place within a social context that is also changing. School demands are more academically rigorous and are increasingly related to career planning. For example, academic success affects whether the teenager goes to college and, in turn, influences future career opportunities. School also becomes an increasingly important social arena in which peer-group pressure accelerates. Lifelong friendships and interaction patterns can be established at this time.

Biological development, academic demands, and peer pressure naturally interact. Adolescents confront a changing self, making it difficult to understand precisely what their needs and capabilities are. Friendship patterns that characterized childhood may suddenly seem inappropriate as young people struggle to find acceptance among their peers. Intellectual capacity, physical skills, and outward appearance are dimensions that heavily influence the kinds of social demands and opportunities available to the adolescent. This is further affected by the youngster's race, ethnicity, and gender. For example, a young woman who matures and grows in size early in her adolescent years may feel awkward and sexually vulnerable, whereas one who experiences these events later may be more ready to integrate them into her social relationships. The reverse is true for young men, who tend to grow and mature later than women. But the young man whose development is late even for his gender often comes to feel weak and unattractive.

As adolescents move closer to adulthood, their life options are affected by cultural influences based on gender and race, as well as being affected by their own capabilities and preferences. Women are moving into roles that have traditionally been dominated by men, such as doctors, lawyers, politicians, and astronauts. However, the great majority of women continue to be channeled by school, family, and peer pressure into typically "feminine" careers that are often less well paid and less secure than male-dominated areas of employment (Dion, 1984: 6–9). Race is also a factor determining length of academic career and employment opportunities, with members of racial minorities having less education and restricted employment options (U.S. Bureau of the Census, 1989). Those with special physical needs can also be deterred by an unresponsive social environment.

The support that adolescents receive has an impact on their development. Parents who experience anxiety over the increasing size, competence, demands, and autonomy of their teenage children may find it difficult to support efforts of adolescents to grow and develop. Anxious parents may try to maintain their control by denying the adolescent's new-found competence or by emphasizing biological changes as a way of increasing the young person's sense of uncertainty and need for parental protection. Other adults, especially teachers, can also reinforce either the adolescent's sense of developing strength and well-being or his or her awkwardness and anxiety.

From society's viewpoint, adolescence is a time of some normative flexibility that accommodates biological changes and sometimes erratic approaches to meeting personal needs. Yet society still expects that by the end of adolescence the developing adult will be ready to assume a relatively stable role in the social structure.

Resources.   The adolescent's physical resources are often prodigious. Physical strength and size are powerful resources, as are the continued strengthening of perceptual and cognitive abilities. Adequate nutrition is an important resource during adolescence because physical growth during this time exerts considerable demands on the body. Sexual functioning matures during adolescence and is a powerful motivator for behavior. Psychologically, adolescents learn how to integrate their new physical abilities with social relationships with their peers and with adults. These become the important beginnings of support systems that will continue throughout life. Perceptual and cognitive resources are especially important for meeting increasing societal demands for achievement in an expanding range of areas, among which school, work, and family are especially important. Through this process, the personality is gradually enriched by increasing mutuality in relationships, a deepening of interests, and a clearer articulation of personal values and goals.

Social-structural resources are those that promote the adolescent's sense of competence and need for individualization. The family continues to be an important potential source of support, and the peer group assumes increased importance. School becomes a possible source of enrichment, while the developing competence of teenagers enables them to participate in a wide range of social activities such as driving, working, and school- or church-sponsored events.

Culturally, values become very important resources for helping adolescents solidify their self-identity and self-image, as well as for helping them order their personal values and lifelong priorities. Decisions about the balance between work and family, self and others, achievement and sharing, and stability and change grow out of cultural values. Robinson and Ward, for example, state that African-American female adolescents are:

. . . engaged in the process of identity formation and self-creation. During this passage from adolescence into adulthood critical attitudes are formulated, behaviors are adopted and life style choices are made. However, African-American adolescent girls are making this passage embedded within a family and a community that is most negatively impacted by a sociopolitical context formed by racial, gender, and economic oppression. We suggest that an African-American female can be consciously prepared for the sociopolitical environment in which she will lie by fostering development of a resistance that will provide her with the necessary tools to think critically about herself, the world, and her place in it. (Robinson and Ward, 1991: 88–89)

Robinson and Ward (1991: 91) further suggest that, "For the African-American adolescent female, the ability to move beyond the internalization of racial denigration to an internalization of racial pride involves a process of confronting and rejecting aggressive negative evaluations of Blackness and femaleness, adopting instead a sense that is self-affirming and self-valuing."

Obstacles.   Biological development can be an obstacle in a variety of ways during adolescence. The biological changes that occur may not be well under- stood and may, therefore, create social difficulties. Changes in size and strength can create appearance and behavior characteristics that are devalued by others: the very tall young woman or the overly enthusiastic and slightly uncoordinated young man are two instances of adolescents who receive such treatment. Illness and accidents are also possible when physical growth is not supported by adequate nutrition or when growth of various parts of the body is not synchronous. In addition, hormonal changes are common and can create fairly rapid and extensive fluctuations in energy levels, moods, and the sense of well-being.

Physical and psychological changes are closely related because the emerging adult body is a critical component of self-image and treatment by others. The ridicule and isolation that may result from developmental irregularities or problems can have powerful effects on feelings of competence and well-being. This is especially true if childhood experiences have begun the process of accentuating weaknesses rather than strengths. However, perceptual or cognitive capacities can be used to lessen the negative psychological effects of physical obstacles. The very intelligent young woman, for example, may be treated with respect even though she does not conform to prevailing standards of teen- age attractiveness.

Social-structural obstacles limit development by restricting access to resources or creating social expectations that inhibit growth. Adolescents from poor families may lack proper nutrition or may need medical care to deal with the nearsightedness (myopia) that often accompanies the rapid growth of adolescence. Families may have unrealistic social or academic expectations for their children, pushing them into situations in which success is practically impossible. Schools sometimes emphasize young people's weaknesses, increasing the likelihood of peer-group difficulties. The peer group itself can be an extremely damaging obstacle if it forces teenagers to conform to stereotyped expectations regarding dress, behavior, and interpersonal relationships.

Cultural values can further exacerbate social-structural obstacles by legitimating disadvantaging expectations. For example, intelligent young women are hurt by cultural values that restrict them to the home, and physically limited males are negatively affected by values that emphasize large physical size and strength. Socialization is a very important part of the adolescent's developing and maturing sense of self. It teaches goals and values that will facilitate the teenager's adjustment to the environment. When this does not happen, the transmission of cultural values through socialization becomes a problem. Such is the case, for example, when gay and lesbian adolescents are not socialized into productive interpersonal relationships that nurture their own self-image and provide the support they will need to function effectively as adults. D'Augelli (1992: 214) states that "the life tasks of adolescents—the transition from dependencies of childhood to the autonomies and intimacies of adulthood—can be severely compromised. . . . much psychological energy is directed to coping with fears of deviance; social energies are devoted to vigilance to avoid disclosure or exposure. Hidden from friends, families, and helping resources, these teenagers may consciously postpone exploring their personal identity until early adulthood."

Implications for Intervention. During any time of change, either personal or social, people are put at risk. Their efforts to understand change and to adapt to it need to be strongly supported. Otherwise, the uncertainties accompanying change can gradually erode the person's sense of competence. Supporting people through change entails providing information, emotional resources, and help in keeping the pieces of shifting institutional relationships in balance. For example, social work practitioners often help adolescents to manage their emerging sexuality, their desire for rewarding interpersonal bonds, increasing autonomy, and the demands of school simultaneously. To accomplish this, the practitioner must involve many systems beyond the adolescent and the adolescent's family.

Social workers are also involved with modifying social expectations for adolescents. Although some flexibility exists in role definitions, teenagers experience many inconsistencies and strains. For example, men are allowed to be more sexually promiscuous than women, so the latter may be punished for behavior that is permitted for the former. Professionals attempt to make social expectations more equitable and to help reduce the severity of punishment when teenagers make mistakes growing out of role confusion and conflicts. This might include helping an adolescent to avoid having a criminal record, being expelled from school, or becoming estranged from the family.

The family can be a significant source of difficulty when its perceptions of, and responses to, the needs of adolescents are inappropriate. This explains in part why social workers so often work with families. Adolescents can appear gawky, resistant, angry, aggressive, and unlovable as they struggle to understand their own bodies and as they seek to establish themselves in their social environment. It is important to try to help individual adolescents and those with whom they interact—especially family, teachers, and peers—to approach each other with greater awareness, caring, and support. Some social welfare resources to help accomplish this include vocational and educational counseling, alcohol and chemical dependency counseling, recreational services, and family counseling.

The emotional turbulence of adolescence may precipitate a resurgence of unresolved conflicts in parents or caregivers (recall the concept of contextual purity), many of whom are dealing with the transitional crises of midlife. These people need help in distinguishing between activities that are focused on achieving their own goals and those that are needed by their adolescent children. As with previous stages, social work professionals must strive toward the elimination of social-structural and cultural values that discriminate and inhibit the growth of the teenager's potential. Academic tracking based solely on gender or physical ability should be of concern to the helping professions. Biases, prejudices, and stereotyping lead to inequities in economic opportunities, poor race relations, and oppression based on sexual orientation and/or gender that are especially hurtful to teenagers who are trying to become productive adults. On a policy and practice level, such obstacles need to be eliminated.

Adulthood as a Life Period

Tasks.   Any attempt at dividing human life into stages is at best arbitrary. Clearly there is much variation in the life tasks that confront adults between the ages of 18 and 75. Indeed, as life expectancy increases (a history-graded influence), what is considered middle age and elderly changes drastically.

Adulthood is a time of accomplishment and productivity, probably the period when people are most goal-directed with respect to their own life aspirations. However, society expects that individual aspirations will mesh with societal needs. For example, rearing children requires resources that are earned—and spent—through the economic system. Socialization in childhood and adolescence is the major mechanism through which adults are prepared to work toward their goals in socially acceptable ways. Individual goals and societal goals, then, are assumed to come together during adulthood.

At no other life stage is the individual quite so oriented toward the performance of societal tasks. Members of diverse groups process societal goals and the means of achieving them through their own particular values, resources, and obstacles. Rossi (1980), for example, demonstrates that the issues confronting women during the adult years differ considerably from those confronting men. These differences, she points out, reflect not only psychological factors but also cohort variables that determine the differential assignment of tasks based on gender. Hammer and Statham (1989) reinforce this view with their analysis of the special responsibility that a woman has to care for others throughout most of her life span—first her children, then her spouse, then her elderly parents, and finally her elderly spouse. In a similar way, Devore and Schlesinger (1981) demonstrate how adult development tasks vary among ethnic groups, while

Sutkin (1984) looks at physical ability as an important variable throughout the life course.

In addition to working toward the attainment of task goals, adulthood is a time when people seek interpersonal intimacy and when some interpersonal relationships may include sexual activity. Marriage is, of course, one pattern, but others include parenting relationships, nonmarried coupling, and selected friendships. The adult's twin sense of accomplishment and well-being are, for most people, heavily dependent on the formation of close interpersonal relationships that provide important social, biological, and psychological supports. Although adulthood is a period of autonomous goal-seeking behavior carried out in the major institutions of society, it is also a time of personal nurturance through the special relationships found in adulthood, for example, marriage or other forms of coupling, parenting, and so on. Thus, adulthood is both outwardly and inwardly focused, a time of both independence and interdependence.

Resources. In adulthood, people usually have as many physical resources as they will ever have. Although physical development continues, gradually moving into increasingly degenerative conditions, adulthood is generally characterized by well-developed physical, perceptual, cognitive, and personality resources. Levels of development vary, of course, but they are not usually substantially changed in adulthood. The use of resources can vary, however. Use is a function of social-structural variables that either facilitate or inhibit adult behavior.

Social-structural resources for adults are found primarily in the major institutions of society that serve to organize people's behavior around the performance of significant life tasks. Through the family and family-like structures, adults solidify their most intimate interpersonal relationships. The economic institution is an important arena in which people achieve their task-oriented goals, although women have also traditionally achieved many task goals through their parenting and other caregiving roles in the family. The political institution interacts extensively with the economic institution and also provides opportunities for significant decision making. The educational, religious, and social welfare institutions may also support task-oriented and personal development goals.

Interactions between adults and social institutions vary for different types of adults. Although the institutional structures support the goal-directed behavior of most adult members of majority groups, the point was made in an earlier chapter that members of minority groups may receive less support. Cultural values strengthen adults' efforts to be independent in specified areas of their activities, although this varies for gender groups and for members of different ethnic groups and subcultures.

Obstacles. Illness and accidents (non-normative influences) can occur at any point in one's life, but higher rates of both begin to characterize middle and late adulthood. This reflects the stresses that accompany adult life tasks, as well as the range of behaviors in which adults engage. For example, work-related accidents and illnesses occur primarily in adulthood because it spans the major working years. Also, a great deal of violence occurs in the context of the family, especially among adults. Moreover, degenerative processes related to physical functioning accelerate, most commonly in the areas of vision, hearing, strength, and cognition. These changes are not usually substantial enough to have a major effect on behavior during adulthood, but their influence grows cumulatively.

A major potential obstacle in adulthood is the gradual deterioration of personality adaptiveness. This may result in part from physical changes that are perceived as modifying appearance and behavior in undesirable ways. Even such relatively unimportant biological changes as loss or graying of hair or changes in skin texture can generate anxiety and defensiveness. Adults sometimes deny these physical changes by using cosmetics, wearing different clothes, or even associating with younger and more "attractive" people. This can have seriously disruptive consequences for long-established and important supportive relationships with spouses, mates, siblings, close friends, and work associates. Loss of these supports can undermine the individual's personality resources and lead to depression or other types of alienation and isolation.

A second assault on psychological functioning in adulthood results from the interplay of social-structural and personality variables. Adulthood is, as has been noted, the principal period in the life course when cherished life goals are sought through such activities as work, peer relationships, and family or family-like relationships. However, it is only in rare instances that all of an individual's life goals are attained, and during adulthood the person has to begin to come to terms with this reality. Social-structural resources naturally play a significant role in an individual's ability to achieve life goals. Poverty, destructive family or family-like relationships, unemployment, accidents or injuries, and the loss of loved ones can all block goal attainment. When these non-normative and disruptive events occur, the individual's own sense of identity, self-worth, and well-being are called into question. Even worse, it may seem that there is less and less time left in life to try again. The sense of personal and societal failure is further underscored by cultural values that stress successful goal attainment.

Psychological responses can include a whole range of defensive actions, sometimes even including changing the place in which one lives so that failure will not be so apparent. Cultural values may be especially inhibiting in the efforts of adult members of diverse groups to meet their needs. For example, some homosexuals respond to negative cultural definitions by hiding their true identity through loveless heterosexual marriages and furtive homosexual contacts. Many women accept physical and emotional abuse rather than endure the stigma of divorce—even today when divorce is much more common than in the past. The cost in terms of personal well-being is extremely high for those who attempt to sacrifice their own needs in order to meet rigid societal expectations.

As the course of development throughout the adult years is examined, it becomes clear that while disorders and disruptions do, in fact, occur, they may result from societal expectations often as a consequence of the negative images of the elderly held by the young (Friedan, 1993). Social work practitioners also need to be sensitive to gender, ethnicity, life style, and physical ability as important variables influencing the package of resources and obstacles that help or hinder the resolution of development tasks.

Implications for Intervention.   As in previous stages, multiple variables govern the tasks, resources, and obstacles encountered in this long and complex period of the adult years. Both age-graded and non-normative critical life events, as well as history-graded (cohort) influences, affect the need for and appropriateness of intervention strategies.

Adulthood is a time of excitement, challenge, change, and stress. Practitioners should be prepared to support adults and help them cope with such stresses of adult life as work pressure, relationship problems, and parenting demands. It is also critical that the social structure reward people's plans and activities. Institutionalized discrimination, for instance, systematically blocks the efforts of certain groups to achieve their goals. In offering help, professionals need to recognize that adults are a very special group with which to work. Adults may strongly value their independence and autonomy if cultural values have taught them to do so. Thus, they frequently resist offers of help from others, even professionals. A sense of competence is extremely important to adults, and utmost care is needed to support and preserve it. Nevertheless, the stresses and challenges of adulthood often lead to the need for personal support and institutional intervention.

Psychosocial themes that characterize adulthood include companionship versus isolation and regrouping versus binding or expulsion (Rhodes, 1977). Major changes in family relationships occur as teenagers increasingly meet their emotional needs outside the family. Eventually the children are likely to establish their own adult relationships and move out of the family home. Spouses may find their relationship with each other revitalized as they no longer have to set aside their own companionship needs in order to meet the challenge of parenting. Regrouping versus binding or expulsion applies when the children leave the parental home. According to Rhodes, the essential task is encouraging the separation of the children as a natural result of their growth and maturity. The ability to accomplish this task rests heavily on developing a strong marital relationship separate from the parenting function.

Increasingly, however, adults are choosing alternatives to the traditional nuclear family pattern. Remaining single, developing an intimate relationship with a same-sex partner, and having a childless marriage are choices more and more people are making. These emerging patterns bring new life-stage demands for which there are few role models. Practitioners must be aware of these alternative approaches to meeting the tasks of adulthood and know how to help people function effectively in whatever pattern they choose. This may present professional helpers with considerable challenges to their own value system, and they may need to stretch their thinking to learn how these alternatives can be integrated into prevailing institutional structures and cultural beliefs.

Before leaving the topic of adult development, we should note that Gilligan (1982) questions the applicability of a male-dominated life-cycle theory to the experiences of women. Gilligan points out that women bring a different viewpoint, different priorities, and an alternative perspective on maturity. The hallmark of this perspective, according to Gilligan, is a moral understanding based on a greater orientation toward the value of supportive relationships and useful networks of interdependence. For example, women may see strength in interdependence and mutual support, rather than the more common male tendency to emphasize independence and competition. This view of the world can be a significant resource for adult women, even though their male partners and colleagues may find it difficult to understand. The effective practitioner must understand these kinds of gender differences, providing support where needed and facilitating communication so that greater sharing of gender-specific resources can occur. In addition, social structures often support oppressive policies. These policies and practices can negatively affect an individual's transition to and success in later periods of life. Perkins (1993) points out that low-wage female workers (Caucasian and African-American) experience more financial difficulty in retirement as a result of gender discrimination in work settings. She suggests that this is because women are subjected to lower wage positions while working and are more likely to be forced into early retirement than their male counterparts. Retirement benefits for women are significantly lower than for men.

Old Age as a Life Period

Tasks.   Just as there is little consensus regarding what is considered adulthood, there is lack of agreement regarding what constitutes old age. Some gerontologists talk of two phases of being old, old age and old-old age, the latter referring to the period from age 85 onward—the most rapidly growing segment of our current population. Technological advancement in health care (a history-graded influence), better nutrition, and the somewhat improved economic status of the average elderly person all contribute to the increased life expectancy of the elderly. For many people this may create two phases of aging: the dramatic change in social role that begins occurring at about age 65 and the increased concern with physical changes and health needs that is likely to develop after age 85.

If gerontologists cannot agree about what constitutes old age, how are we to understand this stage of the life course? Is it a biological phenomenon characterized by physiological decrements? A psychological stage accompanied by sensory and motor changes? A social category defined by an arbitrary chronological age that determines a person's eligibility for programs and services? Perhaps nowhere in the life course is the interrelationship of the biological, psychological, social-structural, cultural, and spiritual dimensions of behavior more dramatically observed.

Looking over one's life in order to make sense of it is one of the central tasks of old age. This need not be a time of morbid reflection about what might have been, nor a time spent focusing on one's losses and decrements. Rather, it can be a time of continued psychological growth and development—an invitation to look more deeply into oneself. Bianchi believes that:

. . . stressing growth through diminishments is not an appeal for a sad and gloomy old age in which one concentrated in an almost morbid way on deterioration and death. Rather, growth through diminishment, based on a willingness to encounter the inner demons of old age with faith, can lead to an authentic joy even among hardships. It is by facing the terrors of old age, by launching out on the final night-sea journey, that a person finds the courage and insight to be profoundly wise for others in adulthood. (Bianchi, 1986: 188)

Obviously, this life stage is one of tremendous change and adjustment, both biologically and socially. Indeed, these two areas interact closely, and the nature of their interaction is the major determinant of whether old age is a time of contentment or desperation. On the other hand, old age may also be a time of freedom from many of the tasks of earlier life stages, such as work. Nevertheless, an increasing number of elderly people continue to maintain active work and professional lives; for them, old age is neither a period of retirement nor disengagement from significant social roles. Whether old age is a time of disengagement from previous social roles and responsibilities or a time of continued interaction with others is related more to a person's individual style of coping throughout the life course than it is a function of chronological age.

Resources.   Although old age entails physical deterioration in a number of areas, most older people continue to have relatively good health and retain most of their perceptual and cognitive capacities until very advanced old age. Age itself, therefore, can be a resource, just as it is a period of continued growth and development. Of course, people age differently, just as they differ in so many other ways. Some people experience advanced physical deterioration at a relatively young age. Nevertheless, most people are able to carry on their usual activities during old age with relatively minor adjustments.

Physical energy may be used differently, however. Some older people tend to avoid the hectic pace that younger people prefer and to think through their actions with more care before doing something. In this sense, the elderly may become more efficient, reflecting once again the strong tie between physical and psychological resources throughout the life course. Looking back on a lifetime of accomplishments, most older people find self-validation and satisfaction and can adjust to lower energy levels by focusing on what is meaningful to them rather than on what society expects. To them, old age is a time of continued social and political activity, and a reference to this life stage as "the golden years," meaning a period of inactivity, might indeed be offensive.

The organization of older people into special-interest groups, such as the Gray Panthers or the American Association of Retired Persons (AARP), has helped strengthen social-structural resources for the elderly. A variety of financial aid programs help maintain income in old age and provide other concrete support services such as housing and transportation subsidies, in-home and congregational meal programs, and medical care services (Ford Foundation, 1989). These services are often needed by elderly people who have limited incomes and who are frail or living alone. Additional social needs are increasingly being recognized and met through self-help groups, the development of recreational programs, the creation of educational opportunities, and the provision of personal counseling services.

Special emphasis has now been placed on structuring institutional arrangements so that older people can retain control over their own lives. Some programs currently being developed are housing that builds in both autonomy and immediate access to help, transportation systems that are more physically and financially accessible to the elderly, and counseling and financial supports that help link the elderly to some type of family or family-like network. Nevertheless, existing social-structural arrangements sometimes impinge on the quality of life of older persons, as when medical care is impersonal and inadequate or when housing does not provide for physical safety and social needs.

Cultural values have become extremely important determinants affecting the nature of old age, and the self-help groups organized among older persons have had a noticeable impact. When the extended family is a common social-structural form, older people are usually taken care of primarily within the family unit.

Other values affect the treatment of the elderly. In a society that emphasizes autonomy and productivity, the elderly may not want to be dependent on family members. They may prefer to be socially and sexually active even if the primary spouse or mate dies, leading to the formation of new families and family-like units among older persons. They may also wish to define for themselves the extent of their involvement with children, grandchildren, and the economic system, rather than automatically assuming roles expected of them by their adult children. All of these structural changes reflect cultural values that are gradually changing to accommodate a much greater degree of independence and variation in the current cohort of the elderly.

Obstacles. Even for the relatively healthy older person, increasing old age brings greater risks of illness, accidents, and physical deterioration. This may progressively limit the person's physical mobility and social participation. It may also strain the financial resources available to the older person. Gradually, the individual becomes more dependent on others. This can threaten a person's sense of well-being. Combined with a commonly experienced gradual loss of perceptual acuity—especially sight, hearing, and taste—the older person may withdraw and become increasingly isolated. This often reduces the motivation for living, which can manifest itself in reduced appetite to the point of malnutrition and a lack of mobility and stimulation that then accelerates physical deterioration.

While there has been greatly increased recognition of the needs of the elderly in recent decades, social-structural factors still make this stage problematic. Young people grow up detached from older people and do not learn how to prepare for this life stage. When grown children move out of the home, sometimes called the "empty nest" syndrome, and when a worker has to retire, abrupt loss of social roles can leave people feeling useless and undirected. The high cost of medical care creates anxiety and the concern that old age will lead to destitution.

These conditions are perpetuated by cultural values that overemphasize youth and physical appearance, as well as productivity and independence. American society values progress and change and is always pushing toward the new with little respect for its own past or those who created it. In such a milieu, it is little wonder that older people feel left behind and left out. We know only too well that these feelings are closely tied to accelerated biological deterioration, social isolation, and psychological distress. Unfortunately, these are realities for a lot of the elderly. Many of these realities are reversible, however, and as the aged gain in political and economic power as a result of their increasing numbers and stronger group cohesion, societal resources may be reallocated so as to meet their needs more adequately.

Ageism is perhaps the major obstacle confronting the elderly in contemporary society. Beliefs about the elderly being unwilling or unable to change, incapable of learning, asexual, rigid, conservative in nature, and dependent and withdrawn are commonly held misconceptions. Unfortunately, these negative images are commonly found among helping professionals (Bloom, 1990). If internalized, these stereotypes become the basis for the self-fulfilling prophesy whereby the elderly come to behave in ways that are consistent with social expectations. Ageism, therefore, is destructive not only to the individual but also to the social order (Barrow, 1989: 10).

Implications for Intervention.   As with any type of diversity, old age has its particular resources and obstacles. Society holds conflicting views about the elderly. On one hand, it assumes that older people are physically and emotionally dependent. On the other hand, it tries to find ways to make them more self-sufficient because they constitute a growing percentage of the population. Social work professionals, as part of their commitment to help people live self-directed lives, must reinforce societal efforts to recognize and support the many strengths of older people. For example, there is a need for many more apartment complexes that allow the elderly to live autonomously and still have access to immediate physical help and social companionship. There is also a need for nursing homes in which older persons' right to, and need for, privacy—including the privacy to express themselves sexually—is respected. Many other services are required as well, especially adequate medical care.

At the interpersonal level, we must be sensitive to the older person's continuing need for friendship, social recognition, and intimate ties to others. An older person may need emotional support to adjust to a radically altered physical appearance or decreased physical mobility. A strong sense of self-respect is as important in retirement as it is at any other point in one's life. Help in meeting daily needs can also be of critical importance. This could include help in such diverse activities as securing transportation to health-care facilities, applying for financial assistance, or filling out medical forms.

Death as a Life Period

Throughout this chapter we have tried to present a framework that is usable for analyzing human behavior in its social context at any point in the life course. We have illustrated this framework with the life stages of conception and birth, infancy, childhood, adolescence, adulthood, and old age. Now we would like to give you the opportunity to use the framework yourself to analyze death as a life stage. It is hoped that this will increase your mastery of the framework and give you greater confidence in its use. To assist you, we will provide some general guidelines.

Before moving to the analytical framework, it may be helpful to think for a moment about your own attitudes toward death. Most children and young people are shielded from death and do not see it as part of life. Hospitals usually do not allow children to visit parents—they have to be adolescents; children are often not taken to funerals, and they frequently have very little contact with the elderly. When something is unfamiliar it often seems strange and even frightening. Many readers may feel this way about death.

Yet today there is abundant literature about death and dying that can help people understand this part of the life course better. As a professional, you will need to feel comfortable practicing in situations that include death or dying. We have already seen that human life and social structures are characterized by diversity, a fact that professional helpers must learn to understand and appreciate. Both death and dying are components of this diversity. As you use the framework to analyze death as part of the life course, remind yourself that it is as important, as complex, and as fascinating as any other life stage.

Tasks.   Think about the life tasks that the individual and society are faced with at death. What does each gain and what does each lose? One way to think this through is to try to imagine what would happen if people lived forever. What problems would be created that death helps solve? Another thought to ponder is why people fear death—what are they really afraid of and how does understanding their fear help explain the life tasks to be accomplished at death? Does thinking about death in terms of life tasks make it easier or more difficult for you to think about your own death?

Resources.   Using the biological-psychological-social-structural-cultural format, determine what resources people have as they try to carry out the life tasks associated with death. Another way to think about this is in terms of those factors that make it easier for people to die. These might be biological factors, such as drugs; psychological factors, such as emotional security; social-structural factors, such as legal procedures to pass on resources to others; and cultural factors, such as beliefs about an afterlife and rituals to help people prepare for death. Resources, then, support people's efforts to die in such a way as to maximize their sense of personal and social well-being. Does it seem a contradiction to think of well-being at the point of death?

Obstacles.   The opposite side of the resource view would be the biological-psychosocial-cultural factors that make it more difficult for people to die. Think about pain, for example. Is it a resource, making it easier to accept death, or an obstacle, making it harder, or is it both? In thinking about obstacles, be sure to include relationships with others. When do relationships make it more difficult to die? When do they make it easier? Do you have difficulty thinking about obstacles, especially in relation to death? Why is this a painful subject for you? Why isn't it?

Implications for Intervention.   To what aspects of dying should professionals be especially sensitive? Remember to think systemically so that you do not overlook the help that those associated with the dying person might need, as well as the help for the particular dying person. As you think about it, are there resources that professionals might need in order to work effectively in the highly emotional situations in which death often occurs? What might these be, and would they include structural supports as well as personal resources? Could you work with someone in the last life-cycle stage? Think carefully about the problems you would anticipate if such a situation were part of your work responsibilities. How does such thinking help you understand the implications of death as a life stage for the helping professions?

THE LIFE COURSE AND THE PRACTICE OF HELPING: UNIVERSAL MODELS AND INDIVIDUAL NARRATIVES

The preceding sections of this chapter summarized selected tasks associated with particular periods in the life course. Readers are encouraged to continue their study of theories regarding the life course to gain a more comprehensive understanding of the complexities of the biological, psychological, social-structural, and cultural influences on behavior. When reading in this area, the helping professional needs to be mindful of possible gender, sexual orientation, racial, ethnic, cultural, class, age, and historical bias. In other words, helping professionals need to be aware of the great diversity in human behavior and development. In addition, traditional developmental stage theories have limited value when considering the non-normative aspects of life. For example, in Chapter 5, Exhibit 5.4, "Everything Happens in Its Own Time," demonstrates how a 36-year-old AIDS patient engages in a life review prior to his death. In traditional stage theory models, such life reflection is considered a task characteristic of old age. Insofar as models of human development throughout the life course assist in conceptualizing human growth and transition processes, they are useful to the practitioner. However, developing a model that encompasses the great diversity of human experience is extremely difficult. Many life-course theorists suggest that even defining distinct chronological periods in the life course is difficult. Certainly, the survival experiences of young "Yummy Sandifer"

(Chapter 1, Exhibit 1.1) would not be considered age-appropriate for a child. Yet, in this age children are growing up in a time of great technological and informational advances in which expectations for them are ever increasing. As science and medicine increase life expectancy, how do we define old age? What tasks are appropriate for older persons who may live 20 or 30 years after retirement?

Neugarten (1982), in addressing the issues of aging, argues that traditional stages are becoming blurred and that an "age-irrevelant" image of the life course must be developed. An alternative to life-course models of development arising in professional literature is the production of material related to specific populations. Monica McGoldrick (1989) and Berzoff (1989) address women's issues in the life course. Freeman (1990) focuses on a strengths perspective when viewing life-course issues specific to African-American families. Boxer and Cohler (1989) and D'Augelli (1992) address gay and lesbian life-course issues. Berman (1986) suggests that old age is an individual subjective experience and that each person defines its personal meaning. These authors and many others focus less on universal models of the life course and explore the variations in human experience. This body of literature creates for the helping professional a way of operationalizing the practice principle of appreciating and supporting diversity. This body of literature broadens our appreciation of the myriad of ways that people grow and develop. It also minimizes views of human development that define normative and deviant behavior according to the values and needs of the dominant culture and class.

In Chapter 1 we discussed various forms of knowledge. Universal theories of human behavior and development represent explanatory forms of knowledge in that they attempt to provide an explanation of how persons develop and interact with the world. These models are usually based on empirical research. However, as we discussed in Chapters 1 and 2, empirical models are not without bias and are often utilized to define normal or appropriate behavior or development. Universal models should never be used in practice to devalue, distort, or pathologize the experiences of the individual, the family, or the community.

How do helping professionals, then, use life-course models? The answer is that helping professionals utilize them as referential material. They provide a general framework for understanding individual human behavior in the context of overarching biological realities and social, cultural, and subcultural expectations. Life-course models assist in developing a broad understanding of the basic biological, psychological, and social-structural resources needed to support individual growth and development from birth to death. This information can be utilized in work with individuals, families, communities, and societies. The content and structure of these models, however, need to be continually refined, updated, and diversified if they are to be of assistance to helping professionals and those we seek to serve. These models should never be utilized to prescribe behavior for persons or to define normative and deviant behavior.

The helping professional best serves individuals and families by seeking to understand their view of their lives and the events in their lives. In Chapter 1 we discussed personal, communal, and subjugated forms of knowledge. These forms of knowledge have not always been fully utilized as a part of the professional helping base. A growing body of literature in social work suggests the importance of personal narration (or "telling one's own story") to the helping process. Stories, myths, tales, parables, and narratives are a primal way of organizing individual and cultural meaning. Brunner states:

We seem to have no other way of describing "lived time" save in the form of a narrative. Which is not to say that there are not other temporal forms that can be imposed on the experience of time, but none of them succeeds in capturing the sense of *lived* time: not clock or calendrical time forms, not serial or cyclical orders, not any of these. . . . Even if we set down *annales* in the bare form of events, they will be seen to be events chosen with a view of their place in an implicit narrative. (Brunner, 1987: 12)

Brunner (1987) suggests that both cultures and individuals develop stories that provide history, guide human interaction, and even structure perceptual experience. Polkinghorne (1988), Norton (1989), and Germain (1990) focus on the importance of facilitating individual's telling of their own stories. Basic to the concept of narration is the idea that human beings strive to apply meaning to the events they encounter. In this sense, narration is related to the cognitive and attributional theories discussed in Chapter 3. Polkinghorne suggests that persons develop "schemes" or plots to their lives:

The narrative organizational scheme is of particular importance for understanding human activity. It is the scheme that displays purpose and direction in human affairs and makes individual human lives comprehensible as wholes. We conceive our own and other's behavior within the narrative framework, and through it recognize the effects our planned actions can have on desired goals. . . . Narrative . . . makes individual events comprehensible by identifying the whole to which they contribute. . . . In summary, narrative is a meaning structure that organizes actions into a whole, thereby attributing significance to individual actions and events according to their effect on the whole, Thus, narratives are to be differentiated from chronicles, which simply list events according to their place on a time line. Narrative provides a symbolized account of actions. . . . (Polkinghorne, 1988: 17–18)

The tool used in human services to gather information regarding a client is called a social history. Health-related services utilize a medical history. The social history is constructed from the information gathered from the client and the client's family, as well as from other sources, such as social service providers. It usually provides such information as an individual's genealogy, physical health and development, social and family relations, education and work history, and utilization of health and human services. The information is obtained through a standard set of questions employed by the helping professional regarding these topics and is written in a professional manner. The medical history is similar in that it details a chronology of the patient's health history, including past illness, a history of family illnesses, and past treatments. This is why Polkinghorne might refer to the social history as a "chronicle of events." In contrast, a **narrative** is the client's own life story. A narrative reveals the meaning that the client attributes to life events and clarifies personal goals, dreams, wishes, disappointments, successes, and failures. Eliciting stories or life narratives from those we serve is an essential part of the helping process. This, of course, means that helping professionals need to listen attentively and patiently to clients as they tell us about the important aspects of their lives through their stories. This active listening also presupposes that we set aside our preconceptions of life as it should be from both our own personal narratives and the professional narratives or models we use to organize the world. Saleebey (1994: 357) suggests that helping professionals "can help serve as a catalyst [to clients or patients] in the reconstruction or reconstrual of meaning as it affects some part of the client's world." The helping professional listens to the stories in order to be able to provide support to clients in attaining their goals. Sandelowski discusses the role of the patient's narrative in nursing practice:

> Incorporating the narratives models or templates available to them in their culture, patients plot their lives as romances, comedies, melodramas, or tragedies in which they are the central protagonists struggling with and overcoming, or failing to overcome, obstacles that impede them from reaching their goals. Like all fictionalizers and, therefore, like all human beings, they select and temporarily arrange events and give them a coherence and unity that the experience they are telling can never have. By incorporating culturally familiar narrative models, stories provide a sense of connection between life events. (Sandelowski, 1994: 26)

Sandelowski further states:

> When nursing intervention is conceived in narrative terms, healing becomes a project directed toward constructing stories that patients can live by and with. The expert nurse-healer not only creates an environment in which patients feel free to tell their stories but also works with patients to (a) make the structure and meaning of their narratives apparent to them, (b) construct a unifying narrative for their lives, and/or (c) reconstruct a more useful or coherent interpretation of past events and future projects. The overall objective of narrative intervention is to transform disabling, incoherent, or overly restrictive narratives to enabling narratives that permit movement toward an integrated sense of self-worth with future possibilities. (Sandelowski, 1994: 28–29)

For the helping person to engage in this process requires a departure from the "expert" role and an ability to listen to the narratives. Baur, a counseling psychologist working with psychiatric patients in a psychiatric hospital, suggests that such a shift is necessary in the helping process. She also affirms the importance of the individual's own narrative as a means of understanding and protecting his or her world:

> This shift in objectives, from persuading patients to get a job or speak more clearly to actively listening to whatever they had to say, encouraged a different kind of relationship. As the "daughter" of a man who believed himself to be a Nicodemosaurus, for example, I became a student whose job it was to learn from the expert whatever I could about this schizophrenic's world. For another patient I became something of an auxiliary memory, holding and reinforcing the few stories he could remember of a happier time. For many I was simply a witness. In all instances, I accepted their aliases, their ideas, their rules (not mine) of communication, and . . . I was rewarded by being transported. . . . Thus over time I became increasingly familiar with the private thoughts of the moderately troubled and grievously ill, and with this familiarity came respect. I was amazed by their bravery and persistence. I was delighted by the ingenious ways in which all of them crafted reality into the shields or canes or costumes they needed to survive. (Baur, 1991: 3-4)

The personal narrative, then, stands in contrast to universal models of development. James Glass's *Private Terror/Public Life: Psychosis and the Politics of Community* recounts the stories of psychiatric patients. Of these narratives, he states:

> No absolutes or universal truths appear in these reflections; each contains its own special commentary on the history of the self and its nightmare world of terror and disintegration. David's reflections on becoming a "particle" and flying through the skies on his way to war, or Ruth's on Auschwitz and the world of 1943, Julia's on cutting and the use of razor blades as teddy bears: each of these meditations, these frames enclosing reality, describes something of being and the origins and the destruction of desire. . . . To have been objective [in studying patients], then, in whatever terms—whether through coding responses, or devising questionnaires, or setting up scales, or somehow systematizing the language—would have been a distortion . . . (Glass, 1989: 13)

The use of personal narratives as a means of professional helping is consistent with social work values that stress the uniqueness and dignity of the individual, the individual's right to self-determination, and the application of a nonjudgmental attitude by the helping professional.

SUMMARY

It is apparent that the life course encompasses a relentless progression of changes. Some of these changes come from within the organism itself, and others are created by the external human and physical environment. Yet amid these changes, some constants exist, including lifelong tasks: physical survival, physical development within genetic limits, attempts to relate to others, developing and strengthening a personal sense of self-worth and competence, and task-focused behavior. We have seen how these constants are shaped somewhat differently at each life period and how there is great variability and diversity throughout the life course based on gender, ethnicity, physical ability, and life style.

Many factors influence the resources and obstacles encountered throughout the life course, and multiple influences (age-graded, history-graded, and non-normative) determine the necessity for, and type of, professional helping required. Using the life course to understand human behavior, therefore, leads back to two important points made much earlier in this book. First, human behavior involves the interaction between people and their environments. Secondly, human beings have common human needs that are elaborated and met in extraordinarily different ways. The next and last chapter will further examine some implications of these two points.

STUDY QUESTIONS

1. Each population of age cohorts experiences similar historical influences as it moves through the life course. However, every person may experience these influences in a different way. What are some of the influences experienced by your age cohort? Discuss how these experiences have shaped your values, aspirations, behavior, and perceptions of the world.

2. Think of tasks normally associated with your present age group. Do you think these tasks are applicable to your present life situation? Discuss these tasks with someone from your preceding generation. Did they apply to that person when they were of the same age? If they are different, what do you think accounts for the change?

3. Discuss some of the resources needed and obstacles encountered by gay men and lesbians in old age. How do these differ from their heterosexual counterparts?

4. Discuss the properties common to all life events (event timing, duration, sequencing, cohort specificity, contextual purity, and probability of occurrence) as any or all of them relate to critical life experiences in your own life.

5. Read the Exhibit at the end of this chapter. How has the death of their children affected the lives of these grandmothers? How has it altered their life course? What resources are needed to support these families at this stage in their lives? What obstacles might they encounter? What are the implications for helping professionals?

6. Narration is a means of making sense of the events in one's life. How do you think the concept of narration might assist you in your professional helping? How might you incorporate the use of narratives into your practice?

KEY TERMS

Age-graded influences. Those aspects of development related to chronological age and including the accompanying age-specific societal expectations.

Cohorts. People born at approximately the same time and therefore experiencing similar historical events (albeit that they may experience them differently).

Contextual purity. The degree to which one critical life event interferes with other simultaneous events in a person's life.

Critical life events. Occasions in a person's life that signal significant milestones and transition points.

History-graded influences. Societal changes brought about by historical events such as demographic shifts, technological change, and employment rates.

Life course. The period from conception to death that encompasses the totality of the physical, psychological, social-structural, and cultural experiences of life at a given time in history.

Life period. Any period during the life course that has distinctive developmental and social tasks associated with chronological age and related biological and psychological abilities.

Narrative. A process by which persons, communities, and cultures organize the events and experiences of their individual and collective lives into stories that provide meaning.

Non-normative influences. Influences on behavior that are unexpected and unanticipated and that show little correlation with chronological age or historical time.

REFERENCES

Baltes, P. (1987). Developmental Psychology. In *The Encyclopedia of Aging,* edited by G. Maddox, pp. 170–176. New York: Springer-Verlag.

Barrow, G. (1989). *Aging, the Individual, and Society,* 4th edition. St. Paul, MN: West Publishing Company.

Baur, S. (1991). *The Dinosaur Man: Tales of Madness and Enchantment from the Back Ward.* New York: Harper Perennial, pp. 3–4.

Berman, H. (1986). To Flame with Wild Life: Florida Scott-Maxwell's Experience of Old Age. *The Gerontologist,* Vol. 26, pp. 321–324.

Berzoff, J. (1989). From Separation to Connection: Shifts in Understanding Women's Development. *Affilia,* Vol. 4, No. 1, Spring, pp. 45–58.

Bianchi, E. (1986). *Aging as a Spiritual Journey.* New York: Crossroads Publishing.

Bloom, M. (1990). *Introduction to the Drama of Social Work.* Itasca, IL: F.E. Peacock Publishers.

Boxer, A. and B. Cohle (1989). The Life Course of Gay and Lesbian Youth: An Immodest Proposal for the Study of Lives. *The Journal of Homosexuality,* Vol. 22, Nos. 3 and 4, pp. 315–355.

Brunner, J. (1987). Life as Narrative. *Social Research,* Vol. 54, No. 1, pp. 11-32.

Clausen, J. (1986). *The Life Course: A Sociological Perspective.* Englewood Cliffs, NJ: Prentice Hall.

Danish, S., M. Smyer, and C. Nowak (1980). Developmental Intervention: Enhancing Life Event Processes. In *Life Span Development and Behavior,* edited by P. Baltes and O. Brim, Vol. 3, pp. 339-366. San Diego: Academic Press.

D'Augelli, A. (1992). Teaching Lesbian/Gay Development: From Oppression to Exceptionality. *The Journal of Homosexuality*, Vol. 22, Nos. 3 and 4, pp. 213-225.

Devore, W. and E. Schlesinger (1981). *Ethnic-Sensitive Social Work Practice.* St. Louis, MO: C. V. Mosby.

Dion, M. J. (1984). *We the American Women.* Washington, D.C.: Government Printing Office.

Ford Foundation (1989). *The Common Good: Social Welfare and the American Future.* New York: The Ford Foundation.

Freeman, E. (1990). The Black Family's Life Cycle: Operationalizing a Strengths Perspective. In *Social Work Practice with Black Families: A Culturally Specific Perspective,* Chapter 4. White Plains, NY: Longman.

Friedan, B. (1993). *The Fountain of Age.* New York: Simon & Schuster.

Germain, C. (1990). Many Ways of Knowing. *Social Work,* Vol. 35, No. 1, pp. 3-4.

Germain, C. (1994). Emerging Conceptions of Family Development over the Life Course. *Families in Society: The Journal of Contemporary Human Services,* CEU article 42, May, pp. 259-267.

Gilligan, C. (1982). *In a Different Voice: Psychological Theory and Human Development.* Cambridge, MA: Harvard University Press.

Ginsberg, L. H. (1975). Normative Life Crises: Applied Perspectives. In *Life Span Developmental Perspectives: Normative Life Crises,* edited by N. Dantan and L. H. Ginsberg. New York: Academic Press.

Glass, J. (1989). *Private Terror/Public Life: Psychosis and the Politics of Community.* Ithaca, NY: Cornell University Press, p. 13.

Hagestad, G. and B. Neugarten (1985). Aging and the Life Course. In *Handbook of Aging and the Social Sciences,* 2nd edition, edited by R. Binstock and E. Shanas, pp. 35-61. New York: Van Nostrand Reinhold.

Hammer, J. and D. Statham (1989). *Women and Social Work.* Chicago, IL: Lyceum Books.

Hareven, T. (1982). The Life Course and Aging in Historical Perspective. In *Aging and Life Course Transitions: An Interdisciplinary Perspective,* edited by T. Hareven and K. J. Adams. New York: Guilford Press.

Harper, B. (1990). Blacks and the Health Care Delivery System: Challenge and Prospects. In *Social Work Practice with Black Families: A Culturally Specific Perspective,* edited by S. Logan, E. Freeman, and McRoy, pp. 239-256. White Plains, NY: Longman.

Kimmel, D. (1980). *Adulthood and Aging,* 2nd edition. New York: Wiley Press.

Lee, F. (1994). AIDS Toll on Elderly: Dying Grandchildren. *The New York Times,* November 21, pp. A1, A11.

McGoldrick, M. (1989). Women through the Family Life Cycle. In *Women in Families: A Framework for Family Therapy,* edited by M. McGoldrick et al., Chapter 11, pp. 200-226. New York: W. W. Norton.

Moen, P. and C. Howery (1988). The Significance of Time in the Study of Families under Stress. In *Social Stress and Family Development,* edited by David Klein and J. Aldous, pp. 131-156. New York: Guilford Press.

Neugarten, B. (ed.) (1982). *Age or Need: Public Policies for Older People.* Beverly Hills, CA: Sage Publications.

Norton, C. (1989). *Life Metaphors: Stories of Ordinary Survival.* Carbondale, IL: Southern Illinois University Press.

Perkins, K. (1993). Working-Class Women and Retirement. *Journal of Gerontological Social Work,* Vol. 20, Nos. 3 and 4, pp. 129-145.

Polkinghorne, D. (1988). *Narrative Knowing and the Human Sciences.* New York: State University of New York Press.

Rhodes, S. (1977). A Developmental Approach to the Life Cycle of the Family. *Social Casework,* Vol. 58, No. 5, pp. 301-311.

Rindfuss, F. with C. Swicegood and R. Rosenfeld (1987). Disorders in the Life Course: How Common and Does It Matter? *American Sociological Review,* Vol. 52 (December), pp. 785-801.

Robinson, T. and J. Ward (1991). A Belief in Self Far Greater Than Anyone's Disbelief: Cultivating Resistance among African American Female Adolescents. In *Women, Girls and Psychotherapy: Reframing Resistance,* edited by C. Gilligan, A. Rogers, and D. Tolman, pp. 87-103. Binghampton, NY: The Haworth Press.

Rossi, A. S. (1980). Life-Span Theories and Women's Lives. *Signs: Journal of Women in Culture and Society,* Vol. 6, pp. 4-32.

Saleebey, D. (1994). Culture, Theory, and Narrative: The Intersection of Meanings in Practice. *Social Work,* Vol. 39, No. 4 (July), pp 351-359.

Sandelowski, M. (1994). We Are the Stories We Tell: Narrative Knowing in Nursing Practice. *Journal of Holistic Nursing,* Vol. 12, No. 1 (March), pp. 23-33.

Shakespeare, Wm. (1919). *As You Like It,* Act 2, Scene 7, Lines 139-166. In *The Yale Shakespeare.* New Haven, CT: Yale University Press, pp. 42-43.

Sutkin, L. (1984). Introduction. In *Chronic Illness and Disability Throughout the Life Span: Effects on Self and Family,* edited by M. Eisenberg, L. Sutkin, and M. Jansen, pp. 1-19. New York: Springer-Verlag.

U.S. Bureau of the Census (1989). *Population Profile of the United States: 1989.* Washington, DC: Government Printing Office, pp. 36-39.

exhibit 4.1

AIDS Toll on Elderly: Dying Grandchildren

"AIDS Toll on Elderly: Dying Grandchildren" by Felicia R. Lee appeared in The New York Times, *November 21, 1994, pp. A1 and A11. Copyright © 1994 by the New York Times Company. Reprinted by permission.*

For a long time, Kathleen Buete feared a telephone call saying that her daughter Florence had died of an overdose. That call never came, but Florence did come home pregnant and with AIDS. She eventually died and Ms. Buete is caring for her 8-year-old grandson, who grows weaker and thinner every day from the same virus that killed his mother.

"I scream sometimes for no reason," Ms. Buete said. "I have my crying fits. I go into the bathroom so he doesn't see me, but he catches me sometimes."

As the AIDS epidemic rages, grandmothers across the nation are increasingly thrust into an old role with a new twist: They are caring for adult children dying of AIDS and for the grandchildren, in some cases also dying, who are left behind.

These women are the unexpected victims of a changing epidemic. Heterosexual AIDS infection jumped 130 percent from 1992 to 1993 (an increase due in part to a change in definition) and experts estimate that as many as 125,000 children will lose their mothers to AIDS by the year 2000. These children are increasingly left in the care of relatives, family friends and social agencies.

In many ways, the AIDS epidemic simply worsens the crisis of American families caused by drugs, abuse, abandonment, prison and death.

In 1992, there were 865,000 children under 18 being reared by their grandparents. Last year, that number jumped to over one million, according to Census Bureau information analyzed by the American Association of Retired Persons. Most of the orphans are in New York, Newark, Miami, Los Angeles, Washington and San Juan, P.R., according to the Orphan Project, a research group that explores policy options for children orphaned because of AIDS.

"We believe AIDS may be one of the categories that will explode," said Rene Woodworth, coordinator of the Grandparent Information Center of the A.A.R.P., which is based in Washington. The center opened a year ago to offer help and information to the increasing number of grandparents raising grandchildren for various reasons.

"We don't have any numbers, but we are hearing the stories," Ms. Woodworth said of the impact of the AIDS epidemic on grandparents forced to raise orphaned children. "You're dealing with the issue of loss, maybe some guilt, maybe some shame. Their biggest concern is taking care of their grandchildren. They are issues the country needs to grapple with."

Many are also struggling financially.

"Some people say, it's very sad, the mother died, but the grandmother takes over without really knowing what it means," said Carol Levine, executive director of the Orphan Project, based in New York City. "The long-term impact is there are sometimes very fragile arrangements."

Carmine Buete, 8, does not remember his mother, who died seven years ago. Now a weary and ailing 65, Kathleen Buete says her greatest fear is dying before her grandson does. In July, she underwent quadruple-bypass heart surgery.

Carmine is the size of a 5-year-old, and tires easily. He recently got a small, bright red and black wheelchair, which he practices driving around their sunny Queens apartment.

"Mom, I'm tired," he said when his grandmother suggested they go out to eat. "We're going to drive there—or I don't eat."

"We could always take my wheelchair," he added. "I'm pushing."

Ms. Buete is divorced and supports herself and Carmine on Supplemental Security Income, a Social Security program for the disabled. His medication is supplied through his participation in clinical trials for children with the disease. Carmine knows he has AIDS and has watched some of the other children in his trials die. For the last 18 months he has had no immune system to speak of. He receives tutoring at home to reduce the risk that he will get infections from other children.

The quiet, tidy household, with a room full of Carmine's toys and games, masks layers of heartache. Ms. Buete's first-born son, Ralph Grosso, died of AIDS five years ago. He was gay. She recently learned that another son is H.I.V.-positive and was probably infected, like Carmine's mother, by sharing needles.

"I never imagined it, not until the AIDS thing came about," Ms. Buete said. "I was thinking about going on a motorcycle and touring the United States, but when it happens, you're there. All grandmothers are.

"There was one grandmother in my situation, but she just lost her granddaughter in August," she said. "We used to call each other once a week. You get upset a lot because you lose a lot of people."

Given the toll the disease has taken on her family, Ms. Buete feels it is important to talk frankly about their experience, and to work with AIDS-related causes like Gay Men's Health Crisis.

Statistics suggest that more grandparents will be caring for children as the disease increasingly affects entire families. Most are families already overwhelmed by poverty and social isolation.

According to the Federal Centers for Disease Control and Prevention in Atlanta, from 1985 through 1993 the proportion of AIDS cases attributed to male-to-male sexual contact decreased from 66.5 percent to 46.6 percent. The proportion attributed to intravenous drug use among women and heterosexual men increased from 17.4 percent to 27.7 percent.

In 1993, there were 9,288 AIDS cases attributed to heterosexual contact, a 130 percent increase over 1992. In New York City, the epicenter of the epidemic with over 70,000 cases, 120 people die of AIDS each week. Most are intravenous drug users or their partners, and many have children.

Studies show that about 30 percent of newborns born to H.I.V.-positive mothers end up infected themselves.

Megan McLaughlin, the executive director of the Federation of Protestant Welfare Agencies in New York, said extended families that care for children with AIDS should be given more support.

"They need money and they need a place to turn when things aren't going as smoothly as they could," Ms. McLaughlin said. "They need mental-health services, after-school services and day care. It's cheaper in the long run than taking kids into foster care."

Support groups are springing up, through hospitals, foster care groups and organizations for AIDS and for children. Some, like Project DEAR in Newark, (Developing Effective AIDS Response) have been around for years. The group of older women who take care of their children and grandchildren with AIDS meets monthly, as they have for almost five years.

Many of the grandmothers are on their own. Some are already caring for the children of other children who take drugs or lost custody. Anecdotes abound about women like Ms. Buete, who have lost more than one child to the virus.

"One woman had a son with the virus whose two kids had the virus," said Earlene Holloway, 67, a vice-president in Project DEAR. "They're all dead now. Most of us right now have lost our children. We're trying to educate, trying to help people who don't know where to go or what to do.

"It's very hard," said Ms. Holloway, who was the foster mother of a boy with AIDS who died at 9. "There were a group of children my child used to go to the clinic with and they're all dead now except two. One after another, they died."

The Family Center in New York City was the first project in the nation to offer assistance in one place for custody plans, disclosure issues and getting health care. It opened this spring. The project also studies various mental health programs for adolescents in families with AIDS and trains students studying social work at local colleges to work with such families.

"If we don't do something, they'll be street kids," said Barbara H. Draimin, the center's director.

Geneva Morrison, a Newark grandmother, watched her daughter Angela Richardson die from AIDS in 1987 at age 29. Ms. Richardson's daughter, Shanti Santana, was also infected. The family believes Ms. Richardson got the virus from her boyfriend, who used drugs.

Unlike many of the grandmothers pressed into duty as mothers a second time, Mrs. Morrison, 55, a retired circuit designer at New Jersey Bell, is married and middle-class. She has private insurance and the support of her church, Shanti's school and Project DEAR. But she said that she is the one holding the family together.

"The men in this family are not dealing with it the way the women are," she said. She said neither her two adult sons nor her husband can easily talk about what happened to Angela or about Shanti's illness.

After Angela died, Mrs. Morrison began caring for her grandson, now 20, and Shanti, now 10. The children have different fathers. Shanti and Angela were both found to have H.I.V. in 1985 after Angela took Shanti to the doctor because of the baby's recurrent problems with diaper rash, fever and diarrhea.

Mrs. Morrison recalled being so stricken by her daughter's diagnosis that she went to her physician and received a prescription for Valium. She only took it for one day, she said, because she needed to stay alert and focused. But a voice inside her head kept insisting it was not supposed to be this way.

"I said, 'Angie, don't get sick and die and leave these kids for me to take care of,'" Mrs. Morrison said, her voice breaking. "I realized she was going to die before me."

Mrs. Morrison became her grandchildren's legal guardian. She enrolled Shanti in Catholic school. She and Shanti's half-brother received counseling after Mrs. Morrison found him using a pin to poke holes in a picture of Shanti's father.

Shanti is of normal weight and height, and takes AZT and an antibacterial drug called Bapsone. She swims, skates and plays basketball. Her grandmother insists that she is a normal child living each day to the fullest.

Yet she is not, as her grandmother is reminded in so many ways. One of the hardest tasks she faced was telling Shanti she had AIDS. Angela's social worker had given her a book, about children with the virus, that they gave to Shanti.

"She brought the book to me one night and I said 'Oh, hell'" Mrs. Morrison recalled. "I said, 'Do you know what the book is about?' She said yes. The next day she said, 'Do

I have the AIDS virus?' I said, 'Yes, but it's a family secret because people aren't very nice sometimes.'"

Mrs. Morrison, however, has found some salvation in honesty and in using her experience to help others. "I've been public for the last five years," she said. "My reason for being public is that I made up my mind that the only way that anything is going to change is you have to come out of hiding. It's a disease. A lot of people look at it as a moral issue."

Shanti says her friends all know about her illness. "One time a kid called me AIDS girl," she said. "I ignored him."

Still, there are days when it all seems too much to bear. "Shanti is a carbon copy of her mother," Mrs. Morrison said softly. "I look at her sometimes and I shudder."

chapter 5

Focusing on Practice

What is always needed in the appreciation of art, or life, is the larger perspective. Connections made, or at least attempted, where none existed before, the straining to encompass in one's glance at the varied world the common thread, the unifying theme through immense diversity, a fearlessness of growth, of search, of looking, that enlarges the private and the public world. And yet, in our particular society, it is the narrowed and narrowing view that often wins.

Alice Walker*

OVERVIEW

The purpose of this book is to provide the beginning generalist practitioner with a framework for understanding human behavior. Perhaps we should say that it is a framework for attempting to understand human behavior, or for understanding some things about human behavior. We say this because so much about human behavior is as yet unknown, and so much more may never be known. The quotation cited above speaks to us about concepts that were presented in earlier chapters and helps us focus as we start thinking about how to apply the material to practice. We began in Chapter 1 with an understanding that as social workers, our focus is the person-in-environment view, a holistic view that has permeated social work since its beginning in the nineteenth century. Allied helping professionals also seek to understand persons in their environments. Public health and mental health workers, for example, look for agents in the environment that

* Walker, A. (1976). Saving the Life That Is Your Own. In *New York Public Library Book of Twentieth Century American Quotations* (1992), edited by S. Donadio et al. New York: Warner Books, p. 142.

promote or obstruct the health or mental health of individuals and groups. We suggested that several screens be applied in the study and processing of the vast amount of information available to us regarding the sources of human behavior. Among these screens are health, growth, ecological, strength, and empowerment perspectives, grounded in the mission, purposes, and values of the social work profession. In Chapter 2, a framework was developed for using systems theory, human diversity, and directionality (purposefulness) as lenses for viewing human behavior holistically, seeing both resources and obstacles as they appear in the complex interaction throughout life of biological, psychological, social-structural, and cultural dimensions of human behavior. Chapter 3 built on the previous chapter, focusing on knowledge that is currently available from multiple disciplines to aid in understanding the interplay of biological, psychological, social-structural, and cultural sources of behavior in individuals, groups, families, communities, and organizations. Concepts that might be most useful to the generalist social worker in fulfilling the purposes of social work and conducting competent practice were selected and given fuller development and discussion. The text presented various approaches to the study of the life course in Chapter 4, focusing on common human experiences but acknowledging multiple influences and validating the extraordinarily diverse ways in which individuals and groups meet their needs and fulfill their goals, as they live out their progression through time, coping with obstacles and managing resources. The text has assumed that the student is familiar from earlier course work with basic psychological theories, developmental theories, economic theories, and systems theory, as well as biological, sociological, political science, and anthropological perspectives. If these theories have not been previously studied, this text will aid and encourage the reader in delving further into such material.

This chapter concludes the book by focusing on the integration of previous material into a framework for practice. It looks at who the professional helper is and what the helper does. It provides guidelines for effective service to people, based on a holistic understanding of human behavior. Just as we acknowledged earlier the great mystery of human behavior that coexists with the vast array of concepts available to explain it, so too we should note that practice is always changing. We will aim to present some of the basics, some of the fundamental issues. However, although this chapter concludes our book, it does not conclude your learning. As you continue in practice, you will be able to apply purpose, values, knowledge, and skills when dealing with the human situations you encounter.

CHARACTERISTICS OF PROFESSIONAL HELPERS

By now in your study of this text, you may be feeling overwhelmed by concepts. Consider F. Scott Fitzgerald's observation: "The test of a first-rate intelligence is the ability to hold two opposing ideas in the mind at the same time, and still retain the ability to function" (Fitzgerald, 1936). Would you agree with us that he underestimates the number of opposing ideas one has to hold in mind simultaneously? Maybe you have experienced the phenomenon common to virtually every student of human behavior, that is, you have found yourself to be a living example of every theory propounded. Imagine, for instance, that you do not know your birthday, and you read a detailed account of each astrological sign; you could conclude that you were a Libra—you are peace-loving and fair; no, on second thought, a Leo—but then again, maybe a Gemini—yes, that is it, the sign of the Twins, that explains your tendency to see both sides of an issue. Some people, when reading about the life course, for example, become temporarily convinced that they have some unfinished business from the infant and toddler life stages. They must attend to it if they are to move on with their lives. But then, they see quite clearly that, in fact, they survived their very early days relatively intact. It was the bombardment with multiple changes in adolescence that posed their biggest obstacle; yet, on the other hand, those changes actually served as resources, presenting practical problems for the emerging adult to wrestle to the ground, only to arise with a strong sense of competence, ready to take on more adult tasks and responsibilities. When they cannot always tell their own obstacles from their resources, how will they be able to assess obstacles and resources in their clients, they wonder. As if that is not enough to worry about, they find themselves vacillating between systems theory and chaos theory views on predictability of outcomes: Is there any hope for them to function as future helpers?

What does this have to do with practice? In preceding chapters you have been reading about concepts and thinking about how they might apply to the people you will serve in practice. Now another element is added—the helper, herself; the helper, himself. Albert Einstein wrote: "The most beautiful thing we can experience is the mysterious. It is the source of all true art and science" (Einstein, 1930). Challenging though it may be to fathom the beautiful mysteriousness of our neighbor's behavior, the human behavior that remains most beautifully mysterious to professional helpers may be their own. If we, as professional helpers, want to integrate knowledge of human behavior into a framework for practice, should we not try to understand our own behavior, as we delve into the mysteries of other people's behavior? We could start by asking, "Who are helpers and how do they get to be that way?" Have people always helped one another? What did people do before there were professional helpers? Did mutual cooperation in the face of hostile physical environments require that our ancestors help one another? Were there people who were what might be termed "natural helpers"?

Numerous perspectives have been offered on the role of helper. The following lines from Robert Frost's poem, *The Road Not Taken,* may evoke feelings and thoughts about your own decision to become a helper:

> . . . Two roads diverged in a wood, and I
> I took the one less traveled by,
> And that has made all the difference (Frost, 1916: 623)

Do you know what combination of elements converged to form your decision to follow a path to a helping profession? The role of "helper" as "healer" within a community is one perspective that has a deep and rich history. The role of the *shaman* in various cultures is well documented. The shaman (male or female) was believed to be "called" to the role within the community, by the "spirits." Usually this "calling" came early in the person's life in the form of prophetic dreams. These dreams preceded a time in the child's or young adult's life when the individual became seriously ill. During this time, the future shaman visited the spirit world and was given knowledge about the sources of both health and illness. Once the youngster recovered and reentered the community, the young person became an apprentice to the tribal shaman to learn the healing arts further.

Having gained knowledge and wisdom from the journey and having completed the apprenticeship, the individual would then complete the appropriate rituals and become a shaman. A fascinating autobiographical account of the process can be found in *Black Elk Speaks* (Black Elk, 1979), which records the life story of a Sioux Indian shaman. Whereas the shaman's primary role was in spiritual medicine and ours, as human service workers, has a more temporal focus, we may learn something about the nature of the helping process and the role of the professional helper by looking more closely at the shaman's healing process.

The archetype of the *wounded healer,* the person who has some "wounding" encounter (spiritual, physical, or emotional) and recovers with increased powers is seen throughout the literature of myth. Akin to the *hero* archetype, the person is called to some quest. The individual separates from the community, undergoes hardships and suffering, gains knowledge and wisdom, and returns home. Exhibit 5.1, at the end of this chapter, tells the story of a nurse named Dusty, who served two tours in Vietnam. Her experiences poignantly demonstrate the concept of the wounded healer. An example of a helper who was both "called" and went through a wounded-healer experience is the Rev. Bernice A. King, whose story appears in Exhibit 5.2 at the end of this chapter. In an interview, Rev. King described a period of time, after her calling in her mid-teens, when she experienced great inner turmoil and felt disconnected from her church and from other human beings, so much so that in young adulthood, even though she had many accomplishments and a strong system of support, she contemplated suicide. She described a dream in which her father appeared to her, after which she felt at peace with her calling in life and clear about her purpose (Norment, 1995).

You may find it useful to stop here and read Dusty's and Rev. King's stories in Exhibits 5.1 and 5.2, then think about some of the issues and questions raised in the introductory paragraphs preceding each story. What similarities and differences do you observe between their stories and the story of your path to the helping professions? Christ, Joan of Arc, and Buddha are some well-known examples of hero or healer archetypes. John Sanford, a Jungian analyst and Episcopal priest, states:

> The shaman . . . derives his (her) power from a personal, direct encounter with the unconscious inner world; he (she) has his (her) own encounter with the unconscious. The effectiveness of the shaman in

helping others stems from the shaman's own depth of experience. (Sanford, 1977: 72)

The concepts of shaman and wounded healer may strike a chord with you and may help you understand something about your own motivation for entering a helping profession. However, perhaps neither of these concepts closely describes the person you are. Some people lean more toward the mystical, others lean more toward the practical. Still others fall somewhere in between, depending on the given day, their circumstances, or their time of life. As we have stated throughout this text, human behavior is influenced by many sources. Keep in mind the concept of equifinality, a principle from systems theory: People may start out at many different points and travel on many different routes toward a similar destination. Also keep in mind the concept of diversity; each person's experience is unique—there are many different paths to helping. Jung's observation applies equally to professional helpers and the people they serve:

> . . . The shoe that fits one person pinches another; there is no recipe for living that suits all cases. Each of us carries his (sic) own life-form— an interminable form which cannot be superseded by any other. (Jung, 1933: 935)

You are now at a place where either you have decided to become a professional helper or you are interested in exploring professional helping as a role you may want to pursue further in your life. In some manner, your life experiences, personal circumstances, and choices, as well as many other factors, have brought you to this point. Sometimes, people are reluctant to disclose motives they have for entering the helping professions, because they fear their motives will not be considered lofty enough. Your reason for entering a helping profession may be a very practical one. You may have needed a job, a helping job was listed, you applied, and you got the job; now you find that not only are you good at your job but you enjoy it, and you would like to do an even better job, so that you can be promoted or licensed. You may be the type of person who feels responsible for doing your work as well as you can, no matter what the task. If the task is providing service to people, then you feel responsible for performing a service that is as high in quality as you are able to give. Perhaps you do not know yet whether a job in a helping profession is the right career choice for you, but you have worked in other fields of employment or study that did not give you a sense of personal fulfillment. Even though you could make more money and have more societal or familial approval, you know you could not stay with personally unrewarding work year after year. It could be that you took aptitude tests that concluded you were well-suited to being a helper, or you feel that you have a natural talent for helping people. Maybe you took a different fork in the road earlier because of family responsibilities, but now you are determined to pursue your calling. This is often the case with many mid-life students who are making career changes and returning to school. On the other hand, you may have a different calling, a dream for your life that you would love to pursue someday, but your dream will not bring income, pay your rent, or buy your children clothes, so your goal is to earn a practical degree in a helping field for which you are suited. You may approach your work with freshness and enthusiasm. Perhaps the study of human behavior simply fascinates you in the same way some of your friends are fascinated with information about cyberspace, or business, or automotives. You may come to study the helping professions with some apprehension or fear. Some people say that they know they would love to be professional helpers and feel certain they would be good at it, but they fear they will be overwhelmed by the pain and suffering they will see. Others say they would like to become professional helpers, but they are afraid they will not be good at it, or that they will never know enough to help all the different people they will meet.

Sometimes, it helps beginning practitioners to reframe their uncertainty into experimentation in living, not in the sense of taking the serious business of helping lightly, but in the sense of understanding that as a human being you are always growing, changing, and learning new things about yourself and cannot be expected to know exactly who you will be in the future. Others are helped by reframing what they see as their ignorance into innocence: they are innocent of much information about many things, but they are setting about to learn, to know more, and they are taking responsibility for learning and knowing what they need to know.

You may have particular interests you want to pursue or types of individuals you wish to help. For example, one woman in her mid-20s who had declared herself a lesbian in high school said that, although she loved her practicum working with elders, she planned to work for a few years in an agency for gay, lesbian, and bisexual adolescents and young adults and their families. She felt proud of her sexual orientation and had been supported by her family. Although she wanted to resume her career with elders in the future, she felt that because of her age and background, she could make a contribution to families who were having a hard time accepting their child's life style. As a member of an oppressed community, you may hold yourself responsible for the well-being of all members of that community. The Code of Ethics of the National Association of Black Social Workers addresses black social workers' responsibility to "marshall our expertise to improve the quality of life of Black people," to "relieve suffering of Black people," and to work for "social change, with particular attention directed to the establishment of Black social institutions" (National Association of Black Social Workers, 1994).

Another example of reframing can be seen in the efforts of several female students who have committed themselves in their professional careers to making changes in the practices of some chemical dependency treatment programs. They found that many chemical dependency programs did not provide childcare for women while they were in treatment or during aftercare meetings. If clients were unable to find and pay for childcare, they were often labeled as "resistant." These determined students obtained grants and lobbied for support in establishing a halfway house for recovering women and their children.

Your own individual wish may be to save the world or to make some small difference. You may have decided simply that you have an obligation to do your part to build a just and loving world to pass on to the next generation. For example, one student returned from Vietnam in the mid-1970s, determined to work toward justice and equality in society. He said he would like to work toward achieving Utopia, and when he was asked what the social work helper's role would be in Utopia, he said, "In Utopia the social worker will be like the Maytag repairman (sic)." Of course, the allusion is to a popular television commercial, which shows the Maytag repair person waiting for a trouble-shooting call, but to no avail; all the Maytag appliances were working just fine, and there were no problems. Other students chimed in and offered that as helpers in Utopia, they would see that all the things that were working to help people reach their potential received good preventive maintenance.

If you are following a human service curriculum, you will take specific courses in practice that will afford you an opportunity to consider your own motives and needs as a helper in more detail, and you will have the opportunity to examine your own human behavior as a helper as you interact with people in a field internship. Many human service helpers tend to be people whose preferred learning style is learning by doing, and sometimes the abstractions of theoretical studies *about* people live in their minds only as unrelated fragments. They want to learn *how* to apply concepts, and frequently the connection between the about and the how to has meaning for them only when they have the opportunity to work directly with people in a field experience.

Marianne Corey and Gerald Corey (1993), experienced counselors and teachers, discuss motives of beginning helpers. Their nonjudgmental approach has much appeal for students. Among the motives they cite are the needs to make an impact, to return a favor, to care for others, to be needed, to have prestige and status, to provide answers, to make money, to have control, and to fulfill the need for self-help. They encourage students not to apologize for having needs of their own but to practice self-awareness, so that their own needs do not get in the way of meeting client needs. For example, if helpers are unaware of working out their own issues through giving help, meeting their own needs can take greater importance than service to the client. If helpers are unaware of their own need to have other people change to conform to their beliefs, clients can be deprived of opportunities to gain control over their own lives (pp. 8 and 9).

Sherrod Miller et al. (1988) describe a kind of relationship dance between two people that falters when one partner pushes or pulls and the other responds with blocking or foot-dragging. A helper who is a one-person powerhouse can risk jumping too far ahead of where the client is, pushing or pulling the client along. In our experience, clients balk not because they reject empowerment, but because they define their goals differently than the helper, resent a perceived threat to their sense of competence and right to self-determination, or believe that the timing is just not right. The helper sometimes cannot believe their clients could turn down such a good plan—it was in place, all set, and ready to unfold; all the client had to do was show up. This can lead a helper to inaccurately assess a client's motivation or give up on a particular client. Then clients may have to push and pull reluctant helpers to get the services they need to meet their goals. For vulnerable families, where parents are at risk of losing custody of their children, there can be devastating effects. In advocacy efforts, where the helper is trying to enlist the support of various systems in the community on behalf of the client, a community system can also resist being pushed, with resulting possible delays in service.

As Corey and Corey point out, another motivation for helping, the need for self-help, can be a powerful energy source for a helper and client. A client may gain confidence and hope from a helper who has coped successfully with the same issues the client is facing. However, there are risks too. Not infrequently, for example, we will hear practice presentations from young adults in their mid- to late 20s who say they experimented with sex, drugs, and rock and roll, learned the hard way, and paid a heavy price. Although they came to see later that one or two suggestions that counselors or other caring adults made had some merit, they say they were determined to make their own decisions and learn for themselves—it was their life. Yet, helpers can become frustrated, wanting so badly to spare their teen-aged clients the pain they see down the road, or wanting so badly for their young clients to see the light—to value themselves, go to school, get a good job, make a nice life. Their clients, who usually genuinely delight in talking things over with their helpers, may see the helpers' frustration and either mollify them with promises to stay in school and get some birth control next week, or shut down, perhaps skipping appointments because "I didn't have anything serious to talk about."

The caveat that "Everything happens in its own time" was impressed on the minds of the authors of this text by a graduate school mentor, Helen Hayward. We have tried to remember that we may not see the results of our efforts to empower clients and to help them build on their own strengths. It is possible that the reward of seeing the positive change to which we have contributed may be witnessed solely by the clients themselves, who make use of our contribution some years later, all on their own, when time, development, and circumstances are different. Your client may make use of your contribution 25 years later, when he or she consults another helper, perhaps about improving communication with a teenage daughter, or seeking advice about a personal desire to go back and finish school. It is that helper, then, who may reap the benefits of satisfaction from the seeds you sowed. As for perspective, think of this: the infant who played peek-a-boo with you over the back of the booth in the restaurant at lunch today may be that very helper. As Kevin Lab, director of Bethany Transitions, reminded a group of older volunteers who work with children: Those children may be the helpers who straighten out our Medicare benefits so that *we* can stay at home, rather than being placed in a nursing home.

None of this is said to trivialize the questions raised by helpers whose work makes them daily witnesses to the enormous physical and emotional suffering people experience: Am I really doing any good? Is what I am doing chipping away, making even a small dent in the mountain of abuse, torture, and exploitation of children or achieving even a small gain in winning equal rights for children? Does my work and my agency's work really empower poor people, or does it offer them just enough to maintain their quietude? We stated in the Overview in this chapter that the professional helper's aim is to *try* to understand human behavior; achieving full understanding of human behavior is not possible. Perhaps the professional helper's aim in practice is to *try* to achieve positive change; the full positive changes the helper desires may not always be achievable, but the trying, the struggle, is meaningful.

Some helpers make a deliberate choice not to enter a field of practice that focuses specifically on pain and problems similar to those they have experienced. For example, one man recently said he would be happy to come back and talk to all our classes about his personal struggle with alcohol, about Twelve-Step programs and how he achieved sobriety and maintains his recovery, but he has chosen a different field of practice. He feels issues around his drinking consumed so much of his life, he simply wants to go on, enjoying his sobriety, loving his wife, being with his children, and using his professional energy in his work to empower people who have developmental disabilities. His situation points to another factor related to such a choice: Our motives for helping may very likely change over time. We find that some beginning helpers are frightened that they will invest their precious time and hard-won educational dollar, only to learn that professional helping is not the role for them. Every year, we hear something like this from one or two early adult students: "This is my third major. I don't know what I'll do if it turns out that this isn't right for me" or "I've been in college for 5 years now; my parents want to know why I have switched, am I sure this is what I want, and when will I be finished." Just as we see helpers who are reluctant to discuss motives that they feel are not as important as the motives of their colleagues, so too we see people who feel that something is wrong with them if they come to feel that they do not want to play the helping role. Sometimes, these helpers compare themselves too much with seasoned practitioners or with colleagues in their classes or at work, whose knowledge, skills, and commitment they admire greatly. In many instances, the fear dissipates as helpers learn to believe in themselves and see their own unique gifts; they come to understand that they are not only good enough but that they will never be duplicated and they must become the helper that only they can be, more knowledgeable and skilled than their colleagues in some things and less knowledgeable and skilled in others things. Having struggled to come to that place, these people may be in a particularly strong position to assist clients in valuing their own strengths and gifts. This is not to say that there are not times when a student or practitioner comes to see that the professional helping role is no longer what he or she most wants. Persons who reach this realization and leave the field, take a different job in the field, or take time out, are to be admired for their honesty and courage.

However, there is another point to consider, which has to do with the multiple stresses placed on many professional helpers today, putting them at high risk for burnout. Especially vulnerable are helpers whose jobs require them to reach out to persons who see little hope and have few resources, to carry impossibly high caseloads, to interact with persons who sometimes behave with violence, or to document gargantuan change within miniscule time frames. Under the worst conditions, even the most caring and committed helper can tire. The changing nature of the profession, especially for the generalist practitioner in public welfare, public health, or mental health, calls out for organizations whose administrators and supervisors are committed to a strengths-health-growth perspective on the human behavior of both helpers and clients, who respect diversity as much as standards, and who understand that all the players (clients, helpers, managers) in systems that offer openness, nurturance, and a free exchange of energy across boundaries have a chance to produce synergy—a whole that is greater than the sum of its parts—and thus avoid entropy-stagnation, loss of energy, and ineffective operation. We note with great interest reports from organizations that adopt a strengths solution-based-on-client-goals partnership model with clients that helpers experience renewed energy and decreased burnout. Such is the case in the experiments described later in this chapter in Exhibits 5.3 and 5.4.

Professional helpers can have more energy and be more effective in helping other people if they also help themselves by treating themselves kindly. There is an old practice truism that the professional helper's most important tool, or instrument, for helping is his *self* or her *self*. Much emphasis in training is placed on what is referred to as "the conscious use of the professional self," including such things as the helper's responsibility for obtaining supervision and consultation, for not exceeding the boundaries of their expertise, for continuing their learning and keeping up in their field, and for holding themselves accountable for ethical practice. These are necessary methods for maintaining the instrument in good repair, but sometimes helpers who would not for a minute shirk their responsibilities in these areas neglect other aspects of maintaining their instrument. Professional helpers can become so immersed in serving others that they forget about taking care of themselves. We are not numbered among those who would label this phenomenon as: "living through others," "loving too much," "codependency," or "enabling" (in the negative sense of contributing to perpetuating another's problems), although there are helpers whose approach might exemplify one or the other of these traits from time to time and might garner benefits from a change in style. We mean it in the sense that professional helping is hard and demanding work, and the instrument, the professional self, gets heavy use, just as a traveling salesperson's automobile racks up a lot of miles or a concert pianist's piano sustains a lot of pressure. By simply working hard at our professions, we risk blowing the occasional tire or popping the occasional string in the form of burnout. Often, a serious student or supervisee in the helping professions needs a reminder: You would never even think about treating another person the way you treat yourself. Some interns who faithfully carry out assignments, want to be sure that they have consulted enough referral sources, want to produce the perfect paper, and want to be accessible when their clients need them benefit from giving themselves an assignment to act as if they were some other person they deeply cared about, and do what they would hope that beloved person would do: get enough sleep, eat properly, make love, play with children, visit friends and relatives, exercise, relax, meditate, pray, or pursue some pleasure or another individualized assortment of activities. Professional helping is a major element in the professional helper's achievement of adult life-course needs for competence, productivity, and mentoring, and a large part of the helper's daily waking hours is devoted to this highly important work. A helper is what Helen Harris Perlman (1957) refers to as a "bio-psycho-social-whole," whose service to people can be enriched by attending to the multiple facets of his or her own system. Alice Walker has an interesting way of saying it: ". . . I'm the kind of woman that likes to enjoy herselves in peace" (Walker, 1992).

Another way to ward off *burnout* is for a helper to temper the need for a client's achievement to be directly, immediately, and solely traceable to the knowledge and skill of that particular helper. A competent, useful, respectful, caring, and effective helper is something a client longs for and deeply appreciates; we should never underestimate how important we can be to the well-being and empowerment of clients. However, as we know when we consider systems, there are as many interacting influences as there are stars in the universe. We are all interdependent elements in multiple interlocking systems; all members of a team; all partners. We share a part of the credit, but we are part of a whole network of helping. Helping, after all, is not about us, it is about the clients. As chaos perspectives remind us, predictability is elusive.

The choice to help others has its roots in your own personal history. As helping professionals who hope to assist others in the growth process—whether individuals, groups, communities, or organizations—we must first try to understand ourselves. Poverty, physical illness, mental illness, discrimination, or some other adversity may or may not have been part of your experience. In some way you have become sensitized to the pain and injustice around you. This sensitivity has "called" you to act in some manner. To begin, however, we may have to follow the path of the shaman and try to become clear about who we are, what forces shaped us, and where we are going. Such a self-examination is continuous, because we are constantly changing.

To comprehend and appreciate our own life course—its sources, direction, and meaning—requires some time for reflection. Indeed, reflection is an essential component in the helping process. The question was long debated as to whether a professional helper should receive counseling or therapy for the purposes of gaining insight into one's self, the argument being that the helper would thus have more freed up psychic energy with which to serve his or her clients. Sometimes, interns say they thought certain issues in their own life were settled, but the experience of being thrown into a practicum in the midst of complex and painful client situations, shakes them up. Other interns find the practicum experience triggers awareness of troubling issues they never knew they had. Some interns decide to take a refresher series of counseling consultations; others enter therapy. How one chooses to reflect is a very personal choice. Horney's perspective enjoys wide acceptance: "Fortunately (psycho)analysis is not the only way to resolve inner conflicts. Life itself still remains a very effective therapist" (Horney, 1945). To reflect on ourselves as we interact with others and to reflect on the experiences of others assists in bringing about the quality known as **empathy**. As stated earlier, the study of human behavior, as well as the attempt to understand even one person, should be undertaken with great humility.

The anxiety you may feel as a beginning helping professional can be minimized as you strive for authenticity in your interactions with others and within themselves. Zen masters speak of "beginner's mind" as being the ideal mental posture. As a novice, all things are new and you remain open to new information and experiences. Experts, however, already have the "answers" and can cut themselves off from new learning. The challenge for us as professional helpers is to gain knowledge, skill, and confidence in our ability to help but to maintain a beginner's mind throughout our professional careers, remaining in awe of all we do not know, curious to know more, and aware that what we knew yesterday has changed today. Assisting others depends on the ability to engage them in some meaningful interaction. To achieve authentic interaction, certain qualities have proven essential: respect, trust, and empathy. Beginning practitioners need to be aware of and accept their own strengths and limitations. Their development of a sense of empathy can be based on their own continuing effort to understand growth, suffering, healing, and change.

Respect for self and for others is paramount. The health model of practice rests firmly on respect for the individual and the belief that people strive toward positive goals. It is helpful to remember that the shaman who misused his or her power was cast out of the community. The role of shaman was only one of many roles in the community. It carried no superior status. Likewise, professional helpers should not see themselves as superior actors in the healing process but as coworkers in healing. The healing—whether within the person, the community, or the social institution—always comes from within. Although forces outside may necessitate change, the process of change is an internal process, in the sense that the change belongs to the person, the community, or the social institution. We as professional helpers can only assist in that change process. Similarly, professional helpers enjoy no inherently superior status to any other member of the community who plays a role in helping people achieve their life tasks. When a client's car keeps stalling, making the whole family late for school and work, a competent mechanic may provide more resources, remove more obstacles, and reduce more stress on a given day than a family session with a professional helper. All kinds of people in all kinds of roles contribute to helping people meet their life goals. Even instructors in the helping professions cannot deny that in a well-made entertainment, a movie-maker of films such as "What's Eating Gilbert Grape" or "Benny and Joon," for example, may communicate more information in a more lucid manner about the meaning of taking a strengths perspective on family functioning than twice (at least) that many of the helping instructor's lectures. Perhaps the importance of the narrative, the need for professional helpers to listen to and hear women's stories as they tell them, comes across at its best in novels such as Margaret Atwood's *Cat's Eye* or Terry McMillan's *Waiting to Exhale,* for example.

Social workers, as professional helpers, assist people in many different ways. In doing so we may assume various roles to help others achieve their goals: broker, advocate, activist, educator, lobbyist, researcher, organizer, mediator, counselor, and outreach worker are just some of these roles. Regardless of the role or situation, the social worker is involved in some interaction with others. While advocating with an income-maintenance worker regarding late benefits for a client, we will always be more effective if we understand the frustrations and limitations that the worker may be experiencing as a result of bureaucratic red tape. While mediating a conflict resolution process between a male supervisor and a female intern, we must understand power, but we may be even more effective in achieving change if we also understand the fears and apprehensions of both parties. Our own values, fears, biases, and attitudes can either assist or detract from our ability to facilitate change in other people and/or in the social institutions in which they live.

As professional helpers in every stage of our career, we need to take time to reflect on our own experiences and the values and attitudes that we hold. The shaman was usually wise enough to understand which illnesses and individuals would be receptive to help. In a similar vein, reflecting on our own life story will clarify our values and attitudes, which in turn will assist in our work with others. Further, we might ask ourselves some basic questions that could improve our helping efforts:

- What attitudes do I hold toward those I serve or with whom I interact?
- What attitudes do I hold toward certain problems with which I am presented?
- In what way do the attitudes I hold affect my behavior toward the people, groups, or institutions I am serving?

These questions—asked in the context of our basic beliefs about human nature, change, and the quality and meaning of life—provide checks and balances in relation to our interactions with and on behalf of others.

To further the analogy between shamanic healing and social work intervention, we can look further into the beliefs of these ancient healers regarding health, wellness, and healing. Shamans were careful not to overstep their bounds. They were clear that they could not prevent the death of an elder person. Death was, in fact, part of the cycle of nature. They did not believe they could heal all physical wounds. Many illnesses, both emotional and physical, were believed to result from the individual's discontinuity with inner or spiritual forces. The shaman's role was to pray to the spirits on behalf of the person (advocacy), to provide a healing atmosphere for the person (trusting relationship), and to assist people to realign themselves with their own natural healing powers (empowerment). The similarities to the helping process of the social worker can be seen easily. The social worker provides a trusting, safe, and supportive relationship through which the client can establish goals and the means of achieving them. Raymond Fox develops the idea of the "safehouse" as a metaphor for empathy and for the helping process:

> In a safehouse there is activity as well as reflection, doing as well as saying, extrospection as well as introspection. Emphasis is placed on the human experience of an active, striving, affirming and potentiating transaction, on recognizing the continuity of the "there-and-then" of the distant past with the "here-and-now" of the immediate present. Both, taken together, establish the conditions for change. The novelty of such integration serves as a catalyst for growth. (Fox, 1993: 46)

Like the shamans of old, today's social worker believes in the positive nature of the human spirit. Social workers seek to empower the person, community, or institution to achieve positive goals. At times, the social worker is called on to intervene on behalf of the person in need.

One further function of the shaman will end our analogy. The shaman was called on to provide some prophetic functions within the community. The shaman was often asked to look into the future to forewarn the community of impending dangers. In this process the shaman provided direction to the community by assessing the wisdom of certain practices. Shamans, for example, were consulted about crop planting, battle plans, and relocation of the community. The shaman's recognized wisdom flowed from the ability to view the situation holistically. Likewise, today's professional helper, viewing people, events, and situations holistically, is able to act effectively. Such a vantage point allows the social worker to intervene at many possible points as a helping person. Social workers may work to assist a particular person, community, or institution solve problems (remediation). They may also intervene to prevent problems and maintain health (prevention) by identifying social concerns, advocating for social policy to address problems, and educating people about healthful and supportive life choices.

When we think about the choice to become a professional helper, we think about Ralph Ellison's words concerning relatives and ancestors:

> Some people are your relatives but others are your ancestors, and you choose the ones you want to have as ancestors. You create yourself out of those values. (Ellison, 1992: 343)

By your choice to become a professional helper, in a sense you choose to join a community of helpers, varied though their paths into the profession, their professional identification, and their areas of practice may be. This community of helpers enjoys an invisible camaraderie. In your imagination, you may call on the spirit, energy, and tradition of this reference group for sustenance in carrying out your helping role, assisting people to attain their life goals.

ELEMENTS OF PROFESSIONAL PRACTICE

In our reflection on the personal narratives of people who become professional helpers, we have seen that they share in common the desire to serve people through their helping practice. However, as we listen to their stories, we hear many different voices: They vary in terms of personal characteristics and backgrounds, they are driven by distinctive needs, and they have traveled widely divergent paths to arrive at helping as their life's work. Now let us turn our attention again to these questions: What is it that professional practitioners do to be helpful? When do they help? Whom do they help? How do they help? Throughout the text, we have attempted not only to explicate concepts for understanding human behavior but also to show how helpers can make use of these concepts in the practical world of giving service to clients. In Chapter 1, we identified five elements that are the basis of contemporary social work practice and suggested that theories of human behavior and practice intervention should possess these elements: health orientation, growth orientation, ecological orientation, strengths perspectives and empowerment perspectives. We noted the congruence between these elements and the primary goals of social work practice: enhancing people's problem-solving, coping, and developmental capacities; linking people with systems that provide them with resources, services, and opportunities; promoting the effective and humane operation of systems that provide people with resources and service; and developing and improving social policy. In Chapter 2, practitioners were reminded that, although systems theory assists in understanding interactions among elements in systems, practitioners must also understand the effects of unequal power among system components. The concept of directionality leads practitioners to recognize that each client's behavior is directly related to the client's goals in life. Taking a holistic view includes recognizing differences between individuals and among and within groups, as well as looking for things a client has in common with other human beings. With respect to diversity, practitioners need to be keenly aware of the connection between the stereotyping and oppression of people on the basis of their diversity and the abuse of power as a tool of oppression. The practitioner can be useful by working for social justice and by supporting oppressed people in their acts of empowerment. In Chapter 3, we said that social work practitioners' commitment to culturally sensitive practice means that a concerted effort be made to design programs around the client's needs and values, rather than requiring the client's adjustment to traditional service delivery systems and services. Given that social work seeks to enhance resources and minimize obstacles to human growth and development, we stated that effective practice requires that social work practitioners strive to improve the social structures that effect clients. Because social structures determine how resources will be made available and to whom, social work intervention at the micro-, mezzo-, or macrolevel requires an accurate and thorough evaluation of the forces that influence distribution of resources. Social work practitioners can serve clients by focusing on psychological concepts that consider nurture as well as nature, take diversity into account, and suggest ways to enhance self-esteem, competence, resiliency, and adaptive and coping abilities. Whatever the biological endowment of each person, social workers are called on to make creative use of resources that support each organism's growth through the life course with optimum health. In Chapter 4, we stated that life-course models can broaden practitioners' understanding of the basic biological, psychological, cultural, and social-structural resources needed to support people in attaining their goals in life. Because the generalist practitioner takes a holistic approach not only to conceptualizing situations but also to carrying out practice, life-course material can be used at all levels of intervention, with individuals, groups, families, communities, organizations, and societies. We emphasized the importance of diversity and the primacy of the individual's narrative or story. Practitioners were reminded that life-course material is not to be used to prescribe behavior for people and not to define normative and deviant behavior.

If the role of the professional helper involves these practices cited in previous chapters and if it includes supporting people in their efforts toward empowerment, assisting them to attain their life goals as free from obstacles and pain as possible, and aiding them to obtain and use as many resources as possible to live their lives as fully as they are able, then central to our task as social work practitioners is the idea of service. Controlling people is not the major task of social work practice. Serving people is the major task of social work. This idea becomes lost as more and more people are referred to social workers by authorities and funders with an accompanying request, expectation, or direction for the social worker to do something to change a person and/or change a person's "faulty" behavior. It is also lost when social workers deny their name and identify themselves solely as clinicians or therapists and limit their practice to finding, diagnosing, and correcting deficits and/or pathologies in people. The idea of service is further compromised as managed care dictates prescribed methods of treatment and goals within a prescribed number of sessions for people with prescribed diagnoses. Such an approach can easily lead the practitioner away from the person-in-environment perspective. When this occurs, the professional tends to lose focus of C. Wright Mills' (1971) distinction between private troubles and public issues, and therefore, they pathologize persons, rather than alter pathologizing social institutions. The latest attack on welfare, as contained in the *Contract with America,* provides an example. Underlying this version of welfare reform is the assumption that the economic system works and that certain people have failed to take advantage of its benefits. Welfare recipients, usually women, are viewed as lazy, promiscuous, and persons whose behavior should not be supported by society. The solution is to cut off benefits to mothers (and their children) when they have not altered these behaviors within 2 years. The focus is not on changing the social and economic conditions that cause and perpetuate poverty. Further examples are provided when we consider the effect of wars on people such as Dusty and the student's family described in Exhibit 5.1 and its introduction. Consider the effects of institutionalized racism and the political assassination of her father on Rev. Bernice King (Exhibit 5.2) or the personal deficit definitions that are made about persons such as Mr. Pollet (Exhibit 5.4), when the issues are political. The nursing home that accepted Mr. Pollet is one of a very small number of nursing facilities that will accept AIDS patients. Care of AIDS patients is very expensive, in comparison with care of many other nursing home residents. Some health care workers refuse to accept assignments to care for AIDS patients. What is the politics or practice wisdom contained in a policy that insists that a terminally ill patient admit chemical dependency and seek treatment?

In this text we have developed suggestions for practice approaches that fit within a holistic framework. Service, in that context, is provided when practitioners seek to assist clients in obtaining their wants, needs, and goals. In many practice situations, the client's goals are ignored or made secondary to someone's expectation that they change some aspect of their behavior. We ask now if you will turn to Exhibit 5.4, "Everything Happens in Its Own Time," and read and reflect on the material in the introduction and in the exemplar. The practice exemplar contains many illustrations of social work practice, which attempts to serve, not change, a client through practice activity that accepts the client's definition of his reality and his life goals, supports his efforts at empowering himself and attaining his goals by building on strengths, developing resources, overcoming obstacles, and working in partnership toward change for the client's benefit at multiple system levels. Charles Cowger's description of promoting clients' strengths and empowerment expresses what the case manager was trying to accomplish in her partnership with Mr. Pollet:

> Promoting empowerment means believing that people are capable of making their choices and decisions. It means not only that human beings possess the strengths and potential to resolve their own difficult life situations, but also that they increase their strength and contribute to society by doing so. The role of the social worker in clinical practice is to nourish, encourage, assist, enable, support, stimulate, and unleash the strengths within people; to illuminate the strengths available to people in their own environments; and to promote equity and justice at all levels of society. To do that, the social worker helps clients articulate the nature of their situations, identify what they want, explore alternatives for achieving those wants, and achieve them. (Cowgar, 1994: 260)

Professional helpers practice in many settings with varying populations who need assistance in multiple ways. The study of human behavior throughout the life course provides some direction in answering this question: Who do we help? The text has provided you with examples of obstacles and resources to positive human development. A systems approach allows the student to view people in the context of the intricate networks with which they interact daily. Behavior is shaped by the interactions with these outside networks, which range in size from the family to society at large. Although the specifics regarding the population we hope to serve varies, our task as social workers is generally viewed as assisting the client system in achieving positive goals. Those who need assistance in achieving those goals because access to them is obstructed or nonexistent become one focus of professional intervention. Social workers also focus on the larger aggregate of family, groups, organizations, and communities.

By working to remove blockages to resources, we perform *reactively*. When we act to create positive supports for persons, groups, and society as a whole, we become *proactive*. A mother of four whose husband has just died may need assistance with burial expenses. She also needs emotional support. As social workers, we react by providing emotional support and by helping the woman gain access to financial resources. Women and children are becoming the fastest growing population experiencing poverty. As social workers viewing the single woman raising three children on either government subsidy or through a minimum wage job, we see the need to be proactive to effect positive change for these women and their children. An example of a proactive intervention would be advocating for legislative changes regarding increases in AFDC payments and the minimum wage. Other examples would be contracting with employers and creating programs to train women for higher paying nontraditional jobs, with assurances of entrance into jobs when training is completed. Accessible and affordable childcare, respite centers, and widespread availability of support groups could ease the stress of single parents and their children. Of course, the present climate of renewed victim blaming, in which women and children are being attacked as the cause of the United States' economic and social problems, shows clearly how social workers often can be diverted from proactive efforts. With the drastic cuts and punitive measures that are being proposed, social workers must react, both to fight against inhumane measures and to assist stigmatized women and children in surviving with decreasing resources in an environment that is increasingly hostile to their needs.

A holistic view of human behavior and the sources affecting it not only allows the social worker many possible reactive and proactive intervention points but it demands their use. Such an approach identifies where problems lie and points the way to where effective solutions are to be explored.

An example may be helpful here. Much concern continues to be expressed regarding the breakdown of the nuclear family and subsequent problems, such as juvenile drug use and teenage pregnancy. Politicians and evangelists alike lay many social problems at the feet of "failing family life." Moralists suggest a diminishing of the traditional values related to marriage and family life as both causes and products of this degeneration. If we define the problems as rooted in moral decay, then it would appear that the solutions should be found within the spiritual realm, and religious institutions would become the focus of intervention.

However, if we define the problem as having social and economic origins, the points of intervention would be quite different. As stated earlier in this text, changing economic conditions based on economic priorities have worked against the family. Marxists, such as Fred Newman (1988), would suggest that the destabilization of the family is an inevitable result of an economy in which persons are considered to be commodities. From this viewpoint, families are unable to cope with the radical and dehumanizing social forces surrounding them.

We could also construct a multifaceted definition of the problem, enumerating all the real or perceived weaknesses and deficits we could think of in families. A different choice would be to take a strengths-based practice approach, which we defined in Chapter 1 as social work practice that *focuses attention on the real strengths of persons, groups, or communities rather than on real or perceived weaknesses or deficits*. Think about the many couples you know who are each working two jobs, who are constantly rushed, who wish they had more time for each other and their children but must keep up the pace, not because they want more and more material goods and not to move up to a higher life style, but because they have to patch together enough income and benefits to maintain themselves and their children at a level that will cover basic needs. Amazing fortitude, or as In Soo Berg (1992), brief solution theorist and therapist, might say to the couple, acknowledging their real strengths: "How do you do that? You are so busy, and it is such hard work; you two must care very much about your marriage and your children to work so hard together to reach your goals." Among the students in the helping professions we meet, it is the rare student who does not have at least one job while attending school full time, maintaining a marriage or partnership, managing a home, and raising children. Those are examples of real strength.

Social workers can work at multiple levels to build on the strengths of families. We can help families to see their own real strengths. In a society and culture that takes *the narrow view* Alice Walker talked about, families as well as individuals are acutely aware of where they rank, both in the public's and the professions' hierarchy of values. They know from year to year which attitudes and behaviors currently constitute either "functional" or "dysfunctional" status, including judgments about whether their particular family's family values are truly "family values," whether they need to enroll in classes on good parenting or whether they meet the requirements for a waiver, and whether their way of living makes them eligible to have their names inscribed on the rolls of "those who take personal responsibility." It is sometimes a more difficult challenge to get people to identify one of their real strengths than it is to get them to name five of their deficits—they have heard all about what is wrong with them, and for many people, they have learned it so well that they risk believing it about themselves and doubting their own worth and competence as human beings; this is disempowering. We can join with families to tell the stories of their strengths to politicians, moralists, employers, policy-makers, planners, and social agencies. As families seek empowerment in this manner, we may be of service to them in a role as translater, translating their stories or narratives to persons and systems in power who speak and listen in only one language: their own. Professional helpers can serve families by acknowledging the strengths of variant family forms. Among definitions of family, Ann Hartman and Joan Laird (1983: 30) cited Arlene Skolnick's use of the expression, "intimate environment," to describe families in which people choose to live. Social workers can recognize as "real" families with differential strengths people who choose to live with their "growing up" family, a two-parent family, a one-parent family, a stepfamily, a family of adults without children, an extended kin family, a family made up partly of related and partly of unrelated individuals, a commune, a same sex family, a multigenerational family, or a family in which a friend's teenage son or daughter lives part time and participates when pressure builds up in his or her first family. "And don't forget my church family, my Alcoholics Anonymous family, and my family of social workers in my class," one professional helping student reminded us. In addition to the human members of the unit, there may be pets who are counted by the humans as members of the family, holding important meaning in the family's life. Professional helpers can take a strengths perspective on families by resisting traditional professional cliches about family functioning. Language is telling. For example, as Marilyn Hecht, a colleague in presenting courses on single parents, pointed out: an *intact* family is a family that is making things work, it has nothing to do with the number of parents in the home. One supervisee, sharing how overloaded she was feeling, described herself as a "married single parent." A child who appropriately assists parents with younger children is not necessarily "a parentified child, robbed of his or her childhood." A mother and daughter who enjoy living in the same neighborhood so that they can see each other frequently are not necessarily inappropriately "enmeshed." The women may be good friends who enjoy attachment with one another. If the women's husbands do not mind at all, it does not mean that they themselves may be avoiding intimacy. One client recently corrected a supervisee, telling her that his divorce was not a problem, it was a solution. The definitions we use as professional helpers are critical, particularly given the fact that our decisions about interventions flow from our definitions of a situation.

Professional helpers can apply a strengths perspective by assisting children in school in coping with new learning. The school social work approach described in Exhibit 5.3 at the end of the chapter shows how one school system stopped focusing on deficits in children's learning and focused on real strengths as a basis for designing new approaches. Other people may seek assistance from professional helpers for various individual concerns: stress, emotional or economic problems, decisions about career changes, needs for information on resources for a disabled child or an ill elder parent. However, helpers may also focus on "macro" issues that negatively affect individual and family life and work toward legislative and policy change. Because of their person-in-situation perspective, social work helpers would utilize micro (individual help), mezzo (intervention in small collectives), and macro (large-scale societal systems) approaches to solving problems.

The question of when to help can be further addressed. In very general terms, professional helpers are most often called upon in times of **crisis** in people's lives. As human beings travel on their life's journey, they encounter demands from the environment that require them to adapt and to cope. Life is never free of obstacles, and human beings develop some process for adapting and coping with these stresses from the environment that works for them, enabling them to keep their system in balance, moving forward with life, growing, and more or less successfully resolving the problems that come up in a person's own characteristic way, using the resources available to that individual. A crisis can be defined as a period when previously adequate resources become inadequate in adapting to or coping with the existing situation. Exhibit 5.4 at the end of the chapter shows how an individual who was coping with a series of crises caused by his grave physical illness sought the services of a helper, who focused on his strong points instead of his weaknesses. A crisis state can occur within a person (job loss), a family (death of a spouse or parent), a community (a hurricane), a society (an AIDS epidemic), or a culture (genocide). A crisis may be acute (a broken leg heals), or it may be chronic (the health care crisis in the United States) with no short-term resolution (effects of poverty, racism, sexism, ageism, ableism).

Helping interventions often focus on **transition points** in people's lives and usually involve role or status changes. People approaching retirement after working their entire adult life may more easily make the adjustment when they have been able to prepare for that event by making plans concerning the productive use of their time, when they have been able to accumulate adequate financial resources, and when they enjoy relatively good health and have social supports. When people are not psychologically prepared, when financial resources are dramatically reduced upon retirement, when health fails, when resources are not available to obtain health care, when people are isolated, or the larger society's devaluation of the elderly accelerates, people may experience severe stress, hardship, and personal crisis. Professional helpers can assist such individuals through counseling and by helping them locate social and recreational activities, economic benefits, health care, and emotional support (the microlevel). They may also advocate for new policies regarding retirement age, Social Security benefits, or health insurance coverage (the macrolevel). These micro- and macro interventions seek to reduce the stresses associated with transitions during the life course. From a strengths perspective, professional helpers can contribute to elders by treating them as adults, not as if they cease to be adults when they reach old age. Adult needs for intimacy, competence, independence, and productivity remain throughout the adult years until death. Older adults should not be "treated like children," but then children should not be treated like children, when being "treated like children" means people are treated as if they do not really know what is good for them, planning is done for and about them, and they are afforded little or no say in determining their own lives.

As professional helpers, we also are asked to help people change behaviors or to cope with certain difficult situations. The welfare worker who works with children is often expected to stop the abusive behaviors of a parent toward a child. The helper may soon discover that poverty, inadequate education, structural unemployment, inadequate housing, and health care are significant stressors, leading to the abusive behaviors. As Ann Hartman points out, situations like these demonstrate the "social control" function of social work; she quotes Bertha Reynolds' suggestion that in situations such as these, the social worker needs to stand "between the client and the community" (1989: 387). This is a stressful position for the social worker when the means are not available for people to reach the goals they desire or goals that are prescribed.

David Wagner (1989) points out that the commitment to social work professionalism and radical change is found to be the strongest at the point of entry into the field and while undergoing professional training. This structural change orientation is gradually attacked by the forces that maintain an unjust society. These forces push the professional helper to focus on personal adjustment, rather than on systemic change.

Maintaining a balanced view of the interaction of personal and societal problems is strongly supported by a holistic study of human behavior from a social work perspective. It helps to accomplish two essential practice goals. One, it provides a "clearer" vision of where problems and solutions lie. Second, it provides a scientific basis for the poetic truism that "no person is an island." A person's fate is strongly influenced through interaction with multiple systems. Empowering people links them with others both for support and strength, so that mutual aid and system change are facilitated. Professional helpers also need to use professional alliances constructively, so as to empower themselves and their clients to produce meaningful and fundamental change. When social workers place themselves "between the client and the community," they will always experience the burden of viewing problems as including personal pain and social-structural components. We can more easily keep on track in our place "in between" when we remind ourselves that the client and the community have unequal power. In assessing systems, helpers can mistakenly conclude that because components of systems are interdependent, the influence of each component on the other is equal. When we stand "between the client and the community," we stand for the client and for the resources that make it possible for people to accomplish their life tasks.

Social work as a helping profession traces its roots to the late nineteenth and early twentieth centuries, the period in the latter half of the century when postindustrialization, immigration, and rural-to-urban displacement placed enormous stress on individuals and families newly arrived in the inner cities of large American cities. Throughout its history, there has existed an uneasy alliance between two prominent strains of helping in social work. One strain grew out of the individual case-by-case help giving of the volunteer visitors of the Charities Organization Society, flowed down through time and flowered in the ideology and practices of the social casework method of the mid-twentieth century, and lives on today in the work of the clinical social worker. Another strain grew out of the social reform efforts of the Settlement Movement, flowed through time through the efforts of group workers and community organizers, reaching fruition in the late 1960s, and survives today in self-help groups and community empowerment efforts. The Settlement (a type of community center) Movement focused on achieving legislative reforms and environmental changes to ease the lives of individuals and families who came into the cities, offering citizenship, language, and job skills training. The Settlement leaders, Jane Addams and her colleagues, spoke out against the inequality of distribution of resources in United States life. Self-help was strongly emphasized. Activity was based on the Settlers' philosophical base. This social reform activity has been termed as "cause," referring to a mission to change society. The Charities Organization Societies' volunteers offered their assistance family by family, case by case, with home visits by friendly visitors, bringing baskets of food and material items and offering advice to families on how they could improve their lives. In addition to their focus on giving individualized service, emphasis was placed on accountability and a scientific approach through supervision, training, and skills development. This form of helping has been termed "function," referring to skills in individuals. Each of these historical traditions made positive contributions to the development of social work as a professional helping profession, but each had certain limitations. As Ralph Dolgoff et al. point out, from a contemporary social work perspective, the charities organizations' approaches "stand out for their judgmental and patronizing qualities and the tendency to blame the victim for his or her problems" (1993: 277). The Settlement houses focused on assimilation and mainstream ideals, the authors also point out, quoting Dorothy Becker (1968: 85): "(The Settlement houses) . . . continued to struggle to teach the poor the prevailing middle class values of work, thrift, and abstinence as the keys to success" (Dolgoff et al., 1993: 278). When you are enrolled in a professional social work curriculum, you will study the history of social welfare and social work in detail in specific introductory and policy courses. Students appreciate Dolgoff's, Feldstein's, and Skolnick's inclusion in their text of chapters that spell out current federal social welfare programs of economic assistance, as well as programs that offer assistance with needs such as health, food, housing, and personal services. There are many other fine texts that address the history of social welfare and social work as a helping profession. If you are pursuing the topics for your own interest, you can get an overview by consulting entries on social welfare, the social work profession, and brief biographies of influential people in the history of the field in *The Encyclopedia of Social Work* (1995). Martin Bloom (1990) presents helpful parallel tables of the development of social welfare and United States history over time and develops an approach to conceptualizing the pushes and pulls clients experience from multiple systems in their environment. Charles Heffernan's (1992) material informs students about particular populations and fields of practice. Karen Haynes and Karen Holmes (1994) pay special attention to developments in social welfare as they have affected women and their rights. You will note as you read the historical development of social welfare and social work that sparse attention was paid to the distinct needs of Native Americans and African-Americans in public policy or programs of service. Social workers need to be aware of the neglect of these groups by the nation and by the profession.

The movement away from casework, group work, and community organization as discrete methods of social work practice toward integrated generalist social work practice methods makes it possible for social workers to make whole their person-in-environment focus and to be trained to act competently to achieve all of the purposes of practice cited in Chapter 1: supporting the problem-solving, coping, and inherent developmental capacities of people; promoting the effective and humane operation of the systems that provide people with resources, services, and opportunities; and linking people with the systems that provide them with resources, services, and opportunities (Baer and Federico, 1978). Whatever their limitations, these purposes and generalist methods take some steps toward resolving the strains between cause and function. In this approach to practice, the mission of the profession for social reform and the skills of professional helpers in supporting an individual's capacities hold equal importance and receive equal attention. The linking of purpose and skill serve to tie the person and the environment together to make a holistic approach to professional helping through social work. Herbert Bisno cited Kaplan's use of the term, "the law of the instrument"; briefly stated, given a hammer, a small child will find that everything he or she encounters needs hammering (cited by Federico, 1984: 241). The application to professional practice is in the possibility that people who come to helpers trained in a very specific method (casework, group work, community organization) run the risk that no matter what service the clients want or need, the approach they are given may be the one the helper knows how to do. Narrowly trained, a helper may be unaware of the world of possible approaches; and when clients also run the risk of receiving what professionals define as their needs, not what they define as their needs, it may not be surprising that some helping efforts fall short of pleasing clients and professionals alike. The generalist integrated methods approach attempts to focus first on the persons being served and their needs. It is assumed that a variety of methods might be needed in human situations, which are always complex and never simple, so that a generalist should be trained in a variety of skills. These are the skills involved in carrying out the stages of the **helping process** (or **problem-solving process**) with people, individually or in aggregates. The terms "helping process" and "problem-solving process" refer to a model of helping that emphasizes a systematic, sequential, and circular process based on the scientific method. In social work, the helper and client are viewed as full partners in the process. In general terms, these skills include: communication, engagement, and relationship skills; assessment, goal setting, contracting, and planning skills; intervention skills; and evaluation, termination, referral, and disposition skills. Each of these groups of skills involves an array of more particular skills. In communication the helper needs to develop the skills of listening, hearing, and feeding back to the client his or her tentative understanding of the content and meaning of a client's verbal and nonverbal messages. In goal setting helpers need to be skilled in assisting the client to specify their desired goals in terms of which goals are most important to them, which are feasible, and which can be achieved in steps and in a time frame that allows the client to experience successes that build hope and confidence that more or greater accomplishments can be attained. As previously mentioned these skills can be put to use as the generalist practitioner acts in the roles of broker, advocate, counselor, educator, planner, administrator, mediator, organizer, activist, and lobbyist, among others. Each of these roles involves particular skills, and more often than not, the helper acts in multiple roles. Consider, as an example, helpers who take a strengths-based practice approach with persons who experience disabilities. Helpers acting in the broker role with university students or industrial workers who have physical disabilities need to be knowledgeable and able to demonstrate their knowledge of entitlement under the Americans with Disabilities Act, be aware that institutions may not know their responsibilities under the law, may not have ready resources to accommodate disabled persons, may have developed intricate methods for bypassing the law, and may have strong legal representation to defend their actions. In the role of educator, the helper can disseminate information about the law to disabled students and workers and/or join with them in accessing the information they need to act on their own behalf. As counselor, the helper will recognize the stigma attached to a disability and how that works on people's sense of self-esteem as competent adults in control of their world; the helper will support people's efforts to resist incorporating a devalued status, which often leads them to blame themselves for their disability or to back away from asking for the resources to which they are entitled. As counselor, the helper will afford persons with disabilities the opportunity to share their thoughts and feelings, assist them to identify and build on their own real strengths, and encourage them to create a reality for themselves (empowerment) rather than to continually adjust to the institution's reality.

Is generalist practice fail-safe? No. It does attempt to honor the diversity of people and their concerns, allows room for putting primary emphasis on peoples' definitions of needs rather than on helpers' definitions, and affords helpers an opportunity to view situations from a systems perspective of interacting and mutually influencing elements in any given situation. Perhaps a major contribution of the approach is that it does not let a professional social worker off the hook; direct practitioners who function as "clinicians" cannot excuse themselves from making an effort to change societal conditions that may lead to their therapy clients experiencing what Helen Mendes (1979) called "psycho-biosocial overload," a term that refers to the stress that results from putting excessive demands on people's internal and external resources. Community activists cannot excuse themselves from attending to the individual or family pain that may lead their community residents' council members to show depleted energy or lack of participation. Does a generalist approach to helping sacrifice depth for breadth? Some social workers would argue that it does. Carol Meyer's perspective is cited by Patricia Ewalt (1994). Meyer advocates teaching about practice with people who are experiencing the most serious and debilitating social problems. She recommends content-based approaches over generalized methods approaches. Her thinking is that vulnerable clients need service from helpers who have specialized knowledge about those clients and their circumstances. Others would argue that generalist social workers foremost must have breadth, because of the diversity of the people they serve, the wide range of needs people present, and the vast number of service areas that a social worker needs to coordinate to be helpful to people. One practice text, edited by Alex Gitterman (1991), combines a discussion of basic social work practice principles and specific information about practice with a series of vulnerable populations. The advantage of such an approach to professional helping students is the presence of material that has direct applicability to their internship duties: working with abused children, battered spouses, or homeless persons, for instance. The difficulty is that unless numerous differing perspectives on serving a particular population are offered, a beginning helper may tend to take an article on practice with a particular population as dogma. For example, material on practice with obese persons that starts with an a priori assumption of intra-psychic causality will likely recommend different practice approaches than material that recognizes variability in body size as primarily an aspect of diversity or material that recognizes the societal pressure for slimness. The response may be that helping practitioners need both generalist methods and a great variety of specialized information.

Current social work practice focuses on the helping process or problem-solving process as a basic intervention approach. As stated earlier, this can be applied in work with individuals, groups, families, or communities. The generalist practitioner will be presented in the course of practice with many other intervention approaches. The choice of approaches used may vary according to client needs, agency or practice setting, mission, constraints, and mandates. Nevertheless, it is imperative that professional social work helpers ensure that their practice methodology is consistent with social work values and purposes.

Naomi Brill (1995) provides a schema that outlines the progression from basic values to technique of intervention (Figure 5.1).

FIGURE 5.1   The evolution of a technique

From: Brill, N. (1995). *Working with People,* 5th edition. White Plains, NY: Longman Publishing Group, p. 138. Reprinted with permission.

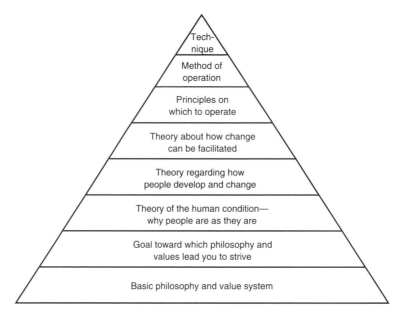

In analyzing the schema, start at the bottom and proceed in ascending order to the top. Basic philosophy and values lead to the determination of basic goals. A belief in the equality of all people would result in a goal of eliminating racial discrimination, for example. An understanding of the negative forces (personal and societal) that trigger discrimination, as well as the positive forces that can be mobilized to eliminate it, will point us further in the right direction. Theories of the change process and methods of encouraging change allow the formation of basic principles, methods, and techniques that can be used toward achieving the goal. Legislative and educational approaches are examples of particular methods that could be used to achieve the ideal of racial equality.

We ask that you stop here in your reading, turn to Exhibit 5.3, "The Principal Goes to School," and Exhibit 5.4, "Everything Happens in Its Own Time." These two examples speak for themselves as illustrations of professional helpers' attempts to put into practice many of the concepts developed in this text. However, after you have read them, it may be useful for you to come back to Brill's schema and reflect on connections you see between the schema and the practice exemplars. For example, is the basic philosophy and value system apparent in each exemplar? What theory regarding how people develop and change led the school intervention team to revise its program? What theory regarding how change can be facilitated guided the case manager's activity?

Another framework for viewing the practice exemplars is an outline we use in practice courses for case presentations. The outline incorporates questions on social work purposes and values, client strengths, diversity, and components of the helping process. It builds on (1) a strengths-based approach and (2) an approach that emphasizes client-determined goals. The list of questions the case presenter addresses includes the following:

1. *What are the mission and goals of your agency, and what match or mismatch do you see between your agency's mission and the values and purposes of the social work profession?*

Usually, the presenter sees a match; often this match is what led the employee or intern to choose to work in a particular agency. This question may help practitioners become more focused on their purposes as they face the everyday encounters with agency paperwork mandates, politics, and problematic case situations. Practitioners can help themselves to refocus in unclear helping situations by asking: What is my professional purpose in being here? In Exhibit 5.3, "The Principal Goes to School," the mission was to help each child achieve his or her fullest educational potential. In the situation presented in Exhibit 5.4, "Everything Happens in Its Own Time," the mission of the case manager's agency was to provide direct support services to HIV-challenged persons and community education and information in an effort to prevent the spread of HIV disease. In both cases, there was a match with social work values and purposes.

2. *Describe the program of service offered to your agency's clients. Does the service offered match the agency's mission?*

This question can clarify for beginning practitioners why they may be feeling uncertain of their role in some practice situations. The confusion may be the result of an incongruity between the agency's stated mission and the services offered or the manner in which they are delivered. For example, a worker may feel that clients are not being treated with respect or given choices of services. The worker may feel that he or she is being criticized by other agency staff for being too trusting or for believing what the client says. At other times, although an agency states that its mission is to provide poor families with basic resources, job opportunities, and personal support, the actual services offered may consist of counseling that focuses on the family's interpersonal weaknesses. Workers can feel more confident if their work roles are consistent with stated agency goals and with basic social work values. New workers or students within an agency are often able to see the discontinuity between mission and program and are at times afforded an opportunity to provide such insights. The principal-social worker (Exhibit 5.3) was able to reassess the school's mission and its program. The intervention team's approach was not working to achieve the school's mission. The changes the team decided to implement in the program of services matched the mission and fit with social work values and purposes. In the situation of the case manager (Exhibit 5.4), her discomfort had to do with the outside system's expectations of how her client should behave and what they thought was best for him. Her situation is an example of the predicament discussed earlier in terms of the helper being "in between" the client and the community. In this situation, social work values were supported by the agency and empowered the case manager to complete her work.

3. *Who are the members of the service team? Which person or persons comprise the client system? Which agency persons are on the team? Which other people have a role in the service situation?*

These questions help practitioners to think in terms of team effort and building a broader base of resources. In Exhibit 5.3, the service team was comprised of parents, teachers, and various intervention specialists, depending on the special learning needs of the individual child. Although not employed in this scenario, the child, extended family, and coaches could also be considered important members of the team. How would you implement that idea if you were a school social worker? In Exhibit 5.4, the service team changed over time and involved outside agencies and extended family.

4. *Please provide some information about your partnership with your client: What do you admire and respect about your client? What has your client taught you that has enhanced your knowledge and skill as a practitioner? What elements in your client's past and/or present life do the two of you consider to be important to your work together? What aspects of your client's diversity need to be given special attention? What are your client's goals— meaning what does he or she want, wish for, hope for? What is working in your client's life? What do the two of you think could work somewhat better? What assessment have you and your client reached together? What plans have you and your client agreed upon?*

The first question in the series means: *What does the presenter admire and respect about the client as a person?* This question takes for granted that a helper honors social work values and has taken seriously the tasks of the early stages of the helping process (communication, engagement, and relationship building) and has begun to develop a full mutual partnership between herself or himself and the client. These tasks are carried out by the helper and client for purposes of reaching a joint assessment of the practice situation at hand. The helper listens to the client's story, consults with the client to see if he or she correctly understood it, invites the client's ideas, and responds to and affirms the client's feelings. Sometimes when professional helpers are asked to identify client strengths, they list such things as: takes medication as directed; shows up for appointments; cooperates with agency rules; or, ironically, demonstrates awareness of his or her weaknesses and limitations. Such a listing does not reflect a deep knowledge of the client or his or her individual strengths. Answering the question "what do you respect and admire about your client" might provide a more thoughtful assessment of the client's strengths. Did it appear to you that the school's revised intervention program took a closer look at what was to be admired and respected about each child as a unique learner who had developed his or her own coping and adaptation skills? Based on the case manager's description of Mr. Pollet, would you say that she admired and respected him as a person? If so, what are some of the things she said about him that indicated this? This question forces a paradigm shift from focusing on what is wrong with a client to what is positive and working for them. It focuses our attention as helpers back to the social work values of the uniqueness, dignity, and worth of each person and away from examining the subtleties of client deficits.

In order to answer the question *What has the client taught me?,* workers need to see themselves as in a reciprocal and collaborative relationship with the client. This necessitates moving out of the role of "expert" and being open to the possibility of a mutual exchange of information. The case manager from Exhibit 5.4 stated that Mr. Pollet taught her a lot that was useful for her personal life about how to live and how to die and for her professional life about the importance of timing; she picked up the client's cues that he was ready for change and that he was capable of making decisions.

The next series of questions from above focus on the assessment and planning process: *elements of the client's life; diversity; client goals; what is working for the client; what could be better; mutual assessment of the client's situation;* and *mutually agreed upon plans.* One way for a helper to be guided in developing an assessment with a client is to reflect on some of the things that go on in a "biopsychosocial whole" person: How does my client define his or her reality? What does my client say he or she *experiences;* what is day to day life like for my client? What does my client *perceive* with his or her senses? What does my client *think?* What does my client *feel?* What *meaning* does my client make out of his or her situation? What does my client *want?* What is my client *willing* to do? What other *systems* interact with my client in the present situation? What elements of the past seem to me or my client to have some bearing on the present situation?

In considering the question about aspects of *diversity,* the practitioner and client can think about which characteristics, strengths, and needs clients share in common with all human beings; which of these elements they share in common with members of their group (Hispanic, Asian, African-American persons; rural, urban, homeless people); and which of these elements they share in common with no other person—that make the client unique. As professional helpers, we need to be aware of the diversity in multiple cultural perspectives. Diversity exists *within* racial and ethnic groups and among women, men, children, elders, gays, lesbians, and heterosexuals. In Exhibit 5.4, for example, Mr. Pollet, as a gay male, understood through direct experience the stigmatization and discrimination gay men encounter in this culture. His identity as a strong person, an independent person, and as a gay man was important to him. His life's work was important to him. Do you think the case manager was culturally aware and sensitive to his diversity? Do you think their gender differences produced social distance?

Consider the question of *client goals* in Mr. Pollet's situation. Despite his chronic illness, he wanted to maintain maximum health for as long as possible and live as independently as possible. Later on he wanted to hold on to whatever independence was left to him. Finally, he wanted to die well, at peace and prepared. Do you think the case manager was committed to helping him achieve these goals?

In relation to the question about *what is working in the client's life* we can go back to Exhibit 5.3 and reflect on how the intervention team began to reframe characteristics of children that had been previously interpreted as not working. An argumentative child was now viewed as possessing good negotiation skills; another child who frequently disrupted class was viewed as an able learner when structure was provided in activities. These characteristics were now viewed as competencies that helped the children adapt and cope and which could be built upon for further growth. Mr. Pollet's life (Exhibit 5.4) was working well for him until his HIV status changed to AIDS; a series of losses ensued: he could no longer maintain his profession and his adult worker role; his income dropped drastically; his body would no longer support his independent spirit and activity; and he needed to involve other people and systems in order to survive. Were there areas in which he might have behaved differently? If you were his helper, how would you have dealt with the issues around his method of controlling pain? Did he need to change?

The question *What assessment have you and your client reached together?* assumes that the helper neither owns the assessment nor is competent to make an assessment unilaterally; the assessment belongs to the client and worker together. Consider a few of the factors that may be involved in an assessment of Mr. Pollet's life situation. Mr. Pollet possessed several attributes that singularly and in combination may have caused him to be stigmatized. He was a gay male who contracted the HIV virus, a drug user, and he was unemployed. How were his life choices and life chances affected by these factors? What mysterious confluence of factors influenced Mr. Pollet to remain true to himself and to hold on to his sense of himself as worthy and competent throughout his ordeal? His defiance can be seen as his struggle to maintain control over some aspects of his life. Do you see examples in which biology, psychology, and social structures interacted with one another through the course of Mr. Pollet's past and present life? What could be more convincing of the concept of adult developmental needs for competency, control, productivity, and independence than Mr. Pollet's fierce determination to run his own life? His case manager seemed to be keenly aware of how many assaults on his selfhood Mr. Pollet was experiencing. She recognized the ambivalence that is felt throughout the life course: Mr. Pollet, like other people, wanted autonomy and closeness; wanted to be independent and in control but wanted to be cared for; and wanted to master knowledge and skills but wanted to learn new information and skills. Mr. Pollet described himself as a survivor and assessed himself as not ready to take on a dependent role, but as he faced the changes in his life, he changed his own assessment of his needs.

The final question has to do with *plans for action:* These include developing tasks or steps to accomplish stated goals, evaluation of the work accomplished, and decisions regarding when the work is completed. A practice wisdom truism states that if you have clear communication, an honest and open relationship, and an accurate definition of the situation, the interventions will follow logically from the definitions. As we examine both practice exemplars, it appears that there are additional factors of importance. In each case, the intervention team and the case manager stayed with the client and the situations through a search for solutions, and all parties engaged in continuous creative thinking about how they could make the systems work.

This has been one format for viewing individual and agency practice. Whatever format is employed in practice should be founded in basic social work values. Whitaker and Tracy (1989) refer to five basic **social work values** that build the framework of practice:

1. Respect for the dignity of the individual.
2. Adherence to a nonjudgmental approach in helping.
3. Respect for the client's right to self-determination.
4. Unconditional acceptance of diversity—racial, cultural, sexual, and political.
5. A passionate and enduring commitment to the poor, to the oppressed, and to the disenfranchised.

Certain practice principles flow from social work values. These values, for instance, are the reason behind the principle of confidentiality. People deserve privacy as a function of their dignity and worth. If they have dignity and worth, they have a right to expect acceptance from the helper, not judgment. If people have self-determination, they have the right to accept or to refuse service; they have the right to ask that we start where they are, not where we are; the right to be fully informed; and the right to be free of the helper's imposition on them of the helper's beliefs.

As the professional helper in social work attempts to integrate the two selves, the personal self and the professional self, the worker must face some basic questions:

- Are my personal values and my professional values the same or different?

Social work as a profession holds the belief that each individual has dignity and worth, *period.* No qualifications. No conditions. No exclusions. These are values that are shared by many other helping professions. Beginning helpers can clarify similarities and differences between their personal and professional *selves* by asking: Do I share these beliefs? Are the personal values I hold values that I assimilated while growing up or values that I carefully examined for myself and consciously and freely chose? Do my values serve me well toward meeting my life goals, appreciating the varied world of people and ideas, enjoying satisfying relationships with others, serving my clients, and practicing my profession? Are my personal beliefs engraved in stone? Do I examine my values from time to time, knowing that I am always learning, growing, and changing? What is my way of deciding which values I want to keep, which ones I want to modify, and which ones I want to discard? Professional helpers recognize these as questions clients find useful in clarifying their values.

- If there is a mismatch between my personal values and professional values, what do I do with my personal values while I am carrying out my professional purpose?

A paradox for the social work professional helper is this: Whereas the principle of self-determination prohibits social workers from imposing their values on others, professional social workers agree to accept imposition of the values of the profession on themselves when they act in their professional capacity. Social work professional values, in conjunction with the framework outlined in Chapter 1, provide the cornerstone on which social work practice is built. Many occasions arise in practice where methods are not easily reconciled with basic values. Human service practice with involuntary clients (such as in psychiatric hospitals, prisons, and juvenile and adult courts) often confronts the conflict between the client's right of self-determination and the various sanctions and methods employed to control behavior. In such settings social workers as well as other human service professional helpers are often placed in dual and sometimes conflicting roles necessitating ethical judgments. Each helping profession has a code of ethics to guide its members in their interaction with various systems. The Code of Ethics of the National Association of Social Workers (1980), the major organization of the profession, spells out principles for guiding the behavior of social workers in meeting their ethical responsibilities to multiple systems, including clients, colleagues, employing organizations, the social work profession, and society. However, the Code of Ethics does not address the social worker's legal responsibilities. Herb Kutchins (1991) suggests the concept of the fiduciary relationship (emanating from the nature of the trust that vulnerable clients must place in professional helpers) as a useful explanation for practitioners' legal duties. Although we have emphasized the idea of working with clients in full mutual partnership throughout this text, we recognize that in many helping situations parity does not exist, for example, when a client who is feeling very shaky emotionally asks for help or when parents are ordered to see a professional helper in order to be able to retain custody of their children. In these instances, the special trust that the vulnerable client places in the helper and the authority the helper has to recommend for or against custody produces a relationship of unequal power, and the greater burden of responsibility is on the professional helper, the person in the relationship who holds the greater power. Kutchins refers to the observation of Gerhart and Brooks that the series of legal regulations that helping professionals need to know are not available for study in a collected form. A few of these legal regulations include informed consent (the right to know what activity will be done, its expected benefits and risks); the duty to warn a third party of dangerous threats from clients; limits of confidentiality; and requirements to report child abuse. The idea of litigation can be alarming to beginning helpers. Many social agencies have gathered information about specific legal regulations that are of special concern to that agency's work. For instance, if you are working in an agency that serves children and adolescents, you should be knowledgeable about legal regulations regarding such issues as parental permission and children's rights to privacy. In mental health settings, the helper needs to become aware of regulations regarding clients' rights to refuse medication or regarding sharing information with relatives or an employer. In an effort to honor the principle of self-determination, the professional helper should be cognizant of systems interactions, realizing that throughout life one system's rights often collide with the rights of another system and require negotiation. When a helper operates in that buffer area between client and community, ethical and legal dilemmas are part of the territory.

Professional consultation and support can assist the beginning helper in these difficult situations. These dilemmas are not easily resolved and can cause distress for the conscientious helper. They point out the need for systemic changes when social forces have negatively impinged on the client's life course so that few viable choices are left. An example is an indigent person unwillingly placed in a psychiatric hospital because of a display of menacing behavior in the community. The professional helper is faced with a client who wishes to leave the facility and the community's concern for safety. The client and the community present conflicting demands, which the helper is called upon to negotiate. Such a conflict might be more easily mitigated or even prevented if more community-based halfway houses for the mentally ill were available. Many professional helpers in the early years of the community mental health movement in the 1960s, in our eagerness to empower persons who were institutionalized, failed to take into account the fact that it is no simple matter to live successfully in the community when one is in the best of emotional and physical health.

Without a full system of multiple supports, surviving in the community is a huge challenge for people who are emotionally vulnerable. Naomi Brill's schema can also be used in reference to public-policy issues. Social policy and public policy should be based upon and consistent with basic human values. Issues such as health care, education, minimum wage, housing, AIDS, and family planning are but a few examples of the policies that helping professionals deal with on a daily basis. As such, social work philosophy, purposes, and values should be essential components in public-policy formulation. Because this has been a text on human behavior and not a practice text, we have not explicated practice fully. When you are enrolled in a human service curriculum, you will take courses that develop in detail the specific skills of each stage of the helping process. In addition to works cited in this chapter there are other texts on practice, each having its own special strengths. Here too, as with the material on social welfare and social work history, you may want to start with entries on practice in the *Encyclopedia of Social Work* (Edwards, 1995). At the end of this chapter, under "ADDITIONAL PRACTICE TEXTS" we have included the titles of a number of texts on direct practice. We hope the material we have included on practice in this chapter will be useful to you in making connections between the conceptual base of professional helping and the application of the concepts in your professional practice.

SUMMARY

The systems perspective developed earlier in the text leads us to conclude that the helping professional who practices generalist social work must seek to influence the systems that affect people in need, making micro-, mezzo-, and macrolevel intervention appropriate. The health-strength-growth, directionality, and diversity perspectives focus our attention on the need to respect the strengths of all people and to honor their definitions of their needs. These perspectives lead us to choose individually and culturally specific approaches. They lead us to serve with sensitivity, humility, and skill. However, as important as knowledge and skill are to social work practice, we conclude this book by emphasizing the primacy of social work values and purposes in guiding social work practice. In conjunction with an ecological and growth perspective on human behavior, values and purpose provide a basis for determining with whom, when, and how we intervene as partners with people working toward their goals of empowerment.

STUDY QUESTIONS

1. Several motives for entering the helping professions were identified, including the need to satisfy intellectual curiosity about what makes people behave as they do and the need to make a contribution to creating a just society. What combination of

various motives do you consider operative in your own decision to enter a helping profession? How have your motives changed over time? How might you expect your motives will change in the future?

2. Working effectively with people requires an ongoing examination of one's motives and beliefs regarding the helping process. How useful is the analogy of the shaman to you in assessing your own motivation for becoming a helping person?

3. Social workers often become involved in the lives of individuals, families, and communities at times of crisis, life transitions, or environmental changes. Think of such periods in your own life. What forces or events precipitated a need for service? What resources interacted to help resolve the problems? What obstacles interacted to hinder its resolution? Consider how professional intervention may or may not have been helpful.

4. Empowerment of individuals and the larger aggregates of families, groups, institutions, and communities often places the human service worker at odds with the prevailing belief and attitudinal systems of powerful elements in the culture and social structures. What resources might you as a human service worker draw upon to strengthen yourself to deal with the problems of racism, sexism, ageism, ableism, and homophobia in both yourself and your culture and social structure?

5. Discuss the quotation from Alice Walker that introduces this chapter, in terms of its implications for understanding human behavior and translating that understanding into professional purpose and practice?

6. There is much to discuss about the account (in Exhibit 5.4) of the joint work of Mary Kay Martin-Heldman and Christopher Pollet. Where would you want to begin? You could begin by asking yourself this: If you or someone you dearly loved had AIDS, would you want a case manager who practiced like Martin-Heldman? If yes, what did she do that you would find useful? If no, how would you want things handled differently? In your own practice experiences, do you sometimes find yourself caught in a struggle between what different professionals expect a client to do and what the client is willing to do? In such situations, what do you find that works for you?

7. Exhibit 5.3 contained a report of program changes in a school system. Have you ever attended a school such as the one described by George Reavis in *The Animal School?* What difference do you think it made that Rosemary Schroeder, who described changes made by her school's intervention team, was both the school principal and a strong proponent of the new approach? If you were a human service professional working in a school system and you wanted to try a new approach, how could you position it in order to gain the commitment of a principal who knew nothing about the approach or did not express interest in change? How do you think the strengths- and client goal-focused approach would work in an inner-city school, or a school with a great deal of diversity, or one that was very poorly funded?

8. Discuss Dusty's story in Exhibit 5.1 in terms of her motivation and choice of methods of helping. What are your thoughts about her ability to be empathetic and flexible in her roles with her patients? Discuss her decision about being honest with her patients regarding their condition. How do these issues relate to your work with individuals, groups, and communities? What are some reasons that Dusty may wish to remain anonymous? What does her story say to you about the nature of the helping process? How do you think events in the present era are affecting both professional helpers and the public?

9. In Exhibit 5.2, you read about Rev. Bernice A. King's path to the helping professions, and in the introduction to the exhibit, you read about a different path to helping taken by other African-Americans, as expressed by social worker Phyllis Bass. If the purposes of social work are to make society more responsive to the needs of people, to help people reach their full potential, and to link people with societal resources, what programs of action could the generalist practitioner engage in to address the inequities Bass recognizes?

KEY TERMS

Code of Ethics of the National Association of Social Workers. Principles for guiding the behavior of social workers in meeting their ethical responsibilities to clients, colleagues, employers, agencies, the social work profession, and society.

Crisis. A decisive state, in which the usual coping strategies are taxed, necessitating a restructuring of behavioral responses. Crises are sometimes divided into developmental, situational, and environmental crises. Crises are often invitations to further growth.

Empathy. The ability to try to understand the situation of another person from that person's perspective. An essential component of the helping process.

Helping process (problem-solving process). Models of interpersonal helping that emphasizes an approach to the intervention process that is systematic, sequential, and circular. In social work, it is a shared process between client(s) and worker.

Social work values. Major beliefs shared by members of the social work profession, including belief in diversity, uniqueness and worth of each person, the right to self-determination, and commitment to oppressed persons.

Transition points. A change in the direction of the life course, brought about by either progression through the developmental stages or by a shift in social status.

REFERENCES

Ansley, L. (1991). Going Her Own Way. *USA Weekend,* January 13, p. 4. Arlington, VA: USA Today.

Atwood, M. (1989). *Cat's Eye.* New York: Doubleday.

Baer, B. and R. Federico (1978). *Educating the Baccalaureate Social Worker.* Vol. 1. Cambridge, MA: Ballinger.

Becker, D. G. (1968). Social Welfare Leaders as Spokesmen for the Poor. *Social Casework,* Vol. 49, No. 2 (February), p. 85.

Berg, I. and S. Miller (1992). *Working with the Problem Drinker: A Solution-Focused Approach.* New York: W. W. Norton.

Black Elk (1979) (told through Neihardt). *Black Elk Speaks.* Lincoln, NE: University of Nebraska Press.

Bloom, M. (1990). *Introduction to the Drama of Social Work.* Itasca, IL: F. E. Peacock Publishing, Inc.

Brill, N. (1995). *Working with People,* 5th edition. White Plains, NY: Longman Publishing Group, pp. 136-140.

Corey, M. S. and G. Corey (1993). *Becoming a Helper,* 2nd edition. Pacific Grove, CA: Brooks/Cole Publishing Co., pp. 2-29.

Cowger, C. (1994). Assessing Client Strengths: Clinical Assessment for Client Empowerment. *Social Work,* Vol. 39, No. 3 (May), pp. 262-268.

DeShazer, S. (1985). *Keys to Solution in Brief Therapy.* New York: W. W. Norton.

Dolgoff, R., D. Feldstein, and L. Skolnik (1993). *Understanding Social Welfare,* 3rd edition. White Plains, NY: Longman Publishing Group, pp. 276-277.

Edwards, R. (ed.) (1995). *Encyclopedia of Social Work,* 19th edition. Annapolis, MD: National Association of Social Workers.

Einstein, A. (1930). What I Believe (In *Forum*). In *Bartlett's Familiar Quotations,* 16th edition (1992), edited by J. Kaplan, p. 635. Boston, MA: Little, Brown and Company.

Ellison, R. (1964). In *Time,* March 27. In *The New York Public Library Book of Twentieth-Century American Quotations* (1992), edited by S. Donadio, J. Smith, S. Mesner, and R. Davison, p. 343. New York: Warner Books.

Ewalt, P. (1994). Visions of Ourselves. *Social Work,* Vol. 39, No. 1 (January), pp. 5-6.

Federico, R. (1990). *Social Welfare in Today's World.* New York: McGraw-Hill.

Federico, R. (1984). *The Social Welfare Institution.* 4th edition. Lexington, MA.: D.C. Heath, p. 241.

Fitzgerald, F. (1936). The Crack Up. In *Bartlett's Familiar Quotations,* 16th edition (1992), edited by J. Kaplan, p. 694. Boston: Little, Brown and Company.

Fox, R. (1993). *Elements of the Helping Process: A Guide for Clinicians.* Binghamton, N.Y.: The Haworth Press, Inc., p. 31, pp. 44-46.

Frost, R. (1916). The Road Not Taken, st. 4. In *Bartlett's Familiar Quotations,* 16th edition (1992), edited by J. Kaplan, p. 623. Boston, MA: Little, Brown, and Company.

Gitterman, A. (ed.) (1991). *Handbook of Social Work Practice with Vulnerable Populations.* New York: Columbia University Press.

Hartman, A. (1989). Still between the Client and the Community. *Social Work,* Vol. 34, No. 5 (September), pp. 387-388.

Hartman, A. and J. Laird (1983). *Family Centered Social Work Practice.* New York: Free Press, p. 30.

Haynes, K. and K. Holmes (1994). *Invitation to Social Work.* White Plains, NY: Longman Publishing Group.

Heffernan, C. (1992). *Social Work and Social Welfare,* 2nd edition. St. Paul, MN: West Publishing Company.

Horney, K. (1945). Our Inner Conflicts, Conclusion. In *Bartlett's Familiar Quotations,* 16th edition (1992), edited by J. Kaplan, p. 657. Boston, MA: Little, Brown and Company.

Jung, C. (1933). Modern Man in Search of a Soul. In *Bartlett's Familiar Quotations,* 14th edition (1968), edited by E. Beck, p. 935. Boston, MA: Little, Brown and Company.

Kutchins, H. (1991). The Fiduciary Relationship: The Legal Basis for Social Workers' Responsibilities to Clients. *Social Work,* Vol. 36, No. 2 (March), pp. 106-113.

McMillian, T. (1992). *Waiting to Exhale.* New York: Viking Press.

Mendes, H. (1979). Single-Parent Families: A Typology of Life-Styles. *Social Work,* Vol. 24, No. 3 (May), p. 193.

Miller, S., D. Wackman, E. Nunnally, and P. Miller (1988). *Connecting with Self and Others.* Littleton, CO.: Interpersonal Communications Programs, pp. 18-19.

Mills, C. Wright (1971). *The Sociological Imagination.* New York: Penguin Books.

The National Association of Black Social Workers (undated). *The Code of Ethics of the National Association of Black Social Workers*. In the University of Cincinnati School of Social Work (1994) Student Handbook.

The National Association of Social Workers, Inc. (1980). *Code of Ethics of the National Association of Social Workers*. Silver Spring, MD.: The National Association of Social Workers.

Newman, F. (1988). The Family in a Time of Social Crisis. In *History Is the Cure: A Social Therapy*, edited by L. Holzman and H. Polk, pp. 126–141. New York: Practice Press.

Norment, L. (1995). New Generation of Kings. *Ebony*, Vol. L, No. 3 (January), pp. 25–34.

O'Hanlon, W. and M. Weiner-Davis (1989). *In Search of Solutions: A New Direction in Psychotherapy*. New York: W. W. Norton.

Palmer, L. (1987). *Shrapnel in the Heart*. New York: Random House.

Perlman, H. (1957). *Social Casework: A Problem Solving Process*. Chicago, IL: University of Chicago Press, pp. 6–7.

Saleebey, D. (ed.) (1992). *The Strengths Perspective in Social Work Practice*. White Plains, NY: Longman Publishing Group.

Sanford, J. (1977). *Healing and Wholeness*. New York: Paulist Press.

Szasz, T. (1973). The Second Sin. In *The New York Public Library Book of Twentieth-Century American Quotations* (1992), edited by S. Donadio et al., p. 341. New York: Warner Books.

Wagner, D. (1989). Fate of Idealism in Social Work: Alternative Experiences of Professional Careers. *Social Work*, Vol. 34, No. 5 (September), pp. 389–398.

Walker, A. (1989). The Temple of My Familiar. In *The New York Public Library Book of Twentieth-Century American Quotations* (1992), edited by S. Donadio et al., p. 504. New York: Warner Books.

Walter, J. and J. Peller (1992). *Becoming Solution-Focused in Brief Therapy*. New York: Brunner/Mazel Press.

Whitaker, H. and E. Tracy (1989). *Social Treatment*, 2nd edition. New York: Aldine-DeGruyter.

exhibit 5.1

Professional Helper Exemplar on Nursing: Dusty

The following account of a nurse's experiences in Vietnam provides a contemporary example of the "wounded healer." It also illustrates empathetic responses to those being helped and the importance of cohorts in understanding human behavior and relationships. How did the Vietnam era affect the United States populace, and how did historical events help formulate attitudes and values that impacted on "Dusty" and others during that period? What historic events have affected the beliefs and attitudes of you and your clients? What events are you and your cohort experiencing now that will affect your behavior and relationships in the future?

One of our students recently drew family diagrams showing how the relationships between the couples and among the children in each generation of her family had been wounded in some way by every action from World War II, to Korea, to Vietnam, to the Gulf War. She showed multiple systems interactions. Her grandparents, very much in love and newly married when World War II broke out, had barely three weeks of living together before her grandfather was drafted. Pregnant and on her own, her grandmother spent the next four years working in a factory, raising her son, becoming competent in her roles and independent in her attitudes. Her grandfather, raised with very traditional role expectations for men and women, returned from the war moderately disabled and unprepared for this woman who was very different from the bride he had left behind. The couple stayed together, but they maintained "a distance" from one another. The husband "began to drink some," and mother and son were "close," according to family members. Our student regrets that her father's childhood was not happier, and she feels badly that her father did not understand what had happened until he was older. Korea took the life of our student's maternal uncle, whose widow was left with a high-school diploma, no paid work experience, and three children to raise. She had dreamed of being the kind of wife and mother idealized in 1950s television families, and it "took a long time" and "a lot of tranquilizers" for her to cope with her situation. Our student's husband returned safely from Vietnam to his job and family but would "never talk about anything that happened in the war." Pretty soon, her husband "didn't seem to have much to say about anything," neither to her nor their children; they became "a silent family in a silent house." Fortunately, they got help through a veterans' couples group, learned that their experience was not uncommon with Vietnam veterans and their families, and "things worked out." The student's worry now is what will happen to her son who was not old enough to go to the Gulf but wants to be a soldier and wants the educational opportunities he can get in the military. The student's story illustrates how people can be assessed very differently, depending on the lenses worn by the helpers who assess them. One group of helpers might argue that if the marital relationship between the grandparents had been characterized by both reciprocal intimacy and open communication, a rupture could have been avoided. Other helpers might believe that intergenerational chemical dependency accompanied by denial was operational. Still others could see unresolved grief. Some might put little credence in the influence of the times and events in which people live, and might consider these people as designers and planners of their own reality. Helpers could see deficits and dysfunction in our student and her family members up and down the line or view them with awe and respect, the way "Dusty" viewed the people she served. A helper might note that the family has lived and survived in perilous times and worked hard to cope with life. From this perspective, a helper might view the professional's task as working side by side with the family as full partners in a mutual effort to harvest and put to use all possible resources for effective functioning. Perhaps this is what Ronald Federico meant when he wrote that a central task of professional helpers is to assist people to "attain their goals with as few obstacles and as little pain as possible" (1990).

The excerpt below, which tells "Dusty's" story is taken from Shrapnel in the Heart *by Laura Palmer. Copyright © 1987 by Laura Palmer. Reprinted by permission of Random House, Inc.*

She went to Vietnam to heal and came home so wounded that to survive she changed her name, her profession, and her past. She agreed to talk about her experience anonymously. "Dusty" was her nickname in Vietnam.

"Vietnam cost me a great deal: a marriage, two babies, the ability to bear healthy children, the ability to practice my life's chosen profession, my physical health, and at times, my emotional stability. After the weight of my postwar trauma reached a critical mass, I changed my name, my profession, my residence, and my past. Silence and isolation allowed me to rebuild a life that for years was outwardly normal."

She is married to a businessman who has no idea that his wife was ever a nurse, in the Army, or in Vietnam.

"When you are sitting there working on someone in the middle of the night and it's a 19-year-old kid who's ten thousand miles from home and you know that he's going to die before dawn—you're sitting there checking his vital signs for him and hanging blood for him and talking to him and holding his hand and looking into his face and touching his face and you see his life just dripping away and you know he wants his mother and you now he wants his father and his family to be there and you're the only one that he's got, I mean his life is just oozing away there—well, it oozes into your soul. There is nothing more intimate than sharing someone's dying with them. . . . When you've got to do that with someone and give that person, at the age of 19, a chance to say the last things they are ever going to get to say, that act of helping someone die is more intimate than sex, it is more intimate than childbirth, and once you have done that you can never be ordinary again."

As a little girl, she adored science, in high school, her guidance counselor suggested that she become a science librarian. She settled on nursing instead, and because she had skipped grades in school, she was a registered nurse and in Vietnam by the time she was twenty-one. She was one of the youngest nurses she knew.

She did two tours in Vietnam, from 1966 to 1968, working in an evacuation hospital as a surgical, intensive-care, or emergency-room nurse. An evac, as these hospitals were called, was the first place the wounded were brought from the field. Once they were stabilized, they were sent on to other military hospitals.

Nurses, it is often said, weren't in combat. It's true they didn't dodge bullets, but they could not avoid the bodies. "The first few times you cut someone's uniform off and the leg falls off, yes, your mind screams, but you stuff that down very, very quickly. You have to. If you lose control, they're going to die. It's as simple as that."

What kept her going then, and what helps a little now, is the knowledge that she was making a difference. She chose to spend a second year in Vietnam because "the wounded kept coming, the war was getting worse, and I was good at what I did." She knew that "these people would have a future because of all of the shit I was going through."

. . . There was an incredible rush that came when someone they hadn't expected to make it through the night went home. Those are the ones she tries to think about. . . .

The horror and the pain come from the memories of the ones who didn't make it. Some never regained consciousness and slipped from delirium into death. Some were angry, knowing they were too young to die. . . .

She never encouraged anyone to deny that he was dying. If a boy said, "I'm not going to make it, am I?" she would usually say, "It doesn't look good." There was a reason for that. She wanted the men to be able to say anything they needed to say before they died.

Intimacy was conveyed in words, silence, and touch. She was never afraid to touch her patients. "Rules don't apply. You're the nurse, the doctor, you're their parents, you're their girlfriend and their wife, you're the only thing they have, and whatever it takes, that's what you give. That's what you're there for. It was just automatic."

. . . David was one of the ones she remembers. Eighteen years later, she wrote a poem about his dying. . . .

There is another boy whose memory was important to her long after he died. She has forgotten his name, but not his face. "He was a little shrimp, probably weighed a hundred and twenty pounds. This kid saved my life. He wasn't even dirty. Not a mark on him. Probably had only been in Vietnam a few days. I don't know what the Army wanted with this kid, a little black kid who definitely should have been thrown back. I picked up his head to turn his head to check his pupils and his brains were running out his ear into my fingers. He had died from concussive blast. I just looked at that brain tissue and thought, 'Whoever this was, he isn't here anymore. He had a mother who loved him and a future and a past and he came from somewhere. It's just such a . . . waste.'"

It was this memory that came back at a time when she was considering suicide. "I thought about pulling the trigger and splattering my brains all over the wall and I thought about this kid whose brains I had to wash off my hands and then I thought about whoever it might be that would have to come into my apartment and wipe the brains off the wall and wash my brains off their hands and I couldn't do that to someone."

The contributions of men who served in Vietnam were, by and large, scorned or ignored when they returned. But the contributions of women, specifically nurses, were simply unknown. The military, which prided itself on the records it kept in Vietnam—counting the number of enemy weapons captured, for example—cannot to this day say with certainty how many women served. The Army that sent them never bothered to count them. The estimate most frequently given is that a total of 7,500 women served in the military in Vietnam. Of these, 83.5 percent were nurses. . . .

[In 1985] there were two anniversaries: the fortieth anniversary of the end of World War II and the tenth anniversary of the fall of Saigon. She was flooded with images of the two wars that had bracketed her life.

Her mother had survived the Holocaust. Dusty was an only child whose grandparents, aunts, uncles, and cousins died in the camps. It was not until she was thirty-six and joined a group of other children of Holocaust survivors that she began to understand how that experience had shaped her. . . .

"I've tried to deny the past, I've tried to run away from it; that hasn't worked and I don't know what will work. Maybe nothing will. I'm just beginning to find out that I am not alone in the pain and I think that perhaps that will be the way out."

It is surprising, perhaps, to some people, but most who have served in Vietnam, despite the hideous aspects of their experience, do not regret that it happened and would go back. Dusty is no exception.

"I have been privileged to see, in absolutely the worst conditions that could exist, exactly how fine people can really be. To see the feeling these men had for their buddies and the things that they did and the caring they had, I think that's a rare privilege. I think I have been very honored by those circumstances."

exhibit 5.2

Professional Helper Exemplar on Ministry: Rev. Bernice A. King

The story of Rev. Bernice A. King's path into helping illustrates the confluence of time, place, and circumstance that affects life choices and life chances as powerfully as one's unique physiological makeup. Consider Rev. King's story in light of the time and place in which she was born and raised; the strengths that were instilled in her by her people; the failure of the dominant culture to respect, let alone acknowledge, the strengths of her people; the events she witnessed; the losses she sustained; her obstacles and resources; her ethnicity; her age; and her gender.

The Rev. King, a Baptist pastor in Atlanta, balances a full schedule of activity including counseling, writing, mentoring children, organizing women's conferences, and developing a ministry for single people. However, her path to helping as a minister was not smooth. In lectures she gives around the country, King discloses personal obstacles she faced. Her father's death had left her angry, and despite loving family and access to resources, her teen and young adult years were troubled, with King experiencing feelings of unworthiness and thoughts of suicide. She was pulled through, she says, by God's grace and revelation of her purpose in life. Many students in the helping professions find personal inspiration from King's story; for them she is a strong, positive role model. Other students acknowledge King's pain, respect her struggle and her courage, and want to "pay her just due" for her achievements—but her story is not their story. Theirs is a story of people who have had "few opportunities and little support" who, in the words of Phyllis Bass, social worker and community agency coordinator, "have had to come up from the depths" of poverty, whose arrival finally at their destination as helping professionals is achieved only after a journey that is by necessity "much longer and much slower," with many stops along the way to overcome roadblocks such as piecing together an education while seeking and holding on to jobs, raising children, and helping out family. Many students echo Bass's concern that if the stories of accomplishments by African-American persons more readily accepted as "mainstream" are the only stories that are told, they can serve to obscure the reality of unequal opportunity and perpetuate the myth that "if they would just get off the welfare and work, any African American could become president . . . easy." For those students, the lesson from King's story is this: Even though she had supportive family and access to opportunities, it was hard for her, she struggled— how hard it must be for someone who has neither support nor opportunity!

What do you think? Do you think that no one's story is quite like any other story, no matter how many apparent similarities there may seem to be? Does each helper, and each client, have his or her own, unique story, his or her own unique path to follow? Do they have a right to their story, a right to their path? Does the human services professional have the responsibility to listen to and to hear and to believe each client's story? Does the human service professional have the responsibility to help clear the path?

The following exhibit is taken from an interview that appeared on the eve of Martin Luther King, Jr.'s birthday, not many months after Rev. Bernice King, at the age of 27, was awarded both a master of divinity and a law degree from Emory University, was ordained a Baptist minister, and preached her first sermon in her home church, Ebenezer Baptist Church in Atlanta, where her father, grandfather, and great-grandfather all had been ministers. The excerpt is from "Going Her Own Way," by Leslie Ansley, in USA WEEKEND, *January 20, 1991, p. 4. Copyright © 1991, USA WEEKEND. Reprinted with permission.*

"Bunny" King's first ambition was to grow up to be a boy. When her mother set her straight, 9-year-old Bunny wanted to be the first female president. Later, she decided to be a lawyer—and the first black woman on the Supreme Court. Two years ago, she announced her intention to be a minister.

Today, the Rev. Bernice Albertine King, 27, wants to go to prison—as a counselor.

Bernice King comes by her ambitions naturally. Born into a family with high hopes and gigantic actions, she is the youngest of Martin Luther King Jr.'s four children, the only one to enter the ministry. Monday, the holiday honoring her father, the nation will remember his dream of mass social change. And Bernice will be working on hers: a teen prison ministry where she can deliver legal and spiritual counsel and change society individual by individual. No such formal program exists, but she has the connections and confidence to get such a program started.

In May, Bernice received a master of divinity degree *and* a law degree from Emory University. The night of her graduation, she was ordained a Baptist minister. Since then she's been working as a law clerk for a Fulton County juvenile court judge, planning for a Ph.D. in pastoral care counseling and fleshing out her prison plan. "I'm trying to take a survey of the land. I think we need some new things, not to forsake old things, but I'm trying to see where *my* gifts can be used."

She travels occasionally to lecture to church groups and other organizations, she sings tenor in the Martin Luther King Choir and, on the first Sunday of every month, she assists in the pulpit of Ebenezer Baptist Church in Atlanta—where her father, grandfather and great-grandfather all were ministers.

On a recent Sunday, homecoming weekend at Ebenezer, Bernice delivered the sermon, her first at her home church as a minister. At 5-foot-5, not much of her was visible above the podium, but her voice was towering. For 40 minutes she preached about "Why the Church Can't Be Silent." She scolded certain members "so heaven-bound that they have no earthly duties" and those holding their noses so high in the air "it appears that they are walking upside down." With a final charge to the congregation to "get busy," she stalked from the pulpit amid foot-stomping and thunderous applause.

Though she had been the one preaching, she knows that many in the congregation saw her father in her face, tone and gestures. Comparisons frustrate her. It was one week after her fifth birthday when her father was assassinated in Memphis.

"When people come up to me and say, 'Ohhh, you sound just like your father,' I don't know what to say. Should I say, 'Thank you'?"

That Sunday, "thank you" *was* her response to several of the well-wishers who shook her hand after services. "It's something I'm going to have to wrestle with for quite some time, but I'm willing to accept it because that's part of the struggle; that's part of being the child of someone who made such a great impact.

"I also realize that people are looking for some sense of hope, and for a lot of people, hope was the civil rights movement. It was Dr. King. . . . They want to get something to take them back to Dr. King."

AN ECHO FOR CORETTA

Coretta Scott King, 63, flew home from a California visit in time for her daughter's sermon. She would go back to L.A. the next day to continue celebrating the 10th anniversary of daughter Yolanda's theater company, Nucleus. Yolanda, 35, spends a lot of time in L.A. and New York City, though Atlanta is home to all four King kids. Martin III, 33, is a county commissioner. Dexter Scott, 29, an entertainment producer, escorted their mother to Bernice's sermon.

Coretta, moving carefully on legs swollen by the combined effects of age and jet lag, seemed unmoved by the sermon. Later she said she was just nervous. "As a parent and mother, one is never totally relaxed. You can't listen uncritically, though when she's doing well you feel very good about it."

And then she said the one thing that would make her daughter wince. "I can't help thinking about her father each time she stands to preach."

REMEMBERING FATHER'S FUNERAL

Bernice is certainly not mimicking her father. She barely remembers him. The Rev. Joseph L. Roberts—pastor of Ebenezer since 1975 and Bernice's mentor and surrogate father since the death of her grandfather in 1984—agrees that comparisons are unfair. "The world is begging to know where the spirit of Dr. King is, as if the world will repeat him," he sighs. "Without a doubt, through genetics and environment, she has been endowed with his gifts. But it's very important for us and for the world not to fall into the trap of smothering a person by the spirit of her ancestors."

By the time Bernice was born, on March 28, 1963, her father already had led the Montgomery, Ala., bus boycott, helped found the Southern Christian Leadership Conference and been jailed, beaten and bombed. Bernice was only 4 months old when he gave his famous "I Have a Dream" speech during the March on Washington, 18 months when he won the 1964 Nobel Peace Prize and 2 when he called for the march from Selma, Ala., to Montgomery—later known as "Bloody Sunday"—on nationwide television. She has been told she was afraid of her often-absent father. "It wasn't until I was close to 4 that I really began to know who he was, and what he meant in my life."

Her memory blurs on specifics, but one incident sticks with her today, an incident wholly responsible for this normally rational adult's fear of dead people:

It began when she boarded the plane that had just arrived from Memphis with her father's body. "I heard, or thought I heard, something like a breathing sound. And I told my mother, 'He's breathing.' She had apparently explained to me that he wouldn't be able to talk. So, in my mind, that meant he wouldn't be able to breathe either, *and I heard him breathing.*"

Her fears were compounded at the funeral, where a tape of King's last sermon at Ebenezer was played. "It confused me, because my mother said he couldn't talk, and then I heard this tape. I started looking for him."

To this day, she has a childish emotional reaction to dead people. "If somebody dies, I'm not sure they're dead. It's spooky. It's like they can come back."

The tape that haunted her was made on April 4, 1967—exactly one year to the day before his assassination. And he was preaching about his eulogy.

NO BARRIERS FOR BERNICE

Nearly a quarter of a century after the civil rights hero's death, racism and discrimination persist. "The reality," she says, "is that, even though we have removed some of the legal barriers, we have not done away with the psychological impact."

Especially on young black men.

Mention their problems and Bernice gets adamant. "A lot of our young people who are locked up in our jails and prisons are there because they don't know who they are, the potential that they have. I want to help them to channel their energy into more positive means. . . . It's easy to hit somebody; it's easy to strike out. It takes a whole lot of commitment to something higher than yourself *not* to do something delinquent."

That higher commitment, that "God-consciousness," is what Bernice hopes to reawaken in kids through her still unformed juvenile ministry. What she has yet to figure out is how to make the dream a reality. An expert has some advice: Learn what makes kids tick, study adolescent psychology.

The need is there, says Don Smarto, director of the Institute for Prison Ministries, a national group. "There are some programs, but they're mom-and-pop, or just very generous people who work out of their own church and probably have other jobs."

Coretta says her daughter's interest in helping young black men is an outgrowth of her childhood; she always played with boys: basketball, softball, street hockey, tennis, you name it. "She was like one of the fellas, really," Martin III says.

At times she thought she *was* a boy. She told her mother that's what she was going to be when she grew up. Her mother told her, "'No, you're going to be a lady. You're going to be like me and Yolanda."

Coretta says: "Her feeling, at an early age, that there were no barriers where women were concerned was a good thing. Bernice had not been a part of segregation the way the generation earlier was. She was aware of it, of course, but she did not have many of the bitter experiences. So she felt things were open to her. Bernice always set her goals pretty high."

"I'm very pleased and humbly proud of her growth and development," Coretta says. "I realize what a difficult challenge it is for her to be in the same field as her father." And she wonders if Bernice studied law so she could have something of her own.

ON GUARD—BUT LOOKING FOR LAUGHS

Bernice mistrusts the press and is quick to say she rarely gives interviews. Her mother tries to keep her distance, too; this interview was the first Coretta has granted in 6 months. Bernice guards her home turf, to the point of not describing her house or even the section of town in which she lives. Nor will she discuss her income from lecturing and work; the county pays a beginning law clerk about $29,000 a year. She's a bit sheepish about her $25,000 Acura Legend, especially since she had just admonished parishioners about the evils of materialism. Calls to the King family are deflected by staffers at the Martin Luther King Jr. Center for Nonviolent Social Change. And Bernice's home phone number is a secret.

Security is a double-edged sword.

"I'm in the ministry, and I've got to have a listed number, ethically," Bernice says. But death threats to members of the King family are continual; a published number could do irreparable damage. Even church-related calls might snowball into unnecessary celebrity-pestering.

"It's real difficult to figure out. I'm not particularly crazy about having to have protective walls up, because I'm just a regular, ordinary person."

Just a regular, ordinary person who wishes people wouldn't be so *serious* around her. Some expect a King always to be profound. As a minister, she's expected to be all things to all people. "It can be a lonely calling, because people are always pulling on you. There are few times when people come to you and say 'What can I do for you?' They're always wanting to *get*."

For comic relief, she looks to her beau, the tall, handsome Tony Frierson. Around him, she's transformed. The Rev. King becomes "Bun," and the two chatter like children. Together they're . . . cute.

Frierson calls King "a very wise and knowledgeable young lady, well beyond her years, chronologically." Funny thing coming from a man 3 years her junior. They've been dating for over a year, but because of his evening work schedule as a master control switcher at Turner Broadcasting Systems, they can't be together as much as they'd like. "We don't do a lot; we don't have much time. We do a lot of dinner—too much. Both of us have gained entirely too much weight."

Both insist—though none too convincingly—that marriage is not in the picture. To Bernice, the marriage equation is complex: "We are two individuals who love each other dearly, but that's (only) right now. Marriage is very sacred to me. It's not like joining a health club. Next to the church, it's the most sacred institution, because from marriage comes family, and family supports society and can ultimately determine where society is going to end up."

And though the path there is uncertain, she knows where society—and she—should end up.

exhibit 5.3

Practice Exemplar on School Social Work: The Principal Goes to School

Rosemary Schroeder, principal of a suburban elementary school, an educator for over 27 years, was a social work student in a practice course the authors of this text taught on combining strength-based, client goal-focused and solution-focused approaches. The combined approach joined basic social work values and practice principles, including strengths-based assessment (Saleebey, 1992; Cowger, 1994) and solution-focused methods (Berg and Miller, 1992; Walter and Peller, 1992; O'Hanlon and Weiner-Davis, 1989; and DeShazer, 1985). Schroeder influenced her school's Intervention Assistance Team to adopt these approaches in their work with teachers and parents. She writes of her experience in putting the concepts into practice in her school. Schroeder feels schools can become so focused on problems that they overlook the strengths children, parents, and teachers already have, just as happens in the fable by George H. Reavis, reprinted below.

THE ANIMAL SCHOOL

Once upon a time, the animals decided they must do something heroic to meet the problems of "a new world." So they organized a school.

They adopted an activity curriculum consisting of running, climbing, swimming, and flying. To make it easier to administer the curriculum, all the animals took all the subjects.

The duck was excellent in swimming, in fact better than his instructor, but he made only passing grades in flying and was very poor in running. Since he was slow in running, he had to stay after school and also drop swimming in order to practice running. This was kept up until . . . he was only average in swimming.

The rabbit started at the top of the class in running, but has a nervous breakdown because of so much make-up work in swimming.

The squirrel was excellent in climbing until he developed frustration in the flying class where his teacher made him start from the ground up instead of from the treetop down. He also developed a "charley horse" from overexertion and then got a C in climbing and a D in running.

The eagle was a problem child and was disciplined severely. In the climbing class he beat all the others to the tops of the tree, but insisted on using his own way to get there.

. . . The prairie dog stayed out of school and fought the tax levy because the administration would not add digging and burrowing to the curriculum. They apprenticed their children to a badger and later joined the groundhogs and gophers to start a successful private school.

George H. Reavis

The following extract was prepared in collaboration with Schroeder and based on her written report.

One of the most challenging tasks facing administrators, teachers, social workers, and counselors who work in today's school systems is that of deciding on appropriate strategies for children who are having difficulty achieving success. Problems in school usually are not isolated. They spill over into homelife through such issues as homework battles or school phobia. Likewise, home problems affect the child's school performance. The school's intervention team has to be keenly aware of both environments and willing to work in both to design strategies to effect changes that will result in a child's being able to live up to her/his potential both academically and socially.

A pattern familiar to schools over the years goes something like this. Problems with children are most often brought to the attention of the school's intervention team either by the teacher or the parents. Often, they are at a point of frustration, frustrated with the child and with their own inability to remedy the situation. There even may be some hostility and anger expressed. Their hope often seems to be that the intervention team will find a way to change the child, so that all will be well and the problems will disappear. The team assesses the problem, then makes recommendations, many of which will not be followed, and there will be little or no improvement in the situation. Eventually, both teachers and parents might give up on the child, blaming the child for lack of results and blaming themselves for failing as parents and teachers. This is exactly what has been happening over the years with results that we in the schools would rather not admit. Strength-, client goal-, and solution-focused approaches, when applied to the school conference situation, reveal several reasons why this approach is not working. Many of the basic tenets of these approaches are reversed in these conferences. Our Intervention Assistance Team studied these approaches and found that we could apply many of the basic assumptions to intervention team conferences by rethinking and restructuring our approach. Now in conferences with parents or teachers, we start by listening carefully to the parent or teacher's concern. We acknowledge their frustration and express our appreciation for the efforts they have been making to resolve the situation. We attempt to make it clear that they know more about the problem than the team does, thus they, not the team, are the experts. We then ask them what is going right with the child and what strategies are working. We encourage them to talk about the strengths, resources, and capabilities of the child, as well as their own. It is often possible for us to see the presenter relax as the negative feelings subside. We find that this opens the way for clarifying their goals and for generating positive solutions. Our hope is that we show our respect for them, validate them, build their self-confidence, and dissipate their experience of frustration. In the past we were fixed on identifying problems; thus, we overlooked strengths, which are so useful, so practical, in developing solutions. The team were the experts who determined exactly what the problem was and offered our recommendations for strategies to solve the problem; thus, we often suggested strategies that did not fit the unique lifestyle of the family, classroom style of the teacher, or learning style of the child. Now, because parents and teachers determine their own solutions, solutions that work for them and solutions they know they are competent to carry out, they are much more likely to follow through. It should be noted here that the team composition varies, depending on the situation. In some instances the team will consist of the classroom teacher, counselor or psychologist, and myself in my role as social worker, not principal. In other situations, the team may be expanded to include the learning disabilities specialist, the speech pathologist, and teachers in particular subjects. When parents request a conference, they, as well as the classroom teacher, are always part of the team. Some examples of the team's efforts follow:

- The team used to recommend such things as a personal desk at home for the child or a designated study hour from 7 to 8 p.m. We now converse with parents about whether or not they find that their child responds to having specific times and places for studying and, if so, what some specific practices are that fit with their family patterns. Here, we want to respect their diversity and validate their competence as concerned parents.

- When a teacher conferred with the team about Nahid, an 8-year-old girl in the 3rd grade who frequently disrupted class by speaking out at inappropriate times, we asked if there were times when the child behaved appropriately. Here, we were following the solution-focused model's practice of getting to solutions by finding exceptions, times when the problem did not occur. The teacher said Nahid behaved well during structured activities and decided she would like to build more structured activities into her classroom.

- Susan, a 9-year-old child in the 4th grade, was not participating in class. Here we combined strength-based approaches with the solution-focused model's practice of asking the presenters of the problem to say how they would be acting differently if the problem went away. The teacher, in this instance, took some time reflecting on the question but finally was able to say that when Susan was participating more, she herself would be offering more praise and would be doing things to build Susan's confidence. She said she thought she could start praising Susan now for strengths she already showed, and she listed those qualities. Eventually, Susan gained confidence and began participating more frequently.

- In a recent conference, a teacher reported feeling fed up with David, a 7-year-old boy in the 1st grade, who frequently hit other children without provocation and always gave the teacher an argument about his punishment. The teacher had been patient but waited almost too long and was feeling pretty angry with David. When this happens, a teacher may describe the hitting as happening *constantly* and *for no reason*. We gave the teacher plenty of time to vent his frustration and then asked whether there were things he liked about David, any strengths he noticed. The teacher smiled and readily commented on David's excellent sense of humor. He reframed David's arguing with him as a negotiation skill the child used as a way to resolve problems. The teacher presently is working with David on ways to use his negotiation skills to deal with disagreements with his classmates.

- In another recent conference, the team heard from Joseph's teacher. Joseph, 13 years old and a 6th grade student, was struggling in class and not performing to his level of ability. He had difficulty retaining and applying concepts, as reflected in his test scores and homework assignments. His comprehension and performance improved when he was actively involved in projects, but during listening times, he seemed to lose his concentration and focus. In addition to the strength he showed when he was actively involved in a project, he was a conscientious student, wanted to improve his grades, and was responsive to teacher support and prompts. Other resources included the presence in the class of a second collaborative teacher and the supportiveness of Joseph's parents.

    In the plans to build on Joseph's strength, each team member accepted specific tasks. The classroom teacher plans to increase prompts to help Joseph focus. The learning disabilities specialist will work with David in math class to enhance his information access skills and will design a sheet of guidelines for following steps in completing assignments. Joseph can keep a sheet at his desk and post a copy at home. Joseph's parents will contract with a private tutor, and the speech pathologist will share information with the tutor about how to teach Joseph mnemonic strategies to enhance his retention of information. The psychologist will assess attention patterns through classroom observation and review of checklists parents will keep at home.

We are in the process of developing a method of documenting and measuring our new approach. With it, we have experienced more success and less frustration. We hold to the belief that teachers, parents and, perhaps most of all, children want to be successful, and we enjoy helping them succeed.

exhibit 5.4
___

Practice Exemplar on Case Management: Everything Happens in Its Own Time

I don't say he's a great man. Willy Loman never made a lot of money. His name never appeared in the paper. He's not the finest character that ever lived. But he's a human being, and a terrible thing is happening to him. So attention must be paid. He's not to be allowed to fall into his grave like an old dog. Attention, attention must be finally paid to such a person.

Arthur Miller[*]

No bird soars too high, if he soars with his own wings.

William Blake[**]

There is no psychology; there is only biography and autobiography.

Thomas Szasz[†]

I want to live my life to the fullest.
Christopher Pollet (pseudonym), Client Goal Statement (1992)[††]

The practice exemplar that follows was prepared in collaboration with Mary Kay Martin-Heldman, formerly case manager and now case management coordinator for a metropolitan AIDS service agency. The exemplar is based on a report Martin-Heldman wrote on her work with client Christopher Pollet (a pseudonym) over a two-year period. From the beginning of their work together, Martin-Heldman and her client enjoyed productive communication and a positive relationship. Martin-Heldman put her client first but sometimes felt caught in a situation many human service workers recognize. Sometimes clients get what professionals think they need, not what clients themselves think they need. Various health professionals as well as family, friends, and the larger community frequently have definite ideas about what is good for a client such as Mr. Pollet and definite expectations about how a case manager should carry out these ideas. In a generalist direct practice class taught by the authors of this text, Martin-Heldman reaffirmed her commitment to the primacy of the client's goals and, in consultation with the instructor, designed strategies for applying principles of generalist practice to mediate the differing views of the people involved, to negotiate their commitment to the client's goals, to sustain her own energy, and above all, to maximize her client's strengths and assist him to reach his goals. Martin-

___

[*] Miller, A. (1949). *Death of a Salesman*, Act 1. In *Bartlett's Familiar Quotations*, 16th edition (1992), edited by J. Kaplan. Boston, MA: Little, Brown & Company, p. 738.

[**] Blake, W. (c. 1793). The Marriage of Heaven and Hell. Proverbs of Hell, line 15. In *Bartlett's Familiar Quotations*, 16th edition (1992), edited by J. Kaplan. Boston, MA: Little, Brown & Company, p. 357.

[†] Szasz, T. (1973). The Second Sin. In *The New York Public Library Book of Twentieth-Century American Quotations* (1992), edited by S. Donadio et al. New York: Warner Books, p. 341.

[††] Unpublished source.

Heldman's agency has since incorporated this approach throughout its case management service and is conducting research on its efficacy. Preliminary reports indicate that clients feel better satisfied with service, and case managers report less burnout as they serve very heavy caseloads (Martin-Heldman served 137 persons living with AIDS/HIV while she worked with Mr. Pollet). If these findings hold up, the approach has very practical applications.

Christopher Pollet (a pseudonym) was referred for case management services by his physician at a local hospital's AIDS Unit. Mr. Pollet, age 36, had been diagnosed with AIDS, severe neuropathy, and cryptococcal meningitis. Damage to nerve endings affected his mobility; he walked with difficulty and needed to rely on a cane for support. His impaired ability to digest food resulted in severe weight loss. The doctor was concerned that Mr. Pollet's living situation was unsafe. Both of them knew he would need home health care as AIDS complications progressed. Mr. Pollet was staying alternately on the streets, with friends, or at a temporary inner-city shelter. He was not receiving the specialized nutrition he needed nor was he protected from the risk of infections his impaired immune system could not fight off. At our assessment, Mr. Pollet told me he wanted both case management services as well as a move to a safer residence.

At the time we first met one another, Mr. Pollet was full of spunk, witty, and very bright. He shared his feelings openly. He had been exercising creativity in making the most of his resources; for instance, he had many acquaintances, and he had been able to exchange his skills for short-term room and board. Mr. Pollet described himself as "a survivor." He added, "I always try to retain whatever independence I can." He characterized his independence as "very important to my identity." Mr. Pollet, youngest of five siblings, was raised in a Fundamentalist faith by parents who died before he was 17 years old; he grew up in a small rural town and was openly homosexual even though the people in his town opposed his life style. . . . He said he recalled "many times when I felt my family didn't love me because of my sexual preference." He heard townspeople categorize gay persons as either "evil" or having "a mental disorder." Despite their difficulty in accepting his difference, people marveled at his creativity with photography, baking, and gardening; thus, he said, "I found my own place in the town." He left his hometown after he finished high school and saved enough money to attend a commercial art school on the East Coast. When he completed his training, he found a job in this city and had lived here since, maintaining a solid work record. Until his illness made it impossible for him to work, he held a managerial position for 8 years with the same company and enjoyed a good income. He had not had a partner nor had he been sexually active for several years.

Mr. Pollet told me he was concerned about his health, saying, "I'm not ready for the viruses to get the best of me." In addition to "retaining my independence," Mr. Pollet stated his goal as: "I want to live my life to the fullest." Obstacles were his difficulty in maintaining a permanent residence, lack of a support system (his family lived out of state, and he did not feel that they would be responsive to him), difficulty in accepting the fact that he was too ill to work, and trouble adjusting to the low income of about $430 a month in SSI entitlement, far less than he had been earning when he was employed.

I understood him to be experiencing multiple assaults on his physical and emotional well-being, and on his role, status, and image of himself as a competent, productive adult. His life course was being cut short in his prime. I wanted to assist him both to maintain his power in managing his own life and to preserve his dignity while receiving the help he needed as his chronic illness progressed.

Mr. Pollet and I agreed to work together toward his goals. I offered support. I brought him information about a group home for persons living with AIDS. He decided to move there but did not abide by house rules or pay his rent for 2 months. Staff at the group home suspected that he was using alcohol and drugs and attributed his behavior to chemical dependency. I discussed the options of establishing a payee or entering chemical dependency treatment, or both, but he refused to accept any of the choices. He said he felt "restricted" in the group home and was "not ready to live by the authorities' rules." The group home evicted him.

We reassessed. He wanted to try living in an apartment alone. I assisted him with the move. Over the next 6 months, he was evicted from two apartments for not paying his rent. I talked about addiction to prescription medication; he agreed he had a problem, was admitted to a drug treatment center, but was asked to leave 2 days later. The center said he was selling prescription antidepressants; he denied the allegations. By this time, his health was deteriorating; he was unable to walk without great difficulty and was incontinent and frail. His physician and I met with him and talked about the reality of his failing health and about the options of involving his family in his care or looking into nursing home placement. He said he was "not ready" to go into a nursing home and wanted to access other resources. I understood that on one level he wanted to be taken care of, but on another level he wanted what other people his age wanted: to be autonomous, competent, and in control of their lives. He agreed to a family meeting, attended by a brother and sister-in-law. Other family members refused to participate because, they alleged, Mr. Pollet was addicted to heroin and had lied to and stolen from them for years. The couple agreed to offer their home to Mr. Pollet and he accepted. I arranged home health care and Mr. Pollet moved out of state to his brother's house. A few weeks later, his sister-in-law phoned, frightened, saying that money was missing and drug dealers were phoning the house. Mr. Pollet denied the allegations. At this point, the medical team felt a need for a psychiatric and psychological evaluation of Mr. Pollet's competence. The person who conducted the evaluation stated that Mr. Pollet was one of the most competent individuals that he had ever assessed.

Mr. Pollet then left his brother's home and returned to this city to stay at the shelter. His health was rapidly deteriorating and his TC (immune-fighting white blood cells) count was down to 0 level (normal range is about 1000), putting him at risk for all kinds of infections. Within a week, the shelter staff brought Mr. Pollet to the hospital emergency room after he had fallen and broken his hip. When he was admitted, both his doctor and I talked with him about his seriously worsening condition—his weight was down to 81 pounds, he had severe diarrhea, and he was virtually immobile because of the neuropathy. Mr. Pollet responded that he understood now that his needs had changed. He said he realized he needed someone to prepare his meals, keep him clean, and give him support. He asked to return to the AIDS group home from which he had been evicted. He said he would now feel most comfortable living with fellow AIDS patients and was ready to accept a structured program, pay rent, and abide by house rules.

I talked to the group home staff who said that Mr. Pollet must complete chemical dependency treatment before being readmitted, but because Mr. Pollet still denied using drugs or alcohol, no treatment facility would accept him. Some of the centers I called also expressed concern about AIDS issues and motivation for change in people with terminal diseases. (This issue of how to address pain, chemical dependency, and AIDS has been a source of continual struggle for me as case manager and for my clients. Many treatment models in use stress the importance of recovery and sobriety for AIDS patients, arguing that it sustains patients' health and helps them resolve inner conflicts. Yet many

AIDS patients feel that they have only a very limited time to live as they choose, and many find their chemical addictions to be their method of pain control.)

Mr. Pollet weighed his options of going to a nursing home, to a hospice, or returning to the streets and the shelter. He chose the nursing home, but he was dispirited. He realized he would be giving up much of his prized independence. He was concerned that without mobility he would lose contact with friends and acquaintances. He felt he would be out of place, a young man in a residence for elders. He worried that he would not have enough financial resources and would lose control of his own money (the nursing home would become payee and he would be allocated $30 a month).

He said he was afraid of dying. He thought he would no longer be needed by anyone, but mainly, he said, "I am afraid I will be isolated and forgotten." He and I agreed to use our partnership to brainstorm ways he could keep as much power as possible in this new environment. The nursing home supported the plans, which included Mr. Pollet's presenting, with his nurse and doctor from the AIDS hospital center, an in-service training session to nursing home staff on AIDS and its treatment. Mr. Pollet thought this was a chance for him to perform a needed service and to make staff more comfortable with him so that they would not fear him or future AIDS patients. He planned to teach the staff portrait photography techniques so that they could take photographs of residents and their families. When he was feeling well enough, he would bake and decorate cakes for residents' special days. Volunteers at my agency planned visits to see Mr. Pollet. Mr. Pollet wanted to continue to meet with me, and we settled on weekly visits and twice-a-week telephone calls. The purpose was to maintain a supportive relationship, review plans, and make changes as his health changed. Mr. Pollet framed his new goal as: "I want to complete the time I have remaining in a safe environment where I feel supported and cared for." We agreed that the time frame for our work would be the duration of his life.

One week later, when I made my next visit, Mr. Pollet had already spent his $30, was out of cigarettes, and wanted more money allocated from his check. A compromise was worked out among him, nursing home staff, and volunteers for purchase of cheaper cigarettes. Mr. Pollet had been thinking about his approaching death and told me he wanted to come to peace with his family before he died, but an obstacle, he felt, was the fact that his family did not visit him, and they had never accepted him for who he was. We practiced ways for him to communicate his feelings to his family and arranged for long-distance phone calls to his brother. Mr. Pollet told his brother that he felt the family had rejected him because he was gay and said he wished his family would come to see him. This was the first time I had heard Mr. Pollet express positive feelings toward his family. His brother responded quickly, visiting the next weekend and bringing clothes and cigarettes.

At the next week's visit, nursing staff said they were upset with Mr. Pollet for throwing his soiled diapers around the residence. They were considering evicting him because of health code violations. Mr. Pollet admitted to the behavior, saying he had gotten angry, feeling isolated and rejected; he said he was the youngest person in the whole place, was very lonely, and had not been involved in any of the tasks we had brainstormed. Together, the staff, Mr. Pollet, and I worked out an agreement. The importance of health codes and Mr. Pollet's ability to take care of his personal hygiene were acknowledged. Bins would be set up with Mr. Pollet's name on them, and he would be responsible for disposing of the diapers in the bins. In exchange for compliance, Mr. Pollet would assist the nursing home in the photo design of its proposed new brochure. The agreement was kept. In addition, Mr. Pollet did get to present his in-service teaching session on AIDS as planned, and it went very well. Mr. Pollet was getting ready now for his approaching death, and on the next week's visit, we completed a life review, including a look back at what his accomplishments were, what he was proud of, and which people had special meaning in his life. He looked forward to it and said it meant a lot to him that anyone would be interested in his story and take the time to listen to it. The review brought out renewed feelings of his love for his parents, the freedom of his early youth, his productivity in his career, and his past relationships with lovers. During this time, he also reviewed his feelings about religion and his fear of dying. He said he had left the church in which he was baptized and raised because he felt ostracized for his homosexuality. He had gone to another fundamentalist denomination but had ceased attending "while I was seeking my independence and when I was angry after I learned I was HIV-positive." Now, as he finished reviewing his life, he felt that he was ready to talk to a clergy member about his spirituality and be prepared to die. I was not able to find a clergyman in the denomination he requested, but he agreed to see a minister from a different denomination, and visits were started.

Mr. Pollet's time was now so precious and so limited. I wondered what I could give him. I decided to write a letter, reminding him of memorable experiences we shared, letting him know how much I admired and respected him, and listing all of the things he had taught me that would make me a better case manager in the future.

Three months after Mr. Pollet entered the nursing home, he died. I saw him for the last time 2 days before his death. Although he was physically very weak, he was still full of spunk, witty, very bright, and as open about his feelings as he was on the day we met 2 years before. He told me that he was "at peace" and would soon be with his parents in heaven. Laughing, he said, "I know I've been fighting. I've been fighting to live, I wasn't ready to go. I'm ready to go now." The way he put it was that he had "laid life out" and "mended" things that needed repairs. I understood him to mean that he saw his life as pieces of fabric that were now a whole cloth. He said he was reconciled with his family, and "I've come to terms with God." He thanked me for my help. I did not know I would not see him again, but I feel we said our goodbyes.

Additional Practice Texts

Compton, B. and B. Galaway (1989). *Social Work Processes,* 4th edition. Pacific Grove, CA: Brooks/Cole Publishing Co.

Epstein, L. (1992). *Helping People: The Task-Centered Approach,* 3rd edition. New York: McGraw-Hill.

Germain, C. and A. Gitterman (1980). *The Life Model of Social Work Practice.* New York: Columbia University Press.

Hepworth, D. and J. Larsen (1993). *Direct Social Work Practice,* 4th edition. Pacific Grove, CA: Brooks/Cole Publishing Co.

Johnson, L. (1992). *Social Work Practice: A Generalist Approach,* 4th edition. Needham Heights, MA: Allyn and Bacon.

Kirst-Ashman, K. and G. Hull, Jr. (1993). *Understanding Generalist Practice.* Chicago: Nelson-Hall, Inc., Publishers.

Maluccio, A. (ed.) (1981). *Promoting Competence in Clients: A New/Old Approach to Social Work Practice.* New York: The Free Press.

Pincus, A. and A. Minahan (1973). *Social Work Practice: Model and Method.* Itasca, IL: F.E. Peacock Publishers, Inc.

Sheafor, B., C. Horejsi, and B. Horejsi (1994). *Techniques and Guidelines for Social Work Practice,* 3rd edition. Needham Heights, MA: Allyn and Bacon.

Shulman, L. (1992). *The Skills of Helping Individuals, Families, and Groups,* 3rd edition. Itasca, IL: F.E. Peacock Publishers, Inc.

Turner, F. (ed.) (1986). *Social Work Treatment: Interlocking Theoretical Approaches,* 3rd edition. New York: Free Press.

Zastrow, C. (1992). *The Practice of Social Work,* 4th edition. Pacific Grove, CA: Brooks/Cole Publishing Co.

Epilogue

The nature of social work practice is by definition performed in a social context. This is true for all helping professions. The text has outlined a framework for understanding human behavior in such a context. From that perspective a practice orientation has been established, which focuses attention on multiple levels of intervention. In whatever field of professional helping, we confront daily the devastating forms and effects of injustice and oppression. It is important for us as professional helpers to do all we can to join with those who are in need of liberation from all forms of oppression. In the beginning of this text, we referred to the *Contract with America*. We would like to leave you with the words of Nelson Mandela:

> "Only free men can negotiate; prisoners cannot enter into contracts."*

---

* Mandela, N. (1985). Statement from Prison, Feb. 10. In *Bartlett's Familiar Quotations*, 16th edition (1992), edited by J. Kaplan. Boston, MA: Little, Brown & Company, p. 745.

Index

Abnormal behavior, 23
Acculturation, 36, 113
Acock, A., 104-105
Addams, Jane, 196
Adler, Alfred, 93, 94
Adolescence period
    implications for intervention, 151-152
    obstacles of, 150-151
    resources of, 149-150
    tasks of, 148-149
Adulthood period
    implications for intervention, 155-156
    obstacles of, 153-155
    resources of, 153
    tasks of, 152-153
Affect, 85, 119
Age-graded influences, 132-133, 167
Aging, 82-83, 95. *See also* Old age period
AIDS
    "AIDS Toll on Elderly: Dying Grandchildren,"
        170-173
    exemplar on case management, 226-230
Allen, K., 105
American Association of Retired Persons (AARP), 157
Anal stage, 93
Anderson, S., 49
Ansley, Leslie, 218
Anticipatory socialization, 132
A priori knowledge, 18-19
As You Like It (Shakespeare), 136
Attention deficit disorder (ADD), 81
Attribution theory, 91-92
Atwood, Margaret, 187
Authority, 101, 119
Avoidant behavior, 88

Baber, K., 105
Baer, B., 19
Bandura, Albert, 88, 89
Baur, S., 165
Becker, Dorothy, 197
Behavior
    avoidant, 88

biological source of, 71-83
cultural source of, 112-118
definitions of, 2, 24
holistic view of, 6, 20, 25
modification, 89
neurotic, 93
psychological source of, 83-98
respondent versus operant, 87
skills needed for studying, 3-6
social-structural source of, 98-112
Bellah, R., 109
*Bell Curve: Intelligence and Class Structure in
    American Life, The* (Herrnstein and Murray),
        78
Berg, In Soo, 193
Berman, H., 162
Berzoff, J., 162
Bianchi, E., 156-157
Biological source of behavior
    debate over, 71-72
    genetics, 72-79
    human development, 79-83
Birth period
    implications for intervention, 140-141
    obstacles of, 139-140
    resources of, 138-139
    tasks of, 137-138
Bisno, Herbert, 198
Black Elk Speaks, 178
Blau, Joe, 112
Bloom, Martin, 197
Blumenbach, Johann Friedrich, 77-78
Boomerang generation, 135
Bouchard, T., 75-76
Boundaries, 42-44, 60
Bourdieu, Peter, 100
Boxer, A., 162
Briar, S., 4
Brill, Naomi, 200, 207
Bruner, J., 112-113, 163
Buber, Martin, 15
Bureaucracies, 110
Burnout, of professional helpers, 183-184, 185